Thoughtful Gardening

The author advances thoughtfully into his Oxfordshire garden in mid-July

Robin Lane Fox
Thoughtful Gardening
Great Plants, Great Gardens, Great Gardeners

**PARTICULAR
BOOKS**

PARTICULAR BOOKS

Published by the Penguin Group
Penguin Books Ltd, 80 Strand, London WC2R 0RL, England
Penguin Group (USA) Inc., 375 Hudson Street, New York, New York 10014, USA
Penguin Group (Canada), 90 Eglinton Avenue East, Suite 700, Toronto, Ontario,
Canada M4P 2Y3 (a division of Pearson Penguin Canada Inc.)
Penguin Ireland, 25 St Stephen's Green, Dublin 2, Ireland (a division of Penguin Books Ltd)
Penguin Group (Australia), 250 Camberwell Road, Camberwell, Victoria 3124, Australia
(a division of Pearson Australia Group Pty Ltd)
Penguin Books India Pvt Ltd, 11 Community Centre, Panchsheel Park,
New Delhi – 110 017, India
Penguin Group (NZ), 67 Apollo Drive, North Shore 0632, New Zealand
(a division of Pearson New Zealand Ltd)
Penguin Books (South Africa) (Pty) Ltd, 24 Sturdee Avenue, Rosebank 2196, South Africa

Penguin Books Ltd, Registered Offices: 80 Strand, London WC2R 0RL, England

www.penguin.com

First published 2010
1

Set in 12.83/15.546 Bembo Book MT Std
Typeset by TexTech International and Andrew Barker Information Design
Printed in Germany by Mohn Media

ISBN: 978–1–846–14289–5

The practising gardener is always a Martha; it is Mary who sits back in admiration, saying how pretty that looks! Mary thinks it has just happened, as a gift from heaven; Mary is a dreamer, overlooking the practical pains and trouble that have gone to the making of the effect Mary admires. Mary can just sit. Martha, if she can spare the time for it, can and must sit and think.

Vita Sackville-West, in *The Observer*, 6 October 1957

Contents

Arnebia echioides, now a rare plant, the 'Prophet Flower'. Satan imprinted his five fingers on its young petals, but Muhammad ensured that Satan could not permanently change the world. As the petals aged, Satan's fingerprints would fade. In my garden they still do.

Preface

Most people begin to garden only when they have a garden of their own, and some people begin only when their most important seedlings, their own children, have grown up. A few of us began gardening much earlier, in our own parents' space and time. I began when I was ten years old and by the age of twelve was a seriously keen grower of alpine plants. I have continued ever since, widening the range of plants which I have known, grown and killed personally. I cannot fully express what gardening has added to my life, ever-present in my mind and increasingly in my muscles, and always adding more to what I notice in the daily course of living. It has also brought many remarkable people to me, a few of whom this book honours. It has deepened what I find in books and poems and in great paintings, the identity of whose flowers is so seldom considered by their curators and historians.

This book aims to look at gardening from many different aspects, swiftly changing as if under a kaleidoscope. So much more could have been included, but I like the variety and balance in what it contains. I believe I have grown all the plants which it mentions if they are plants which grow outdoors on alkaline soil. When I left school I worked for some months in the great Botanical Garden in Munich where I was assigned to the fine Alpinum with its geographically arranged mountain flora and its acres of imported rock, brought in by railway in the first decade of the twentieth century. I have never forgotten the lessons I learned or the human dramas of those days, but I am less willing nowadays to begin work before 7 a.m. and I no longer line up with seventy-seven others to be ticked off on lists kept by the garden's Gruppenführer in a pleasantly earthy seed room. I regret the loss of the edelweiss braces that held up my trousers, but this book recalls subsequent lessons, many of them learned in great English gardens where I have lived or been a frequent visitor. Above all it is based on my good fortune in being responsible for two very different types of garden, the big garden round my Oxford college and the two-acre garden round my house on poor stony soil in the Cotswolds.

Many of my chapters have grown and evolved from articles first written for the *Financial Times*, for which I have been a weekly columnist on gardening for no less than forty uninterrupted years. In January 1970 I was offered a trial column by the paper's legendary editor, Gordon Newton, in the belief that the *FT* needed brightening up on Wednesdays. I even survived my initial observation that the flowers on the great man's desk were plastic, but I did not expect him to become an ever keener gardener, growing excellent fuchsias and much else in his years of retirement. I sometimes wonder where the impetus to write, usually so happily, comes from each week. I trace its roots to my Eton days at boarding school where I used to read E. B. Anderson's superb book on rock gardening by torchlight under the bedclothes, and where my request for special leave to visit the Chelsea Flower Show was known to be genuine and was duly granted, but only with a female chaperone, my tutor's wife, in case I cut loose among the rival attractions of London. I would not even have known how to find them. In Windsor's nearby public library I then tracked down the books of gardening articles by Vita Sackville-West, written for *The Observer* between 1946 and 1961. They remain the best gardening articles which I and so many others have read, and I never imagined that one day I would be asked to re-read her work in full and present another selection of it. After discovering these short masterpieces, which she herself professed to disdain, I became joint editor of the school newspaper, the 'Eton Chronicle', and even then, the writing of casual columns and editorials struck me as something I could do and whose deadlines I enjoyed.

Years of undergraduate terms in Oxford then followed in which active gardening was impossible, although I made up for some of the loss by enjoying the setting of my then college's Addison's Walk, at that time the most beautiful tamed landscape in England. Early Christian desert fathers sometimes hint at the pull of the desert in their ascetic decision to abandon the settled world. Addison's Walk and its meadow's glory, its wild fritillaries, exerted some of the pull behind my realization that I, too, would never wholly live in everyday society. At that time I was writing essays twice weekly for my tutors and I thought that as I could do two, it would be easy to write only one, this time on the gardening I loved. I never imagined that I would write more than two thousand consecutively.

I owed my crucial editorial interview to the interest of Pat Gibson and also to the instincts of Lord Drogheda, such important figures in the *FT* company's life and examples of how to encourage young aspirants to see if they can really perform. I have since owed much to the apt laissez-faire approach of successive editors, especially Geoffrey Owen, Richard Lambert, and nowadays Lionel Barber. For years I contributed in handwriting or by telephone and I thank especially Mary Dorwald and the varied teams of *FT* copytakers, headed by the imperturbable Mandy with whom I, like many others, had the ideal telephone relationship before she emigrated, without ever meeting me in person, while her supporting staff withdrew to new lives in bars across the Mediterranean.

My gardening is done in time stolen from other work, as it is also done in the lives of so many *FT* readers. I owe special debts to helpers and encouragers in the garden, especially my parents and our beloved gardener Leslie Aris in distant years which seem like yesterdays, and those who help me regularly nowadays, Marius Hardiman and Jim Marriott and their respective teams in Oxford, and Marcia Little and Terry Wheeler at my home. Not all the great moments in gardening are solitary and I and my present garden owe much to our duet with Caroline Badger at a crucial time.

As for this book, Stuart Proffitt made me write it, a far more demanding task than I anticipated. Many people in recent years have told me to do it and one or two have tried to buy it in bookshops before it was even commissioned. I am immensely grateful to Tatjana Mitevska for her skilled work in retrieving long-lost bits of text and her ebullient support in so many ways. Neil O'Sullivan deserves special thanks for his intelligent editing over the years and his patience with my anxious transition to a digital future. Nicholas Spencer and Raphael Abraham are worthy successors in the weekly turmoil of *FT* life. My pupils Robert Colborn and Henry Mason skilfully decoded and typed my text, while retaining an amused incredulity at subjects so far removed from their own. Jane Birdsell was the most penetrating questioner as copy-editor and practising gardener and has saved me from several errors. I am particularly grateful for the kind guidance of the many libraries, photographers, nurseries, and Dr Jane Lightfoot who helped me with the business of finding or taking relevant pictures. Dr Claudia Wagner rose to the challenge of tracing so much, so far removed from her expertise in classical art and engraved gems.

I remember my remarkable grandmother Enid wondering why I wanted to go to Oxford and fearing, wisely, that I 'might become a don or something frightful'. Gardening, on the other hand, always seemed to her to be worth encouraging and so, in her wake, I continue to think that I have compensated for the one by combining it with the other.

Thoughtful Gardening

Gardening is a thoughtful activity, but thinkers tend to look down on it. It is practical and repetitive, they think, and it is often very dirty. A few universities give degrees in landscape design and professional horticulture, but their emphasis is on weed-suppression and mass propagation. They do not give degrees in practical gardening and its relation to art and science. I have heard thinkers blame the English love of gardening for England's industrial failure. I have even heard them dismiss gardening as a substitute for proper study, a reason, they think, why women are so keen on it, as many of them, now middle-aged, supposedly never had a proper education 'instead'. When I began gardening, more than fifty years ago, the distinguished Professor of Medicine in Oxford was telling the young male doctors in his department that there were two important rules in life. They must live within walking distance of the hospital and they must not buy a house with a garden too big for their wife to manage.

There are exceptions, including exceptional thinkers. Before I came to Oxford at the age of eighteen I had worked for months in the great alpine garden of the Botanical Garden in Munich, one on a staff of seventy-eight. In my second year of Oxford study, I moved on to philosophy and found a hero in a world of thought which otherwise seemed far beyond my grasp. The famous thinker Ludwig Wittgenstein had the attraction of being described to me by my judicious tutor as 'decidedly rum'. So I tracked down a lecture which the 'rum' Wittgenstein had given in Cambridge in 1929 and marvelled to find him remarking that sometimes he 'wondered at the existence of the world' and at others, that he knew the 'experience of feeling absolutely safe'. He sounded so neurotic to my earth-bound mind. It seemed interestingly odd that he thought, 'How extraordinary that anything should exist.' It seemed even odder that he thought, 'I am safe, nothing can injure me whatever happens,' and believed that others thought so too.

It was hard to believe that he had lived among brothers and sisters, let alone that he was the youngest of eight. Clearly he had not lived my daily life with horses, and surely he had never weeded among nettles.

I then found that he had fought in the First World War, a fact which helped to explain his interest in 'feeling absolutely safe'. I also found that he had thought about 'thoughtful activity'. 'Let us imagine,' he had written, 'someone doing work that involves comparison, trial, choice', constructing something out of 'various bits of stuff with a given set of tools. Every now and then, there is the problem, "Should I use *this* bit?" The bit is rejected, another is tried . . .' Wittgenstein was imagining the 'construction of an appliance', but he could as well have been describing my work in Munich's alpine garden, where I dug with a pointed German version of a straight-edged English spade and planted lemon-flowered trollius among blue Bavarian gentians in the belief that they would go well together in acid soil. Wittgenstein went on to imagine the 'whole procedure' being filmed. 'The worker perhaps also produces sound-offerings like "hm" or "ha!"' : in my German garden, Herr Strauss would burp and Herr Schmidt notoriously farted. Neither in Munich nor in Wittgenstein's notebook did the worker 'utter a single word'. He was thinking, nonetheless: 'of course we cannot separate his "thinking" from his activity. For, the thinking is not an accompaniment of the work, any more than of thoughtful speech.' During my first year in Oxford I had been convinced that I had thought more while gardening in Munich than I had yet been made to think by a tutor in classical Greek. Now, this great thinker, so 'rum' to my teacher, was endorsing my belief. Thoughtful gardening became my creed.

There was still a gap between the philosopher's idea of it and mine. His worker worked thoughtfully, but he did not think long and hard before he started, and he did not put his thoughts into words. His thinking was rudimentary, but when I read on, I learned more. Wittgenstein, I found, had twice worked as a gardener for several months in his life. My hero became a demi-god and though I understood so little, I read whatever I could find of his writings. In summer 1920, I discovered, he had been training to teach in a primary school in Austria, but he had spent the vacation working in the gardens round the monastery at Klosterneuburg, close to Vienna and even closer to the River Danube. While he gardened, no doubt thoughtfully, the abbot of the monastery passed by the flowerbed and remarked, 'So, I see that intelligence counts for something in gardening too.'

It is a pity that the abbot cannot read this book. For thirty years I have had the honour of running the gardens at my Oxford college, New College, in a world of thinkers for whom I also run nine outlying gardens, including some in which they think, but do not work. I oversee the valiant teams of contractors who work for us three days a week from March until December, and I discuss the lawns with the man who cuts them when sent on secondment from the College's grassy sports grounds. Like Wittgenstein's thoughtful worker, I choose, I compare, I try, and perhaps I 'hm' and 'ha!'. Nothing is planted or changed without my orders. The gardeners do the work, but I supplement them at weekends or on evenings when the season is at its most challenging and my own Cotswold garden allows me to be unfaithful. Around me, undergraduates go about their thinking business, without time to wonder that the world exists or the audacity to feel entirely safe. My colleagues, some of them fellow tutors, are paid to think daily too, but I seldom know what they think about the garden beyond an unwondering sense that it exists. Some of them have the oddest ideas about gardening. Our academic year begins in October, and on one such beginning a colleague invited me to drinks in order to celebrate the new year. One thinking guest had just returned from a summer spent testing rats in a foreign laboratory and put a question to me which brought me up with a bump. 'Have you had a good summer too, Robin? Were the flowers all the right colours?'

If gardening has something to do with intelligence, my colleagues sometimes make me wonder where the intelligence lies. The thoughtful gardeners in this book are not people with acclaimed intellectual minds. They include Lady Chatterley's lover and the head gardener of a great house in Northamptonshire near the poet John Clare. For more than forty years my College gardens employed another one, a former prisoner-of-war from Poland who had chosen to live on in England when the world war ended. He worked on the land and ended up weeding in our College grounds. His greying hair grew ever longer, his teeth were reduced to a necessary few, and the upper half of his gumboots remained folded down in all weathers. In the winter months he worked steadily to build a garden cart from wooden planks and when at last it was finished, his fellow gardeners towed him on a lap of honour round the garden paths. He stood proudly in the centre of the cart, holding his garden scythe in a pose which Italian artists ascribe to Death, the grim reaper, in their paintings of his triumphal procession.

The time came for him to retire to the wooden house up a ladder which he had built on a patch of Oxford's allotments and owned after many years of unchallenged occupation. I proposed the usual retirement party, to the scepticism of those who had to organize it, but on the day appointed, the honorand was present, dressed in an unexpectedly smart suit of pin-striped grey. A small group of colleagues waited for the head of the College to attend and make the presentation. We waited, and eventually our head appeared, only to sit down at the piano in the room and give us a stilted version of a piano rag by Scott Joplin. Breaking off, he beamed at the audience over his bow tie and asked, soliciting approval, 'I love boogie-woogie: don't you love boogie-woogie too?' From the back row, the voice of our retiring gardener broke the silence, then silenced us all: 'Personally, I prefer Donizetti.'

Meanwhile, in sunny weather, the thinking undergraduates roll and kiss on the lawns and try to read books with titles like *The Constant Flux*. They are respectful to the plants and are aware of change in the borders without thinking that gardening is only a search for flowers of the right colour. However, as their final year comes to an end they show signs of having caught their thinking tutors' prejudices. They tell me that they do hope I will be around to meet their parents, because their mothers would so much like advice on gardening. When I meet them, what the mothers want is an appreciation of their sons and daughters.

The undergraduates leave, but there is an alarming hole in their knowledge of the world. In more than thirty-five years of teaching them, I have asked from time to time if one of them knows what a primrose looks like. They may have read poetry by Milton or Herrick, and they may even have scored a distinction in plant sciences. Not one of them has ever known a primrose. Recently, there was a moment of hope with a boy from Ireland who told me that of course he knew, it was a pretty flower and it appeared in spring. Expectation soared, but he then went on to say that it was 'sort of rounded and purple, like a cup' which he outlined with his big hands.

I should have given up the question but I tried it one more time on a sharp-eyed young lady, who perhaps evoked it by her choice of scent. In early March, while she read me her essay on changes in classical Spartan society, a cheap scent of bluebells floated on the air. As we ended our hour of teaching, I asked her about her holiday plans, her choice of subjects for next term and, fatally incited by the bluebells, whether she knew what a primrose looked like. She squirmed disdainfully into the sofa and fixed me with a look which had a future in high finance stamped over it. 'That's a really pedantic question,' she replied, 'I see exactly the same flowers as you do, but you just put academic names on them.'

I left for lunch, feeling battered by this young nihilist who had reduced me to a 'superfluous person', like nature-loving father Nikolay in Turgenev's *Fathers and Sons*. I sat myself next to Oxford's Professor of Logic and I retold this exchange, conveying my belief that naming deepens knowledge and encourages closer distinctions in what we see. Philosophical depths threatened to open and the professor fell silent, pushed the last of his food round his plate and looked so uneasy that I thought I had trampled on a logical rule. Eventually he volunteered that he had something to tell me: 'I do not know what a primrose looks like, either.'

Two weeks later I caught him by the sleeve of his pale-fawn mackintosh and took him out into the garden where the grass was alive with primroses and blue anemones beamed under a sunny sky. I even picked a primrose and gave it to him, to which he remarked, 'So, that is it.' Wittgenstein could not have put it more concisely. His ladyfriend then told me that he had put the flower in water and kept it on his desk. There was hope, I thought, but two days later I had a card of thanks and a copy of a famous philosophical article on Meaning and Reference. One of its author's points was that a word seems to have a different sort of scope if it is used by speakers who have differing degrees of knowledge about its reference. The author tried to clarify his argument with an example. 'Suppose you are like me and cannot tell an elm from a beech tree . . .' I was fighting an uphill battle. I can show logicians a primrose, but I can no longer show them an elm tree. Except for a small group in Sussex, mature elms have been killed by beetles.

I returned to reading Wittgenstein, hoping that his months behind a wheelbarrow would have left a deeper mark on his thinking. In his *Brown Book*, I duly found him reflecting on some bedding-out. 'A friend and I,' he wrote, 'once looked at beds of pansies. Each bed showed a different kind. We were impressed by each in turn. Speaking about them, my friend said, "What a variety of colour patterns and each says something." And this was just what I myself wished to say.' It was not at all what I would have wished to say myself. 'How pretty,' or 'How ugly,' I might have said, or 'What a Germanic style of planting.' Disappointingly, Wittgenstein had had no such thoughts. 'If one had asked,' he went on, 'what the colour pattern of the pansy said, the right answer would have seemed to be that it said itself.' The obvious answer seemed to me that pansy-patterns 'say' nothing at all.

I have not called this book 'Talking to Pansies', and even from Wittgenstein's example, I conclude that thoughtful gardening has yet to dig itself in deeply among thinkers all around me. My text and title aim to promote it and answer that young serpent on my sofa. Thinking and knowing do not lead to pedantic labelling from an over-academic mind: they enhance what we see. Thoughtful gardeners think before choosing and planting, so I will share the thoughts on specific plants and their preferences which my own experiments have confirmed. Sometimes I will pass on lessons which expert growers have taught me, because I believe that those who depend on growing plants for their livelihood are most likely to know how to do it, although they are usually too busy to write their knowledge down. Sometimes I have learned through travel, which makes me think less parochially, so I describe my thoughts about gardens which lie far beyond my own. I hope that these gardens will be helpful magnets for gardeners who are fellow travellers too. Above all I have learned from fellow writers and practitioners, to some of whom I pay a posthumous tribute for the impact of their life's work on what I think and do.

The thoughtful gardening of this book is flower gardening, and though practically based, it is linked at times to fiction or poetry. They are not distractions, because they, too, help gardeners to see more. This way of evocative viewing goes back to Chinese scholar-gardeners whose reading and poetry shaped their gardens' names and designs. In the West it began much later with Erasmus, who described and regarded a sixteenth-century garden through associations which the plants acquired from his reading. Erasmus was not a working gardener himself, but reading deepened what a garden meant to him, as it still deepens what mine means to me.

Above all, thoughtful gardening helps gardeners to realize what flower gardening is about. It has become confused with so many other aims, 'saving the planet', 'working for biodiversity', 'reviving a lost world' or 'creating a matrix of linked habitats'. It is none of those things. It means trying to grow plants well, whatever their origins, and placing them in a setting which suits them and us. In pursuit of this aim, it is not wrong to use chemicals and it is impractical and ineffective to use only 'organic' methods. There is no 'organic' killer for bindweed or lily beetles. Nor is it wrong to prefer short-lived, exotic flowers or to love dahlias and chrysanthemums in bright colours, although 'natural' gardening is supposed to despise them. All gardeners cultivate an artificial landscape, even if their minds have modelled it on 'nature' or a 'wildflower meadow'. Artful pretence is rooted in all gardens, but thoughtful gardening practises its pretences in a conscious, independent way. It is not governed by bossy fashion. A classic herbaceous border is not more laborious than a fashionable sweep of rudbeckias and ornamental grasses which pretend to be a prairie. Gardens are not 'havens for wildlife', because 'wildlife' will scuffle in them and uproot the plants. Nor are gardeners 'restoring' a population of threatened butterflies. Gardeners' help to them is infinitesimal in the total picture and is short-lived in the wider context of farming and climatic change with which butterflies must cope beyond the garden fence. Gardening is dulled and limited if defined by moral purposes which are driven by other concerns.

Thoughtful gardening leads instead to knowledge, an asset which is intertwined with gardening's roots. In the first legendary garden stood a tree of knowledge and when our parents ate its fruit, the woman first, the man second, thoughtful gardening was born. The garden, they realized, was no longer the entire world. Ejected from it, they found that plants do not always grow in divine profusion. Hence-forward they had to think while they dug and toiled and made 'comparison, trial and choice'. They thought above all of the garden they had lost, just as thoughtful gardeners still think of gardens they once knew. This thought, too, is explored in this book.

Parterre at Brécy in winter

Winter

Prune Cobnuts and Filberts. Cobnuts and filberts must be pruned as soon as the small red flowers can be seen. These are rather insignificant and you must look closely to find them. It is the male catkins that make the show. The leading shoots of established bushes which fill their space are shortened to a couple of buds each. If there is still room for the bushes to extend there is no need to prune these leaders at all, or at the most only to remove their tips. Side shoots are cut back to the first catkin, reckoning from the tip, or, if there are no catkins, to the first female flower. Some shoots may have catkins only. These should be left unpruned until the catkins fade and then be cut right back to two buds. There is no point in keeping them, as they will not produce any nuts. Badly placed branches which crowd up the centre of the bush should be removed altogether, even if this means using a saw. The ideal nut bush is roughly in the form of a goblet.

Arthur Hellyer, 'February: Fourth Week', in his *Your Garden Week by Week*
(1936; sixth edition, 1992)

Winters respond to thoughtful gardening. They have their short, cold spells, which limit choices for gardens outside warmer cities, and there are also those days of dark rain and gale-warnings, some of which come true. Their boundaries, however, are advancing with the warmer average temperatures of the past twenty years and there are many more days of clear, surprising sunshine than traditional wet in a modern 'fill-dyke' February. Great gardeners have sometimes invited me to see their gardens in late winter, agreeing with Valerie Finnis (whom I honour in my Spring section) that the garden looks its best in February. I now see what they mean. Early camellias, the heavenly scent on upright *Daphne bholua* 'Jacqueline Postill', dozens of *Helleborus* × *hybridus* and as many crocuses as the local wildlife leaves unexcavated: these flowers stand out in the year's first sunshine against the bare tracery of trees, the white bark of a good birch tree (*Betula jacquemontii* being one of the best), and a firm evergreen framework of box, osmanthus and glistening pittosporum.

In late January, I have learned to induce the daffodil season prematurely by planting the excellent *Narcissus* 'Rijnveld's Early Sensation', otherwise marketed as 'January Gold'. It shows yellow trumpet-daffodils at a height of only a foot and persists for weeks even if a sharp frost causes the flowers to lie for a while on the ground. Often, 'January Gold' waits until early February in colder parts of Britain, but it is a superb variety and completely hardy. It is a magical anticipation of spring, rabbit-proof, badger-proof and very easily grown. It has an excellent twin, the pale-flowered 'Spring Dawn' which also has trumpet flowers at this manageable height, but combines light yellow and white most prettily. They are soon followed by the smaller *Narcissus* 'February Gold', another winner except that it flowers with me in March; and then by its bright attendants, 'Jack Snipe' and 'Tête-à-Tête', whose yellow flowers are held in small groupings. I use these smaller narcissi in animal-proof groups for the gaps of bare earth in summer's borders. They are essential accompaniments to the end of winter.

On intervening days, there is time to recall, even to visit, gardens in summer settings abroad. I address this aspect of winter through my memories of the first garden in which I lived as an adult and its remarkable lady owner. I also evoke other thoughtful gardeners, active from Morocco to Texas and back to Great Dixter in Sussex. In winter there is time to travel, and I have learned so much about the range of shrubs which will flower from January to March by travelling to the fine Hillier Gardens near Ampfield in Hampshire, developed by the expert Harold Hillier and maintained so impressively by Hampshire County Council after his death. As I live on alkaline soil, I have dwelt here on shrubs which will tolerate lime, among which I would emphasize the early flowering varieties of *Viburnum* × *bodnantense*, 'Dawn' and 'Deben' being the best-known favourites and 'Charles Lamont' as good as them both. When taken indoors, their flowers have a peppery scent which is sweet but strong. They are essential in the backbone of all thoughtfully planted gardens. The superb witch hazels, or hamamelis, are essential too and well shown in the Hillier Gardens, but are denied to me by the limey soil which they dislike. In the first half of the year gardeners on acid soil have a wider range of choice.

Between reading, reflecting and relishing the early narcissi, I choose the year's half-hardy annuals, usually by sending away for seeds because the seed-racks in garden centres can only display a restricted range. Some of these seeds need to be sown promptly in a heated greenhouse, especially the tall white-flowered *Nicotiana sylvestris*, the tobacco plant which does not catch powdery mildew but which needs an early start and plenty of water throughout the year if it is to develop its big leaves and retain a fresh green. The plants should be potted on into individual four-inch pots before they finally go outdoors, protected by slug bait, in late May. With them, I sow seeds of gazanias, so good in pots and the corners of flowerbeds, especially in the bold 'Tiger Stripe' variety whose yellow-orange flowers are lined with brown. Gazanias profit from an early start because they too can be grown on individually in pots and planted out earlier in May, when they will survive a slight frost. They need direct sunlight for their flowers to open fully.

In mid- to late February I sow the excellent *Antirrhinum* 'Royal Bride' from Thompson & Morgan, a tall variety with long spikes of scented white flowers which repeat well after dead-heading. It outlasts all the others which I have tried in the family. I also start off the mainstays of my bedding-out: tall white-flowered cosmos daisies. The most widely available seed packets contain *Cosmos bipinnatus* 'Sonata', a shorter and duller variety, whereas 'Purity' is taller and bigger-flowered, and the tallest of all is 'Cosmonaut', with semi-double flowers. They too can be potted individually and stopped by pinching out their main stem in order to encourage side-branches and yet more flowers. They respond best to regular watering when first planted out and to constant dead-heading when they flower, a trick which prolongs them until October's frost. At the same time I sow the invaluable rudbeckias, so reliable in any summer. The toughest pretty mixture is still 'Rustic Dwarf', but the best individual flowers come from the recent hybrid 'Prairie Sun', an outstandingly good variety with flat flowers of a sunny yellow and a stamina which keeps it in flower, two feet high, until late October. Rudbeckias are my answer to the unpredictability of modern summers, because they flourish in seasons wet or dry. In late March, lastly, my zinnia seeds go in, because the seedlings grow so quickly and dislike being checked for a while before going out in late May, and so they are best moved only once, directly into individual pots. Zinnias are prettiest in traditional big-flowered mixtures with scarlet and yellow shades. If they are muted or reduced in height and flower-size, they lose their special charm.

None of these plants can be bought cheaply on the market in early summer. By mid-February, active gardening extends beyond the greenhouses to the garden itself. It is accompanied by the first unwelcome patter of four-legged feet, which I describe here not because I dislike animals but because I do not want them in a delicate garden of flowers. Most of them are welcome to proliferate outside the garden's fence, but just as a weed is a plant in the wrong place, so a wild animal in a flower-garden is generally a pest. February causes such animal turbulence, driving elderly badgers into exile and male foxes far afield to find female mates. Gardeners need to be vigilant to survive the symptoms, while taking advantage of the fine-weather days for an early start. Time used early in the year is time freed during the spring

Antirrhinum 'Royal Bride'

rush. I try to weed and aerate the borders by early March, ready for mulches wherever I wish to apply layers of leaf-mould on the soil's surface. It is not an organic food. I prefer to use efficient artificial fertilizer, not inefficient natural compost, as the source of the important chemicals for a plant's roots. The value of a leafy top-dressing is that it opens and improves the structure of the soil, making the roots' life easier. Thickly applied, it will also help to keep in natural moisture, a reason why mulches are best applied after a wet winter or a wet spell in spring. 'Organic' is merely a seductive word, and it was first applied to nature, so far as I know, by D. H. Lawrence. His contribution to passionate gardening will feature in my Spring section, but his ideal of 'organicity' is not one which I share. Nor is it a universal imperative. Sometimes, flowerbeds are better left unmulched, without organic matter, especially if they are made of free-draining soil and planted with plants from stony, poor habitats. Not everything worth growing in nature grows best in the spongy, rotting compost which is pushed at modern gardeners. It is restrictive to be an 'organic' gardener only, and over time I have learned to be eclectic, using inorganic compounds on pests, weeds and plants which

Rudbeckia hirta 'Prairie Sun'

need extra chemicals, and organic materials only where the soil is too poor or too heavy for the plants which I want to grow in it. Both types of material, organic and inorganic, deliver similar chemicals to plants' roots. As 'feeds', they vary only in efficiency.

As in the garden, so indoors, there is profit in making an artful, early start. In the Spring section, I will refer to the willingness of ribes, or flowering currant, to flower early if it is cut when the first buds show on the stems and is brought into a warm room. In winter, even in mid-February, yellow-flowered forsythias will do likewise, opening some five or six weeks early and lighting up a house.

New Year Resolve

My new year is full of good intentions which it would be optimistic to call resolutions. In the garden, I will be more punctual. I will remember to feed everything in pots, even in the middle of their growing season. I will not leave flower bulbs unplanted in brown paper bags. I will try to stake in time, not on the morning after a collapse. I may even check for earwigs. I will not walk on the lawns during heavy frosts. I will remember to sow sweet william seeds for flowers in the following year and I will do the job in the first week of June. I will not throw stones at squirrels. Instead, I will buy a new squirrel-trap and bait it with peanut butter. When I catch one, I will take it in the car and let it out near the garden of the nearest member of parliament who voted to ban fox-hunting.

I will also address the needs of a garden which is in its middle age. It is amazing how things have not grown as I anticipated. The climbers on the walls are mostly too big. I never imagined that my avenues of upright hornbeams and *Pyrus calleryana* 'Chanticleer' would grow so tall and cost so much to cut and shape. I did not expect so many border plants to run wild on such a scale. At lower levels, some of the best small hardy plants have died of old age, a hazard which gardening books seldom mention. None of the dianthus even waited to become elderly, and I am bemused to realize how many I have replaced. I used to reckon that owners of raised beds in a garden had lost the plot when their beds became overrun with the bonfire-red flowers of zauschneria in autumn. Last autumn, my raised beds were a flaming zone of zauschnerias. My old mats of low-growing phloxes have brown patches in their middles. Ants have killed off a little erodium with red-eyed flowers, and something seems to have sat in the centre of my autumn-flowering gentians. I do not want to think about the superb small *Campanula* 'Lynchmere', which was at its best when I dug it up last year and tried to divide it. Its roots are the wrong shape for division and so it has died. I am not alone in finding it difficult to increase as it has now disappeared from many nurseries in the *Plant Finder*, the Royal Horticultural Society's guide to 'more than 70,000 plants and 640 places to buy them'.

The easiest way to treat middle-aged gardens is to leave them alone to become senile. The first sign of middle age is when owners talk about growing only the things which seem to suit them. Then those things get the upper hand and owners start to reclassify the planting as the 'meadow look'. That 'look' involves too many hardy geraniums and valerians and too many seedlings from the previous year's forget-me-nots. If I do not control *Rudbeckia fulgida* 'Goldsturm' this year, I will have to pretend that its border was planned years ago as a prairie. I also have to face the fact that so many of my worst invaders are plants for which I paid good money and which I introduced. Never accept an unnamed autumn-flowering helianthus. The family includes the rampant Jerusalem artichoke whose tubers are so hard to eradicate. Never plant white-flowered *Achillea ptarmica* 'The Pearl' or 'Perry's White' in a bed which is meant to be civilized. They are fine as cut flowers but their running white roots elude removal with a spade.

Here, resolve becomes relevant. Beginners and owners of new gardens start out with all their mistakes before them, whereas middle-aged gardeners live with mistakes already self-inflicted. Try to look at your ageing creations with the eye of an incoming owner. After one such look I commissioned some ruthless cutting and felling. Out went the dull, dusty sycamores and a middle-aged walnut tree which I inherited too near to the house. Half of my trees should have come out years ago, but I forget how I had to make my garden by demolishing a feathery forest. I uprooted more than a hundred tall leylandii cypresses with the help of a mechanical digger's front bucket when I took over the land and had to reopen its lawns and views. It is never too late in life to let in the light.

It is a myth that gardens will age gracefully and become peacefully mature over time. Gardens never stand still and never allow us to buy a season ticket on the line of least resistance. They need as much guiding, reshaping and rethinking in their twenty-fifth year as in their third. The past ten years of gardening on television and in beautifully illustrated magazines have lured many people into trying it as if it is exterior decoration which will be as obedient as a new lamp or sofa

Red *Crocosmia coccinea* entangled with *Achillea ptarmica* 'Perry's White'

cover. When some plants die and others grow out of shape, they learn that the fun of real gardening is that it is never pinned down.

It will never pin me down. I have learned to trust my capacity for experiments which are at least two steps ahead of reality. I am some-one who presented his garden with a laborious new swimming pool and promptly lost interest in swimming. For years Mother Nature has had the pool to herself and has turned it into a dramatic wilderness of self-sown buddleias and bullrushes. They are being sustained on a diet of the naturally drowned hedgehogs which float upwards in the winter months. For years I have been hoping that the water may spontaneously generate human life. Better still, it may prove the Bible right and present me with a female helpmate, a muscular clone of Eve. At least she will not need a work permit.

So far, the pool has produced only a batch of newts. My latest resolution is to restore its former shallow end to clear, rush-free water and plant it with white-flowering water lilies, contained in old car tyres. You know what resolutions are, but I like the idea of becoming that Japanese item, an 'artist of the floating world'. No doubt the lilies will turn out to be the next invaders of my own making.

New Year Resolve

'Tresco on Teesside'

How seriously should gardeners be planning for climate change? It is not an idle question for inactive days in the wake of a New Year lunch. Money is now being thrown at it and the fear of hot weather risks multiplying hot air of a different kind. The Royal Horticultural Society has jumped on a problem which it defines as 'Gardening in the Global Greenhouse'. The National Trust has held conferences on the way forward for the next eighty years. There is a UK Climate Impact Programme and the beginnings of a flood of literature to tell us what to do.

According to the RHS, English gardens can expect to see more loquats, pomegranates, Guadeloupe palm trees and a low-growing North African convolvulus which they have decided to call 'blue rock bindweed'. For hedges, 'good garden management', they urge, will choose oleanders, those dreaded shrubs which flourish round Italian petrol stations. Our gardens, they recommend, should include myrtles and trees of the albizia, which I have seen at its best in Delhi. Do they really believe these recommendations? Have they ever tried to garden in the orbit of Chipping Norton, let alone in unforgiving Derbyshire? Their summary report by two professors produced the airy generalization that 'Tresco has spread to Tunbridge Wells and is on its way to Teesside'. If so, its slipstream is passing many gardeners by. Only recently, we had eleven days of frost in the Cotswolds which killed several of my climbing roses, annihilated the evergreen ceanothus and wiped out established plants of what is considered to be a tough cistus, aptly named 'Snow White'.

In February 2009 and January 2010 we awoke to a deep and beautiful 'winter wonderland' around the dreaming spires of Oxford. It killed off penstemons and destroyed the parahebes. If the National Trust is already discussing the 'impact', not the reality, of climate change, presumably its experts believe that the climate has changed to a new plateau. If they believe in this new plateau, it is only because they are judging it by statistical averages. They are ceasing to allow for the lethal capacity of continuing short, sharp snaps in the wider pattern. Mother Nature is inconsistent and I refuse to trust her, even when she dangles herself in a winter bikini.

We have no idea what the impact of possible global warming will be on Britain over the next eighty years. Some of the most respected experts warn us that one local effect may be bouts of intensified cold. All we know is that for the past fifteen years there has been less frost in most winters, a few very wet winters, more very dry ones and some turbulent storms. What does this variety mean? Whenever gardeners start talking about 'climatic shift', I turn back to an invaluably observed source, 'The Garden Calendar', maintained by the meticulous naturalist Gilbert White from 1751 to 1773 in Hampshire. Between 1757 and 1760 the winters were as mild as ours in the new millennium. On 26 December 1757, 'very mild weather: hardly any frost yet'. In 1758, it 'continued very mild, one short frost excepted, to the end of the year'. In 1759, on 19 January, he recorded that 'many kinds of flowers are got above ground some weeks before their usual times: the snowdrops and some crocuses were in bloom before old December was out'. On 18 December 1760, it was 'very mild growing weather yet: the grass in pastures has kept springing the whole season' and 'soft sunny days like April which brought the flies and other insects out of their lurking-places'. On 1 January 1761, he transplanted a multi-headed narcissus in full flower and brought it indoors. There was no National Trust to tell him to plant banana trees, which was fortunate because there were eleven days of continuous frost in December 1762 and on 31 December 1766 it 'froze under people's beds'. The weather swung between unusual mildness and sudden months or days of frost, just as ours still does. My firm advice to gardeners in the 2010s is therefore simple: do nothing. I refuse to believe that the Texas Palmetto and tender hedges of acacia can be expected to flourish in English gardens in the next forty years. It takes only one night of old-fashioned behaviour by the British ice-demons to wipe them all out.

As always, scares can be multiplied, especially if there are gardening practices which, deep down, the scarers dislike. The National Trust and the RHS have even sent me warning documents about the spread of new insects and pests 'due to warmer average temperatures'. I am sceptical whether the zigzag pattern on our weather chart is the culprit. Bushes of berberis, they tell us, are now at risk of attack by a new type of sawfly which originates in southern Europe. Camellias are at risk from a new Japanese petal blight. The fundamental reason, in my view, is the rise in importing plants for sale in our garden centres. The sawfly entered the Netherlands, and as our world-famous British gardens depend so heavily on the Low Countries to supply the plants in British garden centres, it is not so surprising that this pest is newly arrived in Britain. So, too, is the insect which has infested our horse chestnuts, but it would be just as problematic in a cold phase. It survives more than twenty degrees of winter frost.

The threat of climate change is a convenient scare if, deep down, you hate lawns and lavish flower gardening. Is the weather really so savage in summer that the British lawn is now doomed and the only answer is something called St Augustine grass? Many gardeners will merely invest in pop-up sprinklers fed from their big recep-tacles for rain water. The RHS's professors claim in their study that 'as the climate progressively changes, a much greater challenge to gardeners will be to create the traditional English cottage garden'. They even suggest that lupins will become more difficult. I have never had better lupins than in the recent hot summers and as for the 'traditional' cottage garden, what exactly was it and what grew in it anyway?

As ever, there have been weather catastrophes, but catastrophes are not sound evidence of sustained change. The recent thunderclaps of wind and storms began to blow in 1987 and again in 1990 when they damaged well-established gardens, especially in the south of England. The National Trust can point to the loss of trees at Sheffield Park in Sussex, while others will think of the gales which ruined Tresco or opened up such lovely new vistas at Leonardslee. Were those storms connected with a warming of the British climate and a rising risk of floods? Again, Gilbert White puts the fears into a longer context. 'The year 1751 was one of the wettest years in the memory of man. There were constant storms and gluts of rain from 20 February to 20 May.' 1755 was 'a terrible winter for Earthquakes, Inundations and Tempests and continual Rains, with no frost worth mentioning'. In December 1761 'vast quantities of rain have fallen the autumn

Agapanthus 'Slieve Donard' in my garden

and winter through' and on 23 and 24 December there were 'vast rains and floods'. The 'climate of flooding' is not a modern innovation. It was already buffeting and soaking the mid eighteenth century.

What do the global warmers advise us to do? Their suggestions of myrtle hedges are a hollow joke in Moreton-in-Marsh or Much Wenlock. The RHS is seriously advising us to 'invest in water features and ponds – they will benefit wildlife'. Meanwhile, those who hate efficient, man-made fertilizers lose no chance of telling us that the increased risk of flooding raises the risk that such fertilizers will all be washed out of the soil and instead, we should heap on gravel and organic matter. How organic, though, is all this heaping? In the RHS garden at Hyde Hall in Essex, a newly installed 'dry garden' has already required '260 tonnes of gabbro'. In case you are unsure, gabbro is an igneous glacial rock which had to be transported from Scotland to Essex. The entire project reads to me like ecological rape, involving 800 tonnes of hard core, 460 cubic metres of imported soil and no end of 'crushed red granite'.

Thoughtful gardeners will continue to buy water butts to store their wasted rainwater and will give their gardens a backbone of plants which are totally hardy and capable of withstanding drought. Rock-hardy winter-flowering viburnums remain a wiser choice than mimosas. Spring-flowering hellebores are never killed by frosts and gales. Early flowering prunuses survive drought, cold and wind. Many narcissi flourish in the wild in glacial Russia and its neighbours. In summer, I have learned to trust border plants with chunky, water-retentive roots, the best varieties of day lilies, many of the yellow-flowered inulas and the excellent *Campanula lactiflora*, especially the deep blue 'Prichard's Variety' which arose on the fine nursery of Alan Bloom in Norfolk. At the edges of this backbone there has been a slight shift in reliable hardiness, which has brought many red- and yellow-flowered crocosmias, pink-flowered evergreen abelias and new agapanthuses within most British gardens' range. The reasons are better breeding and more experiment by gardeners, not a reliable shift to a plateau of warmer climate. When this backbone of plants is so solid and varied, who wants an incongruous palm tree, looking brown and increasingly ragged up its thick, ugly trunk? What we need is to dig in with the thousands of plants, still under-exploited, which flourish in the British climate, as ever one of extremes.

Faith, Hope and Charity

While experts debate the effects of a changing climate, gardeners can profit from a clear benefit. Mild winters in Britain are being kind to winter-flowering plants and I urge them on anyone starting a garden or trying to improve an old one. The traditional wisdom of garden designers was that winter-flowering shrubs and plants should be well represented in areas immediately surrounding the house and its doors. I agree. We stray much less farther afield in midwinter and it is heartening to see a pink-flowered viburnum, a winter-flowering cherry or a scented winter honeysuckle from the front door and its nearby windows. Winter honeysuckle is remarkably tough and will even flourish in odd corners beside the dustbins.

The festoons of flower on the yellow-flowered winter jasmine, *Jasminum nudiflorum*, are essential in any garden, and despite the plant's twiggy look in summer, it deserves a sunny place where its colour shows up best in midwinter. Its equals are the many forms of mahonia, another essential plant for beginners or hopeful improvers, and one which may help them to pull their ideas out of a rut. The mild weather nowadays allows the brightest mahonias to flower freely and the accompanying rain suits them too. Most of the family likes a wet season, one reason why such good mahonias are to be found in Ireland. The best known is *Mahonia japonica*, which tends to start flowering in mid-December, frost permitting. The flowers are scented of lily of the valley and open to a shade of acid yellow which is very appealing. The leaves are often a less glossy green than those on their near relations and can look rather drab in the off season or in dry shade, but at least they will grow and flower under light shade from tall trees. They are wonderful shrubs for under-planting a copse or bordering a little walk beneath trees, especially where the soil is unsuitable for azaleas. *Mahonia japonica* also remains one of the first choices for odd corners near the semi-shaded surrounds of the house. It is a joy to pick some of

Mahonia × media 'Charity'

its scented flowers and enjoy them briefly in a heated room in January.

In many garden centres, japonica takes a back seat to the cleaner and shinier hybrid *Mahonia × media* 'Charity'. This excellent shrub has more leaves along its branches and flowers of a slightly brighter yellow than japonica's. It is extremely hardy and eventually spreads into a bush about eight feet high and wide. Great authorities express praise it for its scent but it is not nearly as evident as japonica's brand. Its merits are its cleanness and tidiness, which endear it to shoppers who buy on impulse. 'Charity' was first picked out by Sir Eric Savill from a row of seedlings sent to Russell's nursery near Windlesham in Surrey. They originated from the great Slieve Donard nursery in Ireland, where

Mahonia pumila against New College Chapel's wall

they had been collected from the tall, slightly tender *Mahonia lomarii-folia*, source of 'Charity's' fine evergreen leaves. Two other good seedlings were then raised from 'Charity' by Savill in the gardens of Windsor Great Park and were named 'Faith' and 'Hope'. 'Hope' disappeared altogether in 1964 after the election of a Labour government and 'Faith' has now dropped out of the *Plant Finder*.

'Charity' will still grow almost anywhere and, after five years, will give plenty of flowers and long leaves which reflect the light. I recommend it highly, and its traditional pairing in London with the big-fingered leaves of evergreen fatsia is a splendid match. The easy way to prolong the mahonia season is to choose one of the more recent crosses

Faith, Hope and Charity

which were made between japonica and lomariifolia by the great plantsman Lionel Fortescue in Devon. The best is named *Mahonia* × *media* 'Buckland', and its spectacularly big clusters of flowers are held upright in a bright shade of yellow, usually opening in early February. On 'Buckland's' flowers the scent is elusive, although even here, some admirers detect it. Nonetheless, this variety is an excellent companion for japonica and 'Charity' because it comes later into flower.

I have two particular bits of mahonia wisdom. One is rare and the other surprised me when I first discovered it. The rare bit concerns a very small mahonia called *pumila* which is seldom seen and is unlike the winter flowerers I have mentioned. It is at home in the mountains of California and grows less than a foot high, showing off leaves that are either grey-green or green flushed slightly with a pale shade of brown. I bought this unusual variety about twenty years ago and have left it to make a life in a dry bed at the foot of an ancient medieval wall, conditions which its collectors tell us it likes in nature. It plainly likes them in Oxford and has spread healthily, flowering in late April in a strong shade of yellow. It is unusual and useful against weeds.

The surprising bit of wisdom is that you can cut the tall winter-flowering mahonias very hard into their old wood and do them a great service. As they age they tend to become leggy and show bare branches, but if you cut them very hard in early April, they will surprise you by throwing up young spiky leaves beside the cut and growing away all summer to flower freely again in the winter. Until you are forewarned, you would be unlikely to risk this treatment on a shrub which looks as if it would resent it.

Nancy in Paradise

As you take down your home's decorations after Christmas, perhaps you wonder, deep down, if you really have style. A few people have it, but many more never will. I know, because I knew the best of them, rightly revered as the supreme exponent of the English Country House style in decoration and furnishing. She would have rejected the label with an inimitable aside, but the eye, wit and elegance of Nancy Lancaster live on, as taste becomes more elusive and people even believe that it can be bought by the roll.

American-born Nancy Lancaster designed and decorated some of the most magical houses and rooms in England between the 1920s and the 1970s. She lived in them with a sequence of husbands, maintaining, not unjustly, that for the long haul she was a better chooser of butlers. She was born in Virginia, which remained the ideal landscape in her mind's eye, but 'English' style has often been most successful when conceived by people who are not English. Nancy combined smartness with comfort, everyday wear with wit and fun. She had a genius, as stylish Cecil Beaton observed, for 'offhand perfection'. It showed in her houses but also in her gardens and the smallest details of her dress and vocabulary.

Fortunately, photographs of her homes survive which are classics for designers or owners of a house with class. They run from the 1920s to the early 1990s, spanning Nancy's life which beautified so many special rooms. Her style enhanced the London business which she bought in 1944, Colefax and Fowler, a company which still survives. In it she linked up with John Fowler, her genius of a decorating partner, and together they were well described as the most unhappy unmarried couple in England. Such a marriage of talent and style flowed from their fertile disagreements.

Nancy's Virginian grandfather liked to remark that etiquette is for those who are not well born and fashion is for those who have no taste.

Nancy exemplified his wisdom. Her first marriage was to the immensely rich and handsome Henry Field, grandson of the founder of the great Marshall Field store in Chicago. Henry died tragically within six months and Nancy then married the rich and cultivated Ronnie Tree. He was an ideal match for her talents and together they made interiors which were the acknowledged masterpieces of inter-war taste, above all in the great house at Ditchley in Oxfordshire where traces of Nancy's decoration survive. When they parted, Nancy told me how she went over by agreement to collect her remaining furniture from their house, in which her former husband was entertaining weekend guests with the young lady who duly became his wife. A Visitor's Book lay open in the hall and as Nancy left, without intruding on the party, she wrote in it in big letters, 'How is Puss getting on in my boots, then?' Puss was surprised to discover the message when she invited her first guests to sign their names in the book after lunch. Nancy, meanwhile, remarried briefly the owner of Kelmarsh in Northamptonshire, for the house as well as the company. When she left, she moved in 1954 to Haseley Court near Oxford, where she transformed an eighteenth-century house into yet another masterpiece, her final, happy home, and laid out gardens which were a fascinating tribute to her skill and eye.

More needs to be put on record about Nancy and this final garden. I know it, because I lived on the place in her last two years of ownership of the entire property and I gardened with her on many charmed days in the years when I was first writing columns on gardening. When she sold the main house she gave me many of her practical books on gardens and flowers. Gardening, she would say, is best done on your stomach, weeding with your teeth. We crawled and chewed, even when she was seventy-five, and almost every plant, its position and its partners in her garden remain imprinted on my mind.

By the time I knew her, Nancy had lived the grand life and spent money as freely as water from her garden hose. Nonetheless, she worked outdoors whenever she could, alarming my wife and myself by tugging the hose through the ground floor of the cottage which we rented from her and calling at six in the morning, 'When are you going to have babies or shall I come upstairs and show you how to do it?'

Nancy Lancaster with her hose at Haseley Court

'I water in the mornings,' she told me, 'when I cannot sleep, so it is for you to see that I have not caught pneumonia when you wake up.' When we then had the babies, she compared the colour and texture of their cheeks in cold weather to ripening nectarines. Meanwhile, it was for me to accompany her with the long-handled pruners and to listen to the stream of memories, down-to-earth comments and questions which came at me from the middle of an over-sized deutzia or a favourite lilac which needed dead-heading.

'I have had the best of it,' she would tell me, 'when the best was worth having.' It still seemed pretty good to me, and I must adjust the published impression that the distinguished adviser Graham Thomas left a lasting imprint on Haseley's famous walled garden. Nancy respected his knowledge but was wary of his taste. It was not Graham Thomas who first taught her about many of the roses which she chose for her garden, from 'Mme de Sancy de Parabère' to stripy 'Leda' and climbing white 'Sombreuil'. She gave me a neglected book, *The Charm of Old Roses* by Nancy Steen, in which she had made copious marks and notes. It was her springboard, whereas there are many fewer such marks in her copies of Graham Thomas's classic works on old roses which she gave me too. Unwary readers of garden historians might think that her garden depended on two colour schemes, one of pink roses and after a crossing avenue, one of yellow roses. She certainly included those colours and when her sister complained that pink and orange did not go together, Nancy typically told her that, 'In time you'll begin to like anything with anything.' Green, she knew, helped harsh colours to blend, but I knew the garden at its height and, by then, the combination of pink and orange had long disappeared. It was replaced by a palette of a wider range which was Nancy's own.

How much I learnt from her, much more, even, than from my previous spell as a trainee gardener in Munich's botanical garden. Sometimes on winter evenings I still walk my mind round the details impressed on my memory: the Italian cypresses whose leaves smelt of paper in old books, the Canadian lilacs pulled over to make an arbour, the honeysuckles grown as standard trees, the patterns of silver *Artemisia splendens* and golden creeping jenny which evoked the pattern in a mosaic floor at Torcello in Venice's lagoon. She had a decorator's sense of staging and a boldness rooted in her own good

'Offhand perfection': Nancy Lancaster by Cecil Beaton

taste. She grew big trees of the tender *Sparrmannia* and put them in cleverly shaped boxes which were painted in her favourite Confederate shade of grey. The plants had been grown from cuttings, she told me, first given her by Laurence Olivier. She trained huge plants of grey-leaved *Helichrysum petiolare* on wires in pots. In other pots she grew wisterias like trees, and for years afterwards I treasured the standard wisterias which she gave me. Everywhere there were rare roses which her eye had picked out as a match for Haseley's sandstone walls. I first learnt from her about the unusual rose 'Ash Wednesday' which has flowers of her favourite grey. She liked modern varieties too, the stronger pink 'Aloha' as a climber, tumbling yellow 'Golden Showers', the powder-scented 'Constance Spry'. Her main garden path was lined with the low box hedging which she had loved since her youth in Virginia. She acquired most of it for nothing when the National Trust threw it out from other gardens in a fit of labour-saving drabness. It was she who knew that old, leggy bits of box will grow bushily again if the bare bits are buried below the soil. She was always alert to practical wisdom.

Her fellow American, the admirable Lanning Roper, was an important source of advice in the garden's early years. Nancy was always a great magpie: 'I am not a decorator, I am a percolator.' Lanning Roper helped with ideas for her walled garden's planting after a first fallow year in which she cleaned it by growing potatoes all over the ground. He taught her to plant grey-leaved phlomis against the walls of the house or to plant *Campanula persicifolia* among bearded irises, but she taught me to love the stripy *Syringa vulgaris* 'Sensation', to cut Rosa mundi roses down to ground level after flowering or to interweave alstroemerias with silver-leaved *Senecio viravira*. My word, she made us laugh. One afternoon, two learned Oxford experts in Roman history came up to call from the village: she asked these confirmed bachelors how landowners had survived the farming depression of the 1880s. The more learned of the two replied, 'That is not my period', with a caution which young beginners abominate. 'Periods,' retorted Nancy, 'were the one thing I thought that professors like you never had.'

In the hot July of 1971 I used to walk in her heavenly garden in the cool of the day when the roses were falling everywhere and she was about to sell most of the ground she loved. She wrote at the time: 'Now it is gone, but life is a series of Grand National jumps. It is like the end of a party.' In her mid seventies she withdrew to the Coach House beside her former home and made yet another enchanting garden as if the party had merely changed its scale. She planted evergreen yews and clipped them, brilliantly, into a circular sofa with green arms. She contrasted them with a golden-leaved robinia and multiplied the regale lilies which she grew on canes in pots. 'Better at choosing butlers', she was sustained by her last choice, Fred, who learned how to make her whisky sour with the juice of fresh limes and how to remind her whom she had invited to lunch. As her years declined he would go out and record the chorus of early morning birdsong in her walled garden and play it to her while she lay in bed.

For me, the move from her house was like an expulsion from paradise. Others had shared this feeling. In the 1920s, a footman of hers remarked that 'Nancy sitting side-saddle on her horse before hunting, immaculate in her top hat and veil, is a picture I shall take to the grave with me and if afterwards I see her looking the same I shall know I am in heaven.' So shall I; but meanwhile, I look back with total recall on the garden which closed behind us. Over it stands an angel with a flaming sword, turning this way and that, but not because its lady owner had eaten its forbidden fruits. With characteristic Virginian wit, Nancy once sent a photo home to America, showing herself in a magnificent evening dress. She wrote on the bottom, 'How we apples float . . .'

Scenting Winter

In warmer winters, my best shrub beside the house is the excellent sarcococca. It makes a neat evergreen edging which varies according to the form planted. The leaves shine, the plants grow anywhere and they flower profusely, scenting the entire approach to the front door. I bless the day, twelve years ago, when I planted them by the dozen. I now have a solid hedge, about three feet high, which is covered in scented flowers, asking to be picked and taken indoors. Not enough is said about the value of these early, hardy shrubs as decoration inside the house. Their popular American name is Christmas box, honouring their shiny green leaves and small flowers. One vase of sarcococca scents an entire room, saving the expense of buying throwaway lilies.

I do not regret the form I chose. *Sarcococca confusa* is distinguished by its modest height, pointed leaves and black berries. Eventually, it might grow up to five feet but I clip my plants hard after flowering and find that a limit to their height increases their width. The smallest of the sarcococcas is *hookeriana humilis*, which grows about a foot tall and is willing to spread by its own suckers. However, it does not have the berries of other varieties – black on *confusa* or red on *ruscifolia*. As these two varieties can be controlled by pruning, they are first choices for a difficult corner in a garden. They thrive in cities.

Gardeners are more familiar with the sweeter, sickly scent of the skimmia. Well used, it is another charming shrub, but its sex life has to be sorted out. Unless you mix a male with females, you will not get the best berries on the best forms. One male can cope with up to five females in its vicinity but I tend to plant smaller groups of three, two females to one male. Among the females, the most profuse crops of large red berries come from *japonica* 'Nymans', closely followed by 'Veitchii'. I pair them off with the male *japonica* 'Fragrans', which is less tall and should go in front of them. There are other possibilities but I am not so fond of the varieties with red-purple buds or leaves which go yellow-green. All skimmias will grow almost anywhere and respond to pruning and shaping. Unexpectedly, they root with extreme ease from cuttings taken in spring after flowering. They make the most obliging green mounds for awkward, shaded situations. They also pick well, especially when in berry.

The superb winter honeysuckle is in every way the skimmia's equal. It is so easy, so free-flowering and so powerfully scented that I cannot imagine living without it. It hides the sort of dustbin on wheels which our local council gave to its ratepayers as if to help the environment. My winter honeysuckle has helped it far more than their green plastic. There are two varieties, of which the earlier, *Lonicera × purpusii* 'Winter Beauty', is better. It retains many of its leaves in most winters and it bears small cream-white flowers which are scented with a slight sharpness to their sweet base. Familiarity has taught me two extra possibilities. You can prune 'Winter Beauty' as hard as you like so that its eventual height and width of five or six feet will never be a problem. When you prune it, you can take whole branches indoors, where they will last for weeks and be very cheering. The other variety, *L. fragrantissima*, is almost as good as 'Winter Beauty' but it flowers later when it is less welcome.

The best of all early scents is a mimosa's and here, urban gardeners have the advantage. Mimosas never survive outdoors for long in chilly parts of Britain but they have become a spectacular sight in London. They are listed botanically as acacias and two of the best and hardiest sights are the pretty blue-green leaves of *Acacia baileyana* and the clusters of yellow flowers on *Acacia pravissima*, whose shoots tend to arch forwards. If you prefer mimosas with ball-shaped heads of flower in yellow bunches, ask for *Acacia dealbata*. Even in modern mild winters, I would still plant them with their backs against a south or west wall, remembering that they reach a considerable height very quickly. They soon race up to twelve feet or more and are an excellent choice for impatient urban house-owners. Their display in the garden is only part of their charm. Heads of mimosa are the most exquisite of scented plants for use indoors.

The only rival to these powerful scents is the exceptional winter-sweet, *Chimonanthus praecox*. Most of the forms available in the trade take a long while to flower, at least five years from the year of planting, but this slowness should not put you off. I prefer to see wintersweets grown as free-standing bushes, which will develop up to seven feet high and wide with a favourable wall near them. If you train them against the wall itself, you cramp their style and lose the impact of the pale straw-yellow flowers, which do not show clearly against most colours of walling. A wait for up to seven years is infinitely worthwhile. All over the bare branches the flowers then give off such a heavy, spiced scent that not even a French scent-maker can recapture it. The flowers' pale, watery colouring remains remarkably robust during slight bursts of frost. If you shop carefully, you may even be lucky and alight on one of the quick-flowering forms. One such early flowerer was available recently through the nursery at Christopher Lloyd's home, Great Dixter in Sussex. Others are now reported, but they remain in short supply and are not yet available in general nurseries' lists.

Available but overlooked is the shrub with the sweetest sugary scent when it flowers in late February. *Ribes laurifolium* is over-shadowed by its grander, red-flowered relations, but it remains a lovely plant, growing up to four feet tall and especially good when fixed against a low wall, even against one of those awkward low walls beneath a window. The flowers are pale green, noticed above all for their scent, and selected varieties are neater and even more generous in bud. 'Mrs Amy Doncaster' is still scarce, but commemorates a brilliant Hampshire gardener who died in 1995 when over a hundred. 'Rose-moor' is easier to find, but the basic *laurifolium* is just as beloved by bees.

A Hunter's Hand

Beyond the sarcococcas, I have finally achieved an aim which I
announced nearly twenty-two years ago in the optimism of late
youth. In the lower part of my garden, where the ground slopes gently
downhill to a muddle of confused greenery, the goal was to imitate a
formal pattern of avenues copied from great French gardens and
known, four centuries ago, as a 'goose-foot' or *patte d'oie*. At the time
the illustrator in the *Financial Times* provided a picture of geese
heading outwards with strings in their beaks; twenty-three years later,
have they run wild and flapped off into chaos? The answer is 'no', but
at a cost.

I now have five clearly defined avenues at a height of more than
twenty-five feet and a length of more than sixty yards. They could be
called a goose-foot, or they could be compared to the five fingers on
my right hand, whose outer edge has become splayed after a collision
with the ground in Leicestershire during an excellent day's fox-
hunting. I prefer, therefore, to claim I have planted a Hunter's Hand.
It is impressive, but every impression has its price.

Its composition was based on a guess. Others might have chosen
tightly clipped horse chestnuts, trees which were used as an excellent
formal hedge by the late David Hicks when he transferred his skills
from interior to exterior design. If so, their hedges would now be
brown, ruined in summer by the chestnut's new insect-predators. For
my outer fingers, or alleys, I began by thinking of sorbus trees, one of
which still survives as a memorial. It is impressive but I withdrew the
other two avenues after hearing a lecture by an expert who predicted
an epidemic of fireblight from the West country, targeted at the very
variety which I had planted by the dozen. The withdrawal was wise,
but for the wrong reason. The sorbus family is still waiting for this
supposed attack from the West, but anyone who wants to imitate a
goose-foot design should consider no more than two varieties of tree.

I already had two. I had opted for a central avenue of hornbeam and outer avenues of an evergreen pear, *Pyrus calleryana* 'Chanticleer', chosen at random from a book. If a well-known garden centre had not supplied me with two back-up pears of the wrong variety, the outer avenues of 'Chanticleer', now four in all, would be perfect. Their combination with a central avenue of hornbeam is also good, but the hornbeam developed in unanticipated ways. Each tree was planted about three yards apart and between them I put a temporary filling of the scented *Philadelphus* 'Belle Étoile'. After twenty-two years, the philadelphuses are still only three feet high, hating the poor soil and the competition for water with the trees' roots. Last year, they were at their best, flowering freely near ground level before the trees put on a spurt in August and almost obliterated the light.

The downside is unexpected. In late April, the new leaves on all these trees open by the thousand in shades of fresh vivid green. They look unacceptably hectic in the middle distance until they mature and tone down. I had never expected the garden to be over-greened in this way. The visual counterweight should be strong red flowers, best found in oriental poppies or a vigorous Darwin tulip called 'Oxford', but they struggle to compete because the trees have matured, drying and shading the soil.

Before this excessively green phase, the pears flower so prolifically in early spring that at night they add an extra pale dimension to the light of the moon. Life with 'Chanticleer' pears is never dull. They lose their leaves very late in the year, and turn a brilliant shade of ruby, like an ageing professor after dinner, in a 'fall' which is often delayed until early December. Individually, the trees are stiff and upright in habit, but in groups they respond excellently to light clipping and will branch sideways into a continuous avenue if they are planted at intervals of three yards. Their best phase is from late July until November, when they have toned down and developed a charming, glossy sheen on their plain green leaves. Accept no substitutes for the 'Chanticleer' form of pear tree and enjoy watching its lower trunk swell with age, like the lower leg of a hard-worked horse.

My hornbeams are the regular *Carpinus betulus* 'Fastigiata', which is said in books to have an upright, fastigiate growth. In a way it does, but only after developing too much of a middle-aged spread. I have had to

My 'Hunter's Hand' avenues after a July trim

clip hard to keep the hornbeams upright and stop the width of bulge which develops in old specimens on roadsides. Nowadays, there is a truly upright hornbeam, *Carpinus betulus* 'Columnaris', which grows more slowly and would be more manageable. My original supplier, Landford Trees at Landford Lodge, Salisbury, Wiltshire, offers both varieties nowadays, but the choice was not available in 1987.

The formal patterns of these avenues look their best on ground which slopes gently away from the viewer so that they can be surveyed from a higher point. Maintenance was simple in the early stages. As I am not a believer in the organic fantasy, I made free and healthy use of weedkillers based on glyphosate, which are safe to apply between young trees because they are inactive when they fall on soil, not directly on leaves. The main commodities needed were patience and stability. It takes at least ten years for the effect of an avenue to develop and then you must allow time to cope with it. I fear I have now created a monster I cannot control. I am not willing to go up a ladder which is balanced on a fragile pear tree in order to cut a regular line for each avenue at a height of more than twenty feet. The more the trees are clipped on their sides, however, the more they grow up to the sky. The attempt to level them off has been the long-running drama of the past two summers and almost any equipment available for hire has a drawback in this situation. It is either so large that it squashes the intervening garden, or it refuses to work on a slope. I have come to rely on two expert tree-cutters whose jeep draws an ascending, powered platform for use among the central hornbeams.

On paper it may sound simple, but the hoist tends to sink into the ground in wet weather and the entire job takes a week, once every eighteen months. It is not cheap and for the workmen it is not pleasant. I am not giving up, because a *patte d'oie* or Hunter's Hand brings months of developing beauty and only a brief bout of spring frenzy. It is not an asset for anyone's old age and it leaves me wondering how our unmechanical Georgian ancestors cut the high hedges in their avenues so neatly. At Chiswick House or Versailles, they did not have a mechanical platform, but neither did they have officials for health and safety. When labour was cheap, standards of risk and expendability were ominously cheaper too.

A Year's Itinerary

While I wait for the first flower-buds on my avenues of pears I ask myself on cold wet days, if money and distance were not obstacles, what would be a good itinerary for a garden visitor in each month of the year? Fortunately I can think of so many different itineraries. They would begin in January and February with the sub-tropical gardens at Abbotsbury, near Weymouth, Dorset, a favoured site which has fine shrubs in flower throughout the early months. Maintained by the Ilchester Estate, the garden draws on more than a hundred years of intelligent planting, little of which we can grow in our colder gardens. I would also visit the Eric Young Orchid Foundation on Jersey, which deserves its prominent place on the island's postage stamps. The standards of flower and cultivation in this collection are unsurpassed, and if you coincide with the slight scent which rises from its slipper orchids, the paphiopedilums, under glass in early February, you enter paradise in your imagination. The next stop would be Cornwall. In our warmer winters the gardens at Caerhays near St Austell tend to hit their peak as early as mid-March. They remain the most stunning sight in the exotic world of magnolias, camellias and rhododendrons, because they include so many of the original collections from the Far East. They are also the home of many of the williamsii hybrid camellias, which have transformed the spring season of sheltered urban gardens. Despite the sea winds, a visit is unforgettable. On the return journey you should drop in at Trewithen, the masterly Cornish garden of the late George Johnstone, whose central walkways show the loveliest displays of camellias and mature rhododendrons.

In April, the destination would have to be Sissinghurst Castle in Kent. Repetition never stales the impression of the spring flowers in the section of the garden which Harold Nicolson regarded as his 'life's work'. In mid-April, you can admire the mixtures of so many small spring bulbs in the little beds beneath his long walk of pleached limes.

You can then go on to the superb clumps of white trilliums near the hazel trees, an area which used to be bedded out with polyanthus. In April, the coach parties, too, are fewer.

Further afield, I would hunt out the enchanting garden at Castello in Florence which is accessible from the city on a number 28 bus. It is open only in the mornings, but is closed on Mondays. Much of the enlarged plan which was laid here in the sixteenth century by the Medici family has vanished nowadays, but the box parterre has charm and the wide range of lemon trees in their terracotta pots are a memorable sight in their shelter-house in April. In the warm greenhouse on the east of the garden, the most sweetly scented variety of tender white jasmine was first cultivated. Nowadays, azaleas and some showy peonies brighten up the place, too, but it remains evocative and under-visited.

In May, my first choice is the Botanischer Garten in Munich, accessible by the city's number 2 tram to Nymphenburg. By mid-May, its enormous alpine garden is a mass of flowers on almost every outcrop of rock and in the main garden the central beds show a brilliant scattering of tulips and bedding in colours which we would not always risk in England. It remains the outstanding botanical garden in continental Europe. For a wilder note, my trail turns south to the matchless garden of Ninfa, two hours' drive to the south-west of Rome, when it is dripping with wisteria and the purple-blue flowers on its paulownias. American, English and Italian taste met as nowhere else here in the Caetani and Howard families across nearly a hundred years and made a garden among the ruined buildings of a medieval Italian township. Helped by the site's constant springs of water, it is still Italy's jewel.

In the third week of May, you may be beginning to dread the prospect of another Chelsea Flower Show. If so, prepare for it at the exquisite garden of Bagatelle in Paris, within easy reach of the city's centre and the Bois de Boulogne by metro and then a number 246 bus. From about 20 May onwards, the iris garden here is beautiful and already, the early roses will be bursting into flower while the fine Japanese peonies are open, too, on the far side of the house, leading down to the lake.

I recommend that you stay at home in June and celebrate, perhaps, with a visit to the impressive long borders at New College, Oxford,

The double borders at Kiftsgate Court in June

open every afternoon. As I plant and oversee them, I like to think they are a comfort to the suffering souls in the college while they sit their final exams. By late June, you should move on to Hampshire where the pair of long herbaceous borders at Bramdean House, near Alresford, mirror each other's colours and contents. They show you that much 'modernist' gardening is uglier and more boring than traditional herbaceous planting in the classic style. From mid-June onwards you should also go up to the great garden on the edge of the Cotswolds, Kiftsgate Court in Gloucestershire. Now in the third generation of the same family, it has been raised to even higher levels of sensitive planting by Anne and Johnny Chambers. The alstroemerias flower while the Chinese deutzias are setting buds in the formal Pool Garden. *Campanula latiloba* 'Highcliffe Variety' persists under tall trees, the Rosa mundi rose-hedge is magnificent and the rampant Kiftsgate rose is in full white flower on overpowering branches which run high up the trees and cover a width of hundreds of yards. This rose is a spectacle to be admired, but not imitated in gardens with less space for its aggressive vigour.

In July, I would go off to my favourite small garden, Helen Dillon's walled garden at Sandford Road in the Ranelagh district of Dublin. At that season her drooping dieramas are at their best and her two differently coloured borders complement each other down the length of what used to be the Dillons' perfect lawn. Go and see what the acknowledged queen of small hardy plants has done to her garden's grassy axis. At every turn, the small groupings of plants here are works of genius, beautifully grown and understood.

In August, I would choose the peaceful atmosphere and neat formality of Iford Manor near Bradford-on-Avon in Wiltshire, the Italianate garden of the thoughtful Edwardian architect Harold Peto, which I describe in more detail in my Autumn section. In the third week of September, I would go to the great sanctuary of the Michaelmas daisy, the Picton Garden at Old Court Nurseries, Colwall, to the south of Great Malvern. Its one-and-a-half acres are densely planted with autumn flowers, and on Michaelmas Day the huge sweeps of asters and accompanying daisies and rudbeckias provoke immediate envy. They are a brilliant example of a wild style of planting which is not confined to short-lived British wildflowers or stale shades of pink and mauve.

In October I am sure the trail ought to lead across to America to Vermont, but I know its maple forests only from television and cannot suggest more than a drive down the highways which are best known for the fall. In England, meanwhile, I am content to visit the changing colours at Westonbirt Arboretum in Gloucestershire. In November, the route bends back to the RHS garden at Wisley in Surrey to see the greenhouse-displays of formally trained chrysanthemums which tumble on wires in the shapes of sprays and fountains. They set the standards for all growers who have the energy to fight off whitefly in a cool chrysanthemum-greenhouse.

December is in no way a postscript. In the weeks before and after Christmas, the spectacular gardens at Longwood in Pennsylvania remain the most brilliant display of indoor plants and exterior lighting in the world. Longwood is twelve miles north of Wilmington, Delaware, and although it has the resources of the Dupont Foundation to support it, it sets a yearly example which justifies every cent of the $20 million expense. It reminds us that darkness is not universal in winter

The double borders at Bramdean House in June

Poinsettia patterns in one room of Longwood Garden's Christmas display

in the world of gardening. In its East and Main Conservatories the bedding-out for Christmas is a thoughtful revelation. Multi-coloured cyclamen and unusually coloured poinsettias are massed with brilliantly unseasonal white snapdragons, the rare plume-flowered *Euphorbia fulgens* and an enchanting heather, I promise, called *Erica canaliculata* with tiny white flowers. Running through them is one of the garden's hallmarks, the spikes of true blue flowers on lovely *Plectranthus thyrsoideus*, not displayed in British botanical gardening. From the showers of wild orchids to the Brazilian plantings of the great Burle Marx, Longwood is the pinnacle of practical, artistic gardening.

If you follow this trail, you will be horticulturally broadened and financially stretched. Alternatively, you could make these visits one by one over the next few years. Meanwhile, I will have regrouped and, like you, come up with another twelve which are irresistible too.

I Spy a Hyena

For those of us who stay at home, heavy snowfalls are increasingly rare in British gardeners' experience of late winter. When one hit our gardens recently, it gave them a fortnight of night-time visibility, like an x-ray in reverse. For the first time I saw what really goes on in my garden after midnight. I did not like the look of it at all.

The action began sweetly and for the first two days I felt sentimental. In the snow on the lawn two unidentified animals, surely fluffy and furry, were imprinting their uninvited tracks. From opposite ends of the garden they drew irresistibly closer. They described two little circles and over-lapped under one of the garden arches on which a white-flowered wisteria flowers in May. I pictured two happy rabbits taking time off work because snow had blocked their usual commute to their feeding-grounds. I even imagined wisteria as the animal equivalent of mistletoe under which the two of them had stopped and lovingly brushed whiskers.

On the third day there were yet more signs of these visitors. Snowed into my home, I went out in gumboots to investigate and I need only say here that it seemed they had not stopped at kissing. Feeling slightly envious, I trudged back indoors. I expected that the evening would see a snow-melt and that the cumbersome traces of my gumboots among the lovers' footprints would have disappeared by dawn. Instead, snow fell so deeply that even a buck rabbit abandoned the joy of sex in a snowdrift.

The snowfall glistened so crisply on the following day that I should have brushed it off my ceanothus. I did not, because I wanted to see another print-out in white of the garden's lovelife without human foot-prints to spoil it. In my mind's eye I remembered the classic Alfred Hitchcock film *Rear Window*. Signs of disturbance in the garden alerted Hitchcock's onlooker to a crime in his backyard. I would be a front-window detective on the morning after, not a voyeur from the rear.

The night-time duly saw some action but not of the kind I expected. Tracks proliferated from all directions and love had evidently taken flight. There were two hares, three rabbits, some impudent foxes, and the tracks to and fro of a badger. A cluster of paw-prints converged on streaks of blood and feathers where the corpse of a pigeon had been ripped open. No respect had been shown to the flowerbeds. A gang of beasts had run straight through my Michaelmas daisies and had relieved themselves on my favourite *Cistus × laxus* 'Snow White'. Are our gardens treated in this way every night while gardeners are peacefully asleep? These tracks make a nonsense of the Royal Horticultural Society's promotion of the garden as a 'haven' for wildlife. I want plants in my garden, not bloody-minded badgers, and I do not see how a haven is the right description for a space in which wildlife rips its fellow members to bits. Suspicions intensified when I bent down on one knee and started to analyse the tracks. Badgers are unmistakable and after fifty years of chasing foxes I am not going to be deceived about them. The problem was a deep-clawed imprint. It was not a cuddly squirrel. It had led the assault on the pigeon and had dragged the carcase away from the crime. I sketched the footprint on an old seed packet and went indoors to check in a book.

It was no use looking in books about Winnie-the-Pooh. It was certainly not a Wizzle and the claws ruled out a Woozle. From long ago I have a chart called *I-Spy Tracks*, a relic of the days in newspaper history when Big Chief I-Spy set competitions from his wigwam in central London and asked for them to be solved by young readers like myself. Big Chief I-Spy agreed with me that the claws were not a badger's. The near-perfect fit was a hyena.

I know you do not believe that hyenas live in the Cotswolds. Are you sure? Yellow-eyed big cats have been sighted in Wales around Lampeter and nobody knows what they are. Mad enthusiasts are trying to introduce beavers into the north of Britain. Sadists want to re-establish wolves in Northumberland. One of my Oxford colleagues even wants to release lynxes to kill off competing animals in the Home Counties. Has a human scientist already let out a hyena? Sabre-toothed hyenas were only too active in prehistoric Somerset, because their bones have been found in the caves at Wookey Hole. In the 1820s Oxford's Reader in Geology, the thoughtful William Buckland, used to mesmerize his undergraduates by waving the bone of a hyena to illustrate his lectures. Kirkdale Cave in Yorkshire had just been opened and found to contain teeth and bones which Buckland recognized as relics of elephants, rhinoceroses, hippos and hyenas. Biblicists argued that the animals had been sheltering from

God's Flood, but Buckland pointed to the toothmarks on many of the bones. They belonged, he argued, to a den of antediluvian hyenas who had dined on the beasts in the cave. Where are those hungry hyenas nowadays? Only the print-out of a rare snowfall allows us to see what animal games go on after midnight. Hyenas may well hide by day and come out at night when badgers invite them to a cocktail party with canapés dipped in blood. With due respect to the RHS, I do not want a haven for hyenas. I want happy gentians and my own spinach.

As the light faded I was ever so slightly nervous inside my barricaded home. I listened to Prime Minister's Question Time on the radio and I think the exchanges must have drifted into my dreams. After dawn I woke to find yet more claw-tracks and churned snow, two more headless pigeons and a trail of cloven hoofprints on top of the best agapanthus. They had arrived in the week of the stimulus package for failing financiers. Evidently, the animal kingdom had taken a stimulus package of its own. What, I wondered, are the political affiliations of these animal offenders? It may have been Prime Minister's Questions which caused me to pose this problem, but I found myself recalling a classic exchange in the first of those parliamentary debates about 'hunting with dogs'. The late Nicholas Ridley began it with a chilling description to the House of Commons of a stoat in his Tewkesbury constituency. Ridley had witnessed it, he told them, mesmerizing a rabbit and then shredding it to pieces in cold blood. His conclusion was that animals of such brutality should be hunted without scruple. He was answered from the far left by Tony Benn, congratulating Ridley, a Thatcherite apostle of jungle law in economics, for realizing at last that the jungle needed regulation.

There is no regulation in my garden after midnight and plainly the law of the jungle lives on. My academic colleagues in Oxford liked to equate Margaret Thatcher with C. S. Lewis's White Queen, ruling in Narnia in a realm of frozen snow. If you have been wondering where Thatcherites have gone in the latest economic crisis, the answer is they are out there in the wilderness, celebrating in our garden-havens when a snowfall reminds them of their Queen's old days. I know you still find the hyena hard to credit. Admittedly, Big Chief I-Spy's chart was printed before the muntjak was known in British gardens and its hoofprints may need to be taken into account. Meanwhile, I am sticking to my hyena theory, and a right-wing hyena at that. Naturally it is laughing the whole way to the nearest unregulated bank.

On the Dutch Dealing Floor

During the animal activities of this early February, cut flowers sent me on a different track. After flowering for four incredible weeks since Christmas, the pollen and petals of my pale pink lilies at last collapsed and went from their vase to a well-earned grave. Where do these prolonged performers come from? I discreetly asked their provider and traced them back to their source.

The trail took me at 6.30 a.m. through driving rain to the heart of Europe's floral industry, the sheds at Aalsmeer in Holland. They are just down the road from Amsterdam's Schiphol airport and are not a usual haunt for an Oxford don who has not yet had a cooked breakfast. Aalsmeer is the biggest warehouse area in Holland, with a floor space of more than a million square yards, criss-crossed by ten miles of railway lines under cover. It supplies many of the cut flowers which in Britain we believe to be fresh. It makes Covent Garden Market look like a secondary parasite.

Ever alert to the problems of a female readership, I believe I have hit on the perfect solution for grumbling husbands. Suppose you are married to an over-age broker, the sort of man who is still unable to accept the Big Bang, that shockwave which eliminated face-to-face dealing on the floor of the old London Stock Exchange and the lunch hours which followed with his male friends. What can you do with him when, deep down, he is still expecting you to cook him a three-course lunch as graciously as the debutantes who used to enliven his London office? Here is the answer. Enrol him in a crash course in the Dutch language and pack him off to Aalsmeer.

He has no idea what heaven awaits him. There are eight old-fashioned dealing rooms, each with 200 traders who long to test their wits against new arrivals. They will give him his own personal red and yellow button and expect him to revive his skills of mental arithmetic without use of the dreaded computer. Every plant and flower on offer

The pricing clocks in the dealing room at Aalsmeer

is propelled through the dealing room on a sort of adult train set. He can bid for the coaches one by one, placing his bets according to a fast-moving clock whose face is so big that even middle-aged eyes behind spectacles can make out the numbers. They will look bewildering at first, but he will soon realize that the numbers on the lower right refer to the cut flowers' quality and length of stem. The middle bands give the numbers in each lot and a rapidly travelling light marks the bidding price by zooming round the face of the clock.

There is one further advantage. The prices are agreed like the prices of investments when one tries to sell them by telephone. They go downwards, not upwards. At Aalsmeer, if he misses the first press of the button, he will get a second chance. Quite often the price is still falling and he will gain by having made his mistake. No smart little jobber will then bid him up to teach him a lesson. If he presses the wrong button and buys a load of flowers which he does not want, he will have a big bunch of Valentines to take home for the wives and girlfriends in his flirtatious history.

I now come to the part which he will find irresistible. Every single dealer in each of the clock-rooms is a man. Two women, Riet, say, and Anya, stand down on the stage, pointing out the loads on offer to the males in the seats above. Most of the bidders are early-to-middle-aged Dutchmen who seem to be doing almost nothing. After doing it they go out into the waiting room and smoke like chimneys.

Prices tend to stabilize after the first hour, and from 8 a.m. until 11 a.m. the dealings in cut flowers run within an established range of day-trading, settling into limits for which new bidders are not wholly responsible. Do not underestimate the scale of the operation, although entry is for dealers only. They pay €650 for a yearly card after proving the existence of a cash-pile in their bank accounts, and in a single morning they help about 21 million flowers and pot plants to find new owners. The Aalsmeer market recently merged with its only equal, Flora Holland. The merger began in 2008 and the joint venture now turns over the huge sum of €4 billion of perishable stock.

Naturally, some of it is hideous. As I watched, truckloads of my worst floral enemies were being sold off at prices between €0.29 and €0.24 per stem. If you are buying in thousands, those marginal points make a difference. On stage, Anya and Riet point to truckloads of sea lavender and a merry sort of sunflower called *Helianthus* 'Sunrich'. They sell in 20 seconds and the next carriage-load is full of *Solidago* 'Tara Gold'. From the Netherlands, the British import about €650 million worth of cut flowers each year, but even so, they are beaten by the insatiable Swiss, Norwegians and Austrians. Perhaps the British total should be increased by adding all the flowers which our super-markets fly in from Kenya, Uganda and Israel. Even so, there is no escaping the Dutch. Flowers come to Aalsmeer from these same sources, because Dutch growers are out there organizing the trade. More than 16,000 varieties pass through the Dutch sheds every year, and it is impressive how much of the stock at auction still originates in the Netherlands, where more than 6,000 growers specialize in cultivating it under glass.

In 1997, there were fantasy plans for a link by underground tunnels between the flower market and Schiphol airport so that flowers could travel even faster to and fro. This Dutch tunnel vision has never been realized. Meanwhile, like the Dutch, I hope the streamlined enterprise continues to thrive. The business is run as a cooperative, which would normally fill onlookers with foreboding, but the structure suits the Dutch temperament. It caters for yearly variations in profit and the likelihood of a small return on most years' turnover. About 3,000 members submit to careful controls of quality and pay transaction costs of about 5 per cent on the value of loads which are bought by their buzzers. This flower market is the least promising business for a private equity buy-out, but in confidential rooms I saw the secrets which keep it ahead of rivals in China or Dubai. Seventy quality inspectors grade and assure the classing of all the goods which go up on the clock. Any new variety must be submitted by its grower for testing before stock is auctioned. On long benches I saw specimen vases of the new cut flowers of the future which were being controlled at room temperatures and observed for their ability to persist. Nowadays, I found with regret, cut-flower roses have to be bred without scent if they are to last long enough for their demanding clients indoors. I can well understand why my Dutch-auctioned lilies persist for four weeks in water. Breeders and judges have been striving to establish such long-lasting varieties.

Would I consider premature retirement to one of the floral floors? I hate an early start and I hate cigarette smoke. I will stay put because I like the mixed smiles of male and female pupils beneath the non-commercial clock of an Oxford library.

Wild on the Broadwalk

Like those dealers in the Dutch market, we all divide our lives into separate compartments. In our biographical cabinets, one drawer is for family and others for friends; one for facts, now partly forgotten, and others for fantasies, perhaps more than we recognize. What happens if we break down the barriers which keep the compartments apart? We have heard so much about joined-up government, and yet the results seem even more detached from reality. What about joined-up living?

In 2003 I joined up three of the least-related compartments in my personal space. They are not an obvious unity. One is gardening, especially in botanical gardens. Another is horses, especially with stirrups, and the third is my lifelong fascination with the history of Alexander the Great. In sweaty Thailand, I galloped wildly on horse-back for Alexander's sake through a big botanical garden, unlisted and unrecognized by Britain's RHS. I have not lost my grip on reality. It truly happened, thanks to that queen of illusion, a motion picture for the big screen. First in Morocco, and finally in Thailand, I played my part in Alexander's cavalry, loyal to my superstar Colin Farrell, under the guidance of our god Dionysus, the inimitable Oliver Stone, director of the epic Alexander film.

I doubt if any other gardening columnist has left hoof-prints among the trees of a botanical forest. They have certainly never made them to camera, surrounded by the cavalry of the King of Thailand. Our location was described in my script as 'jungle', but Dionysus never told me that his jungle would be man-made and that he was asking me to attack an enemy concealed by the work of 150 gardeners who had been planting and watering the venue for three months. I shared in the attack from the back of a horse, first a black one, then a chestnut one, complete with leathery horse-blankets made from the hide of an 'upholstery cow'. We charged in the Phukae Botanic Garden, a gigantic park some sixty miles outside Bangkok.

On days of duty, I would gallop into battle for my squadron leader Hephaestion, while his beloved Alexander urged us onwards for the sake of immortal glory. I detest almost every form of ornamental grass, but as our squadron waited to career through the woods, workers with mattocks and pitchforks bedded clumps of chunky grasses along our route to make its course seem even more rough and natural. While stuntmen bumped into the tree trunks, I had time to check the botanical labels which were whizzing past my horse's bridle on the intervening branches. In Thailand, January is the dry season, but the botany of the Phukae garden has a scope and range which leave my expertise floundering. Specimens with names like spondias and diospyros mean nothing to an English provincial mind. Even if you have seen a schleichera in leaf, I bet you have never galloped through one so that the tips of its branches brush your silvered cavalry helmet.

Western gardeners know nothing about this extraordinary botanical garden. In the Saraburi province, it is a vast expanse of state-maintained greenery, divided in two by a busy out-of-town road. On one side, I explored on foot its huge expanse of clipped box topiary, in which grey boulders were arranged like units in an oriental army. In the intervening spaces there was nothing but pine trees and vivid bougainvilleas. Elsewhere I recognized a tamarind tree, but the rest of the planting baffled me, not least because a cohort of busy Thai ladies continued to spray it with hoses while failing to grasp my questions in sign language. The only guide to this side of the garden is a big green model at its entrance which shows acres of unnamed treetops. Across the road, however, the trees in the other section are arranged in orderly botanical families, ranging from Ebonies to Guttiferous and Leguminous plants. Our army's base camp was beside the section of Euphorbias, the family whose plants squirted juice into the eyes of Alexander's horses in the ancient Iranian desert and rendered them blind. My black cavalry charger kept his head up and I think from the map that we had to gallop in the section which the garden-model called Dilleniaceae.

Perhaps I will now be asked to gallop down the Broad Walk in Kew Gardens. I am not sure that I recommend a close exploration of a jungle imported for Hollywood. The danger is not that the green bananas and accompanying bamboos will begin to turn brown when the season warms up. It is that their jungle was the cover for an array of elephants, equipped with tusk-extensions and ferocious female mahouts. The plants in the man-made jungle had been chosen to be elephant-compatible so that the beasts would not uproot and eat them on their first battle-charge. Instead, they sheltered in its canopy of vivid green until they emerged towards our horses and dared us to take them on.

The film shows some of the results, but it does not show the botanical labelling. Nor does it show how a horse gallops off to the left when an elephant begins to charge it. It also does not show a thoughtful gardener's fury in battle. On flights to Thailand, the airlines show a film to passengers about animals in films, entitled *Wild on Set*. It is now obsolete. It has nothing about the latest wild animal, a historian on horseback, charging through trees which he cannot recognize despite fifty years of English gardening.

The Lettuce Farm Palace

More than thirty years before this cavalry service in a Thai botanical forest, I had visited Thailand and reported on my visits round private Bangkok gardens. I met and learned from their presiding spirit, the expatriate American William Warren, who held the honoured position of gardening columnist on the *Bangkok World* newspaper. My visit fell in Thailand's rainy season and for much of the day my wife and I were marooned in a small hotel room, at whose bare wooden table I wrote my account of the crowning victory against elephants which was won by Alexander the Great in north-west India. In the afternoons, I would meet with Thailand's most perceptive gardener, Pimsai Amranand, sadly now dead from a random attack in her house by an armed intruder. My text on Alexander has been more fortunate. It played a part in the filming of *Alexander*, for whose sake I returned to Bangkok to re-enact the very elephant-battle which I had written up in the city.

After my first visit I remembered how my garden hosts had regretted that it had not been possible to meet Thailand's most distinguished gardener, a princess of the royal house. On my return visit, Alexander's filming schedule took a break on a Sunday and the cavalrymen were left to amuse themselves. I chose a trip to the first place which my guidebook to Bangkok mentioned as a garden with a 'tranquil retreat'. Its name was Wang Suan Phakkat, which means the Lettuce Farm Palace. The one keen gardener in the film production was the set decorator, whose last assignment had been on *Seven Years in Tibet*. Together, we set off for three hours in a Lettuce Farm.

If I believed in the gods, I might think that I was being guided. Here I had returned, fighting for a film-army in the very battle whose history I had first written up in Thailand. Here I was, too, pushing open the gate of what turned out to be the lovingly tended garden of the late Princess Chumbhot, the princess whom I had missed on my previous visit. The Lettuce Farm Palace has a heartening origin. In 1932, the Thai royal family was deposed and the family members had to go into exile. Among them was the young Princess Chumbhot, who left with her parents for England and stayed there for the next five years. Most of the family's properties were taken away from them, and when the surviving family members returned to Bangkok, they chose to reside on ground surrounded by simple allotments, a virgin site. They bought a few of the neighbouring plots and over the years they developed their ordinary surroundings into the separate houses which now cluster around their Lettuce Farm residence. Their plot of ground received a pavilion from a temple site in the countryside, and around it four groups of traditional houses became filled with items from the royal collection and relics of the prince's passion for music. There was also a garden in which the young Princess Chumbhot decided to work with her own hands.

Among the allotments on a Bangkok lane, the influence of gardening seen in England has left an unexpected mark. During her exile in England, the princess had learnt that English gardens like to show off their flowers and trees. Her love of flowering plants blossomed and during the next forty years she assembled a variety of trees, shrubs and courtyard gardens in Bangkok which are still a credit to her taste. She had a Far Eastern love of rocks and artistically arranged stones. She planted brilliant water lilies in tubs. She imported flowering specimens which Thai gardeners had never seen. Each of her visits abroad led to an addition to her garden's collection. I found myself struggling with botanical families which I had never encountered before. Quassia is a striking plant with scarlet spikes of flower, and if only the weather in Oxford was warmer, I would cherish an ochua with rounded cream-yellow flowers.

By a roundabout route, I had returned to the missing piece of my previous visit to Bangkok. What was the princess like? In the small accompanying museum, I found the final piece in the jigsaw, an appreciation of her by my previous host in Thailand, the gardening columnist of the *Bangkok World*. William Warren emphasized how she worked in the garden herself and knew and planted everything in it. She would call herself, laughingly, the simple housewife, Mrs Wigg of the Cabbage Patch. There was nothing of the Castle of Mey about her

Tabebuia chrysotricha, Princess Chumbhot's pride and joy

or the arm's-length extravagance of England's Queen Mother. In William Warren's view, the princess resented the lack of education which had befallen her as a Thai princess. She corrected it by constant reading, travelling and talking. In 1976, Bangkok was shaken by a student revolution which was repressed very forcefully by the police. William Warren remembered calling on the princess in her garden house that afternoon and finding her weeping over a tin of Iranian caviar. As she watched the events unfolding on television, she exclaimed through her tears: 'Idiots, dumb idiots.' He then realized that she was referring to the police.

From palace to cabbage patch, the princess's route turned out to be one of enlightenment. Exile turned her to gardening, England inspired her and she returned to lay out the neatest town garden in a Bangkok setting which would have worn down a less flexible mind. If we had met thirty years before, I might perhaps have recognized orchids like *Cymbidium simulans*, which is still growing in her trees. It would have been fun to learn about the blue-flowered eranthemum and to discuss the very different art with which she arranged her personal rock garden, so different to ours in the English tradition.

Some twenty-five years after her death, the gardens are still open daily from 9 a.m. to 4 p.m. If you can decipher Bangkok's number 3 bus, it stops right outside the gate. There are always good things in flower, but I doubt if you will recognize more of them than I could. You will certainly not recognize a wonderful yellow-flowered variety of the pink trumpet tree, which is otherwise known as tabebuia. Only a week before Princess Chumbhot died, she was delighted by the flowering of this yellow beauty. It was the only one known in a gardener's care. As my two trips to Bangkok joined up and came full circle, I honoured the thoughtful gardener who transferred herself from a throne-room to a simple allotment and left a permanent mark of beauty on her world.

Christopher Lloyd

For even more years than Bangkok and its elusive princess, a great
fellow garden writer has been a guiding force in my life. In his absence
I share with many gardeners the sense that there is a hole in the mixed
border of our lives. Christopher Lloyd died in February 2006 after
nearly eighty years of gardening. He was the acknowledged king of
garden writers and one of the most influential masters of practical
gardening in all its forms. He was the most thoughtful of gardeners
and his thoughts had a frequent edge to them.

Lloyd's Sussex garden at Great Dixter remains a living testimony
to his distinctive eye and tireless mind. He wrote profusely, delighting
weekly readers of *Country Life* magazine for more than forty years.
His admirers multiplied in the last twenty years of his life, as he set an
inspiring example of the irrelevance of 'retirement' to serious human
beings. Like the ancient wise man Solon, Christopher grew old,
'always learning much'. He delighted in the company of the young
and made his home an open house for younger visitors, whatever their
background, if they loved plants and nature. He even became an
American icon, a status reinforced by his own visits to the States and
his lucid, but unpredictable, lectures.

He was a distinctive person formed at a distinctive time and his
death left me with a sense that one of the last titans in the field has
gone. People always think that, a younger colleague consoled me,
when the masters of their earlier days have died. I do not think this
view is correct. There were unrepeatable reasons why Christopher
was a commanding example. His distinctive eye and style led to scores
of distinctive anecdotes. I fielded or caused quite a few of them in my
years as a writer on gardening.

Christopher Lloyd began with an advantage enjoyed by few
gardeners nowadays. He lived throughout his life in the fine house
in which he was born and so he never had to lay out a garden from

scratch. One of the concerns of his later life was to keep this property together and pass it on through a complex web of family ownership. The main beneficiary was his niece, who then sold her part-share to a Trust backed by a big grant from the Heritage Lottery Fund, matched by funding from other sources. Nearby Dixter Farm has now been bought for teaching and the housing of students, and an extra car park is now available too. Christopher would be pleased, because he had capitalized on his fame for the sake of the garden's future, remaining both coy and amused by the results. In later life he auctioned superfluous items from Dixter and made himself inconspicuous in his gardening clothes in the garden during the sale. Nonetheless he was not displeased that even his trowel, though almost defunct, went to an American buyer for £200.

Christopher was born in 1921 and was brought up, the youngest of six children, in a strict household. He rapidly found his life's work outdoors. His father, Nathaniel, was an able architect, and was very close to Sir Edwin Lutyens, whose designs were important for the Dixter house. His mother, the remarkable Daisy, makes sporadic appearances in Christopher's gardening books and left a lasting impression on his personality and outlook. He was twelve when his father died but he continued living with his mother until her death in 1972: there were moments of petulance, but their relations remained very close, central to each other's lives. Daisy had an independent spirit too. After a visit to Austria in her early years, she surprised surrounding society in Sussex by wearing an Austrian dirndl for much of her remaining life. Daisy was an extremely keen gardener and she recalled how her son soon began to work with her outdoors. At the age of seven he could name many plants in the garden. She and her husband were friends of the great Miss Jekyll and used to visit her famous Surrey garden where Christopher was presented to her as a keen boy-gardener. Inadvertently Miss Jekyll authorized him, commanding him to 'go on with the good work'. She gave Dixter four fine plants of the spiky *Yucca gloriosa* but his mother moved them away for fear that the pointed leaves might damage one of her children.

Christopher grew up to be extremely sharp himself. He benefited from a clear mind and a Cambridge education but he combined them with a practical devotion to gardening, not just to garden-watching.

Christopher Lloyd with matching *Verbena bonariensis* at Dixter

His classic book is *The Well-Tempered Garden*, still one of the funda-mental texts for gardeners. The imperious designer Russell Page was one of those who remarked to me that it was a pity that it was a book by such an ill-tempered gardener. Nothing could be less true. Chris-topher was not bad-tempered. He was irreverent and mischievous but was always prepared to give credit where he owed it. In reply, he described Page's own admired book, *The Education of a Gardener*, as an education in arrogance, not gardening.

Visits by Christopher to one's own garden were unpredictable and were famous for leaving a sting behind. Eventually he paid a visit to one of the few practising gardeners who is a match for him, Helen Dil-lon in Dublin. She let him go out alone into her stunning garden at the back of her town house in Sandford Road and watched while he went down on one knee, ignored its brilliant planting and merely looked over the garden wall. When he came inside, he told her: 'Helen, your neighbour has a very interesting kind of holm oak.'

She was not deterred: 'Christopher,' she replied, 'I have a friend in America who has two dachshunds. She has named one "Christopher" and the other "Lloyd".'

Christopher loved dachshund dogs and made the reputation of his own beloved Tulip through fond references to him in his writings. 'I am very honoured,' he replied.

'So you should be,' she retorted, 'they are both bitches.'

I heard the story in similar terms from both of them. It was the beginning of their much-appreciated friendship.

Christopher was impatient with garden-owners who presented themselves as great gardeners even though they were busy with another main occupation and employed gardeners to do the work. In several pointed newspaper articles, he would describe his visit to a well-known owner's garden but mention the owner only in passing, if at all. Instead he would describe in detail the working gardener who was really in charge. He then took his readers round the garden in the gardener's company, as if the owner had nothing to do with it. Some-times, he underestimated the owners' commitment and how much they had contributed in spite of the pressures of other work. Once he described in dry detail a visit to the excellent garden of a former managing director of Pearson, the owners of the *Financial Times*, during which his host drew aside to clip a dead-head off a pink 'Frau Dagmar' rose and put it into an accompanying basket. 'I admired the pretence,' Christopher wrote, unjustly. His comment was still remembered with irritation ten years later.

Underneath these barbs lay the fact that he was a gardener who believed in gardening, at a time when gardens were fashionable but when practical, detailed work in them was in retreat. In keeping with this belief, he liked opinionated writing if he felt that it was based on observation and so I was pleased to receive an encouraging letter from him only two months after beginning to write in the *Financial Times*. I was a young nothing and he was already the experienced master but he was taken with my heartfelt assault on the nation's fondness for heather, a plant I detested in gardens. Both of us, he kindly added, owed our jobs as journalists to the support of Arthur Hellyer, then the maestro of practical journalism who wrote both for the *FT* and *Country Life*, where he had helped to appoint Christopher as a columnist. Time passed, however, and tetchiness took over. There was even a phase when whatever I wrote in the *FT* was challenged at length by Christopher in the next issue of *Country Life*. I continue to dislike the prickly purple-leaved form of berberis, but I bless it for one unattested virtue. I had written that it was a dreary plant, best suited to the gardens of a provincial hotel, whereupon Christopher wrote at length in defence of hotel gardens and purple leaves and against people who put other gardeners off. I had just bought a house with an over-developed berberis of the purple kind, so I dug it up and sent it to him by Parcel Post, telling him that I hoped he would appreciate the prickles. I had a letter back saying that he would now apply for en suite bathrooms and turn Great Dixter into a hotel.

The skirmish, which only he sustained, then fastened at random on my approval of a low-growing carpeting plant called *Phuopsis stylosa*. Christopher protested in his *Country Life* article for the following week that I had never even mentioned that it smelt of foxes but that he was not surprised as I was only a university lecturer at Oxford and had no idea what a fox smelt like. It was a badly aimed shot because my life has been divided between gardening and fox-hunting and I have scented many more of the furry adversaries than Christopher had even seen in a picture book. A truce was called and ten years later I accepted his generous invitation to Dixter.

In late August, I coincided there with the last hours on earth of his famous dachshund Tulip, who was wrapped in a blanket and looking doleful, like his master. Even so, it was not all a time of melancholy. In later age, Christopher flourished on duets with his own working gardeners, one of whom, Romke, marked a new theme in Christopher's writing. He began to feature in Christopher's articles as a foil for Christopher's own sparring. When Romke left, there was a bleak winter and a slight downturn as the ageing Christopher had to cope with a garden on heavy clay and a vacancy at its head. In 1988, the gap was wonderfully filled by the young Fergus Garrett. Christopher told me he had first noticed Fergus while showing a party of students round his mixed border. He had made a characteristically teasing remark about the colour of Fergus's hair. Fergus gave a smart reply and, on seeing his talent, Christopher ended by bringing him to work at Dixter. It was an inspired combination, which also spilled over into the weekly articles, where Fergus acquired an ever-stronger presence. He transformed his patron's remaining years.

No sooner had I arrived at Dixter than I was taken out to visit the garden with the likelihood of a testing question while we walked round. Christopher had grown up when good taste in colour in gardens was being set by a country-house class who dismissed many shades as fit only for the lower orders. He had a principled objection to such narrowness and linked it to his intelligent war on convention. The colours in Dixter's longest border could be challenging, one reason why his first book, *The Mixed Border*, published in 1957, took some years to make a mark.

As we walked around, I held up my end, but marvelled at the exact, short answers which he gave to almost any question which occurred to him or me. He had the eye of a practised naturalist, alert to capsid bugs on the young shoots of a fatsia, and no less to the reasons why some, but not all, shrubby hebes have a hardy strain in their breeding. Dixter's old orchard was an early example of natural, 'meadow' gardening long before 'wildflower gardening' was pushed at us as a fashion. Christopher's supreme virtue was his exploration of the line between garden plants and plants regarded as 'wild' or only fit for nature. His range of knowledge here was encyclopaedic. He was able to look at neglected plants like woodruff or the lovely low-growing paris with sharp discrimination. He insisted, as I do, that all gardening, even wild gardening, is basically a pretence. We simulate 'Nature', our own human concept. We do not obey it.

In summer at Dixter mornings started early, with a pre-breakfast survey of the garden before 7 a.m. On my visit we stopped beneath a magnificent clematis, *flammula* I think, and Christopher told me with typical mischief that Graham Thomas had dismissed it as a second-rate variety. It looked stunning, and from the surrounding greenery Fergus emerged, weeding skilfully. We talked amiably but, as we turned to go, Christopher remarked that the tips of the left-hand edge of this enormous wall-plant were showing the first signs of wilt and should be sprayed in the next few hours. I had never even noticed them. He exemplified the view that you get as much out of gardening as you put into it. As a boy he had asked the great Miss Jekyll why her clumps of the lovely blue poppy were so big. 'Because I water them twice a day,' she replied. Bits of these poppies lived on for years in his own beds at Dixter.

Lunch, as usual, was cooked on an unmodernized stove with an obsolete buff finish. Christopher grew to love cooking, often with ingredients from the garden, but as Tulip approached death under his dog blanket, his owner drew aside and consoled himself by telling me why women are 'never any good' as garden designers. They cannot see the middle distance, he claimed. The result is a muddle of flowers without form in the foreground. I do not think that his dog's plight was clouding his sincerity.

People had a way of playing into Christopher's hands. I cherish the article in which he corrected Miss Jekyll at her most famous. She would describe how, every year, she would go out into her wood and say thanks to God because 'June is here, lovely June'. Christopher justly observed that June is a poor month in woodland as it is full of flies. The late spring shrubs are over and she really ought to have gone there in May. Women, however, could take their revenge. I once went with an enthusiastic American lady to Dixter who found Christopher by the cold frame and greeted him effusively, 'Mr Lloyd, when I last came I bought the most marvellous tin of beeswax polish for my banisters from your lovely lady wife: may I meet her and buy another?' 'She's not here,' Christopher replied with glee. Her very existence was out of the question. That same summer, I had heard how in his late seventies Christopher had been in an elevated botanical group which was assessing some of the garden beds at Kew. A young gardener with his shirt off was digging nearby, and Christopher peeled away from the group and kissed him wholeheartedly. He returned to the botanists as if nothing had happened, and made the most penetrating observation on the classification of ornamental grasses. Shortly after, the tails on his big topiary peacock birds at Dixter were docked by an intruder. Many of us enjoyed speculating who had done it and why.

Christopher loved the *FT*, especially when the music and opera critics were prominent. During one recasting of the Saturday paper, I investigated whether he would like to write on the same page, side by side with myself. The purple berberis had ceased to prickle. He said he would be delighted, but the then page editor had never heard of him and decided that a writer over seventy would be past his best. He even wrote bluntly and told Christopher as much. Christopher then refuted him by writing better than ever in *Country Life* for the next fifteen years. I regret it, because I would have been teased, corrected and greatly improved each week. He would have learned to keep off the subject of foxes.

Jardin Majorelle

Like the sale of Great Dixter and its owner's gardening accessories, the sale in Paris of the designer Yves Saint Laurent's effects in February 2009 did not pass quietly into history. The prices soared above anything so mundane as a global economic crisis. The Chinese then disputed the legal title to objects which once stood in the royal palace in old Beijing. Myself, I remembered an item which never came under the hammer: the garden in Morocco.

The Villa Oasis in Marrakech was acquired by Saint Laurent and his partner Pierre Bergé in 1980I. It stood in what was the quarter then known as Serenity and came with seven acres of grounds. In 2008 Saint Laurent died after more than a decade spent largely in the villa's calm. By 2006 Bergé was estimating that the small part of the garden which is open to the public had attracted 660,000 visitors in a year. It has become one of the most visited gardens in the world.

When I saw it five years before Yves Saint Laurent's death I was almost alone among rare cactuses and bamboos, figs, cycads, and flowerpots painted in a famous shade of blue. The paths were discreetly designed beside canals and pools of water and the latticed garden pavilion to which they led had a certain charm. In the burning heat of Morocco it seemed delightful that someone so famous had made a garden with such intelligently chosen plants. I had never worn anything in the least Saint Laurent but my opinion of his taste rose with my awareness of his garden.

When I visited I had no idea that the garden is not all about Yves. It belongs in a distinctive phase of his life but it also belongs in the story of a previous French expatriate, the artist Jacques Majorelle. Remarkably, it connects with each of their boyhoods, a time which is so often a source of the best-loved gardens. Majorelle used his boyhood to escape from his dominant father, whereas Saint Laurent never fully escaped his admiring mother. The Morocco garden connects, too, with the years of sadness and despondency which each of them lived through and confronted in its grounds.

Bergé once said that Saint Laurent, his long-term lover, was 'a man of exceptional intelligence practising the trade of an imbecile'. If so, the imbecility is remarkably interesting. Much of what I know about it derives from the excellent biography by Alice Rawsthorn, former *Financial Times* correspondent in Paris. In 1996 she published the story both of Saint Laurent's life and of his financial involvement with Bergé, his devoted promoter. I like the timeline with which she concludes. It is not a gardener's usual reading but it enables me to state that the Marrakech garden was acquired thirteen years after Saint Laurent's safari look and his designer duffel-coats in honour of Paris's student rioters (1968), ten years after he posed naked except for his spectacles (1971) and six years after the failure of his 'genderless scent' Eau Libre (1975). He bought the villa when *Le Smoking*, the male dinner-jacket, was a central theme in his female collections. In that year (1981) Yohji Yamamoto was showing prêt-à-porter in Paris for the first time and Bergé voted for Giscard d'Estaing before swiftly changing sides. In 1989 Saint Laurent's company went public on the Bourse and in the mid 1990s Bergé was fined for insider dealing.

Rawsthorn's subject was not gardening and only recently can we follow in print the clues to this garden's early life. In 2007 a philosophy teacher in Toulouse, Alain Leygonie, published an excellent book-length study of the garden and its first maker, Jacques Majorelle, who died in his mid seventies in 1962. To write it, he interviewed the surviving family and the admirable head gardener, Abderrazak Benchaâbane. I remember discovering from the villa's working gardeners that they were part of a core team of at least eight. The small enclosed area on display nowadays is very well tended but I am unable to name many of the cactuses on view, as some of them flower only every thirty years and there are no labels.

Majorelle was born in Nancy in 1886 to an artistic father whose sizeable house and garden lived on as vivid memories in his mind. He emigrated to Morocco in 1919 and four years later began to buy the ground which now includes the garden. It took another three purchases of land during nine years to round off his house and home. The style of the place was initially his vision, a combination of

Cacti and the blue pavilion in the Jardin Majorelle

well-understood Moroccan vernacular style, modern architectural fashion, and traditional details and façades. Majorelle was a bold traveller in the Atlas mountains and an early admirer of the style of its village houses, from which he copied the strong 'Berber blue', now on his garden's pots and walls. It was a bold colour to import into red and ocher Marrakech In 1931 he extended his paintings to another subject, what he called his naked negresses. The girls used to swing their hips and breasts and pose for him in what is now the Villa Oasis garden.

When the novelist Anthony Burgess interviewed Yves Saint Laurent in the 1970s, he asked him what he thought of women. He took the answer to be 'dolls', at least until Saint Laurent apologized for his franglais and explained that he had actually said 'idols'. Saint Laurent liked women and never imposed on them the homoerotic lines of clothes and body which rival designers favoured. He even used to say that women are only truly attractive as they age and their character shows in their faces. One of his models, however, remembers him pointing to her breasts and asking disapprovingly: 'What are those?' I do not think he would have wanted Majorelle's naked negresses to be reinstated in his garden.

Majorelle had a fine eye for local plants which would grow in a

Moroccan garden. He also admired the colours painted on Moroccan houses. Majorelle Blue is still a recognized colour in modern paint-boxes and the famous blue of the garden began in Majorelle's time. At its peak he employed twenty gardeners but between his death in 1962 and 1981 the garden went into a serious decline. Saint Laurent and Bergé then bought the house when a French company was about to develop it into a hotel and pool. With the help of two designer friends, Bill Willis and Jacques Grange, they decorated it meticulously, taking nine months to mix the right shade of red paint. Saint Laurent insisted: 'The last thing I want is a palace. I am against ultra-splendour.' He bought chairs for $5 each and local carpets which dated from the 1930s. He was guided by the wish to realize Majorelle's dreams for the garden as they were known to him through Majorelle's widow and servants.

For Majorelle the garden was the scene of a hard divorce, then a new love in his sixties for Maithé Hammann, half-Haitian and half-German, whom he finally married. Sadly, money worries beset him, compounded by a car accident when not insured on a Moroccan mountain road which led to his loss of a leg. Yves Saint Laurent began his tenure more happily. As he had been brought up in Algeria, Marrakech took him back to childhood memories which he enhanced with the seductions of drugs and sex. His first house in Marrakech in the 1960s was known as the Villa of the Snake, where the wild parties included the young Gettys and the rock star Mick Jagger. He moved on to the Villa of Happiness, just beside Majorelle's garden, but by then his life owed more to despondency, drink and drugs. It was Bergé who renamed Majorelle's house the Villa Oasis after a favourite novel by Eugène Dabit. In the Oasis, however, Saint Laurent lived in saddened seclusion. He was most at ease there with his succession of French bulldogs.

Whereas Majorelle had had an impetuous temper, Saint Laurent struck many of his friends as childlike, before he seemed to enter old age suddenly while still only in his forties. Both of these artists deserve to be remembered for the garden in which, successively, they sought solace. When the actress Lauren Bacall appeared at a Manhattan opening wearing a smart black trouser suit, she snubbed the inquiring columnists by telling them 'if it's pants, it's Yves'. Visitors to the Villa Oasis need to understand more clearly how 'if it's plants, it's Yves' but it is also Jacques who planned the garden before him.

'Oh dear, I do love gardens!'

As the Saint Laurent garden exemplifies, flowers and gardens do not spring from our heads without a history. There are memories in us all: memories of flowers seen long ago or ideal gardens from a childhood which we can never revisit. I wrestle with my own dreams, knowing that the underlying images will never be fully realized in hard daylight.

These memories of flowers and gardens stay with us to the end. In the face of approaching death they surface with a new intensity when bunches of flowers from visitors activate these old and immovably deep memories. Quite often, the onlookers, too, turn to flowers for consolation. Édouard Manet found inspiration in vases of flowers as his life reached its end and the flower paintings of his final months are the supreme tribute to the comfort of flowers near death. Like painting, literature has its list of flower-lovers in their last days to which distinguished names continue to be added. One of them is the novelist Katherine Mansfield. She lived for four years with a diagnosis of probable death before she succumbed to tuberculosis in January 1923. Nowadays she is most widely remembered for her *In a German Pension*, a work of her youth which she later refused to have reprinted. As she realized, it does not do her justice: she should be valued as a writer who never lost her penetrating eye and critical standards. She also never lost her deep-rooted love of flowers and gardens. They are entwined fascinatingly in her published letters.

In summer 1919, she was living in her new home, 2 Portland Villas in Hampstead, turbulently married and suddenly aware of the true nature of her illness. Her friend Lady Ottoline Morrell was sending her baskets of flowers throughout the seasons from her garden in Oxfordshire, 'exquisite tulips and some sprigs of rosemary and verbena', 'peonies and delphiniums and lilac (I half expected to find the infant Moses under the irises)' and above all, the roses of which 'I am saving the petals to dry'. In mid-June, 'the sound of the wind is very loud in this house . . . Now it is dark and one feels so pale – even one's hands feel pale . . . I feel one might say anything – do anything – wreck one's own life – wreck another's.' In a note at this time she certainly spoke out: 'the red geraniums have bought the garden over my head,' she wrote, 'They are there, established, back in the old home' and 'quite determined that no power on earth will ever move them again': was she looking up at them from the lower ground floor? 'But why should they make me feel a stranger? Why should they ask me every time I go near: "And what are *you* doing in a London garden?" They burn with arrogance and pride. And I am the little Colonial walking in the London garden patch – allowed to look, perhaps, but not to linger.' Katherine Mansfield had been born in New Zealand: if she lay on the grass, she continued, the geraniums 'positively shout at me, "Look at her, lying on *our* grass, pretending she lives here . . . She is a stranger and an alien. She is nothing but a little girl sitting on the Tinakori hills and dreaming: 'I went to London and married an Englishman . . .'"'

Later in 1919 she left England for the Continent, fearful for her health, 'in the condition of a transplanted tree', as she quoted from Chekhov, 'which is hesitating whether to take root or begin to wither'. We can now follow some of her impressions through the magnificent edition of her letters. In earlier volumes there are some flowery moments as she thoughtfully emerged from the years of the Great War. She confronted that war's pervasive effects and complained, acutely, that they were not addressed by her contemporary Virginia Woolf in her novel *Night and Day*, published in 1919. In autumn of that year, flowers came to the fore in her own thinking. The life-sentence of tuberculosis had just been passed on her and in the hope of a remission she went to Italy and southern France where welcomed the fields of anemones and the local narcissi. She was delightfully happy watching the men who came to help in the garden. In north Italy, 'a big kind grey old dog in a cap' came to speak bad French to her about violets 'savage and mild' and roses that flowered in 'le mois de Noel' and a lily as big as a villa. In January she enjoyed the scent of double-flowered stocks. She walked in a floral heaven near Menton at a time when its coast was still teeming with wild flowers. It is fascinating that this young genius of a writer, exiled by her health, was lodged near Menton in months when the great Lawrence Johnston, creator of the garden at Hidcote Manor in Gloucestershire, was attending his mother in a rest-home nearby. They never met.

Katherine's excellent letters from these years are explicit about the roots of her love of flowers. They went back deep into her childhood in faraway New Zealand where her cousin Elizabeth also grew up, later Elizabeth von Arnim, made famous by her marriage to her German garden. 'When I was about the height of a garden spade,' Katherine writes in March from Menton, 'I spent weeks – months – watching a man do all these things and wandering through canes of yellow butter beans and smelling the spotted speckled broad bean flowers and helping to plant Giant Edwards and White Elephants. Oh dear, I do love gardens! I had better stop.' Constantly, her letters show her responding to cut flowers and the floral baskets which were sent to encourage her. Even under the threat of death she was dreaming of the outlines of a future garden. In January she was thinking of 'little curly blue hyacinths and white violets and the bird cherry. My trouble is that I had so many flowers when I was little. I got to know them so well that they are simply the breath of life to me. It is no ordinary love. It is a passion.'

By October 1922 medical treatments had failed and Katherine arranged to be accepted into the Institute of the legendary guru George Gurdjieff, whom her letters' editors succinctly present as 'a widely travelled Armenian Greek'. This prince of baloney had the most imposing presence and his theories of cosmic rays and curative dancing only helped to enhance his mystique. It was in Russia that he first established his Institute for the Harmonious Development of Man. After the Russian Revolution he transferred his blend of communal living, 'healing' labour and Far Eastern carpets to the Priory at Fontainebleau with the help of his newly found French supporters. Katherine Mansfield learned of him through a lecture in Paris by his accompanying fantasist, P. D. Ouspensky. In later years the famous landscape gardener Russell Page also knew Ouspensky, just as he knew Gurdjieff, whose natural daughter he married when she was already pregnant. The Fontainebleau Institute and its bogus theories of 'harmony' underpinned Russell Page's abstract ideas about the natural world.

There is a special poignancy to Katherine Mansfield's final letters from this farmhouse of Russian exiles and souls in need of help. 'According to Mr Gurdjieff,' she writes, 'we all of us have our "illness" and it takes very severe measures to put us right.' For Katherine he prescribed a hideaway above the cows in the farm barn where she could sit 'and inhale their breath'. She duly sat up there on a pile of carpets. Life was appallingly cold and, away from the cows, the main business seems to have been cooking, cleaning and simply staying alive. Hearty Russian dancing punctuated a life spent peeling carrots. Her letters' editors propose that the company and social grouping were what most appealed to her, and as authors live isolated lives, I can well believe it: 'they are all very different but they are the people I have wanted to find – real people – not people I make up or invent.' They were so real that before long, they had stolen all her underclothes.

What did 'cosmic harmony' do for her love of flowers? Wonderfully, that love was still with her despite the hours in the cowsheds and the intense cold and damp. The autumn of her entry to the Institute had been a 'marvellous' year for dahlias: 'big spiked red ones, white ones and a little bright orange kind – most lovely'. As she left Paris, she was still recalling in letters the 'Michaelmas daisies on a solitary bush in Acacia Road. I like them. They have such very delicate petals.' In the Institute for Harmonious Development, in early January 1923, she was 'looking for signs of spring already'. 'Under the espalier pear trees there are wonderful Xmas roses . . . and somebody found four primroses the other day.' Within a day or two she was dead. She was thirty-four years old.

The deeply felt memory of flowers had sustained her for so much of her shortened life. Three years earlier, in Menton, she had written home about her 'fifteen cinerarias in Italy' and how 'they grew against the sea'. 'I hope,' she added, 'one will be able to call these things up on one's deathbed.' I strongly believe that she could and did.

Snowdropping

Back in the English countryside, the February fashion nowadays is snowdropping. Hundreds of suitably wheeled vehicles descend on selected snowdrop collections. The dress is traditional: tweeds, waterproof jacket and a walking stick if you are still young enough to need one, not two. Snowdroppers are persons of mature experience and a battle-scarred financial history which stretches back to the 1970s. The scars are not strong enough to stop them handing over £20 for a single snowdrop which catches their fancy. I have been snowdropping with the best of them and the results have caused a slight adjustment to my views. I used to picture snowdrops on the edge of woodland or in leafy soil of a good depth where they are partially shaded and sheltered. Instinctively I would not plant them in open flowerbeds or on dry stony soil.

Visits in two directions changed my practice. The first was a visit to the poetic collection of snowdrops which was carefully accumulated near Oxford by the poet and author James Fenton during the 1990s. In his garden snowdrops were not tucked away in shade. They were started in twos or threes in raised beds, borders and cultivated ground at the base of a wall. In these places his snowdrops grew into serious clumps and allowed themselves to be divided and scattered under old-fashioned roses and between specialized alpines. The great botanical authority William Stearn considered that snowdrops hate farmyard manure and will die if they are covered in it. If Stearn had been wholly right, there would have been no future for Fenton's initial plantings of snowdrops under roses which were manured and top-dressed. In fact, snowdrops will survive mulching and manuring in moderation, although they increase even more rapidly when the manuring ceases and has been absorbed into the soil. In an Oxford Professor of Poetry's keeping, highly priced snowdrops multiplied among manure and became a portfolio of carefully chosen growth stocks. Perhaps they prefer the Muses to the rotted manure, but I had not expected to watch such distinguished selections as *plicatus* 'Colossus' or 'John Gray' increasing and allowing division after only a few years in the ground. It was unexpected to find a summer border under-planted with the excellent *nivalis* 'Anglesey Abbey' and to see old roses carpeted with a tall, early charmer called 'Limetree'. This variety's academic credentials are impeccable. It is said to have been discovered under the very lime tree beneath which the keen mind of R. A. Butler used to relax while writing his Education Act, the framework for Britain's post-war teaching.

The lesson from Fenton's garden of the Muses is that a collection of snowdrops will develop steadily in ground which has been well manured, away from shade or grass, and will enliven bare flowerbeds in a changeable February. Individual bulbs of named varieties are expensive, but they are not feeble and as many of them spread quickly, they soon seem a reasonable buy. I noted down the large-flowered 'Mighty Atom' and the early 'Castlegar' from Ireland which starts to flower just before Christmas, a wondrous sight. There is a particular charm in 'Neill Fraser', a single Scottish variety with rounded flowers which were greatly admired by the connoisseur E. A. Bowles. With Fenton it flourished in a flowerbed in open sunlight. For vigour, 'Galatea' and 'Magnet' are unsurpassed, even under a well-manured rose hedge.

My second instructive visit was to the supreme collection of snowdrops maintained at Colesbourne Park, Gloucestershire, off the A435 between Cirencester and Cheltenham. The collection goes back to the great tree planter and gardener H. J. Elwes, whose great-grandson still lives in the house, and in February it attracts hundreds of snowdroppers willing to follow its signposted trail. The surrounding arboretum and water are a fine sight, especially from vantage points carpeted with yellow aconites. A sharp eye for a tree has continued to run in the Elwes family and a visit to Colesbourne is pleasant enough even if you look upwards into the trees' branches rather than downwards at *Galanthus elwesii* around your feet.

The initial part of the visitors' walk runs under tall trees beside carpets of Britain's native snowdrop, *Galanthus nivalis*. A spectacular mass of the vigorous snowdrop 'S. Arnott' is one of the sights of this

top left: *Galanthus* 'Colossus' in James Fenton's garden
top right: *Galanthus nivalis* 'Anglesey Abbey' in James Fenton's garden
above: Snowdrops carpet woodland in Burford, Oxfordshire

part of the garden and shows what a superb choice this old Scottish variety is on almost any soil. The provost of Dumfries sent bulbs of it down to H. J. Elwes in this very garden. It is fine to see their descendants flowering by the hundred in this same home and giving off a sweet scent in the sunshine, to those who kneel down and check it out.

The second part of the trail leads round the house into less expected territory. In sunny beds beneath walls or among border plants, fine snowdrops are also flowering freely and forming divisible clumps. I do not think that poetry runs in the Elwes family, but many of the most expensive snowdrops are happy here too with a life in the open rather than under the canopy of tall trees. The soil at Colesbourne is no better than mine and refutes the view that special snowdrops insist on special leafy conditions. Mrs Elwes told me how some of the best clumps in the woodland grow on Cotswold brash without any depth of soil beneath. As proof she pointed to her special discovery, the old snowdrop 'George Elwes', which is named after her son. She found it among tree roots and had to dig destructively in order to acquire large bulbs for transplanting and eventual re-sale.

Among such diversity it is hard to name the flowers accurately, let alone to tell a double 'Cordelia' from a double 'Hippolyta'. My success rate at naming was only four varieties out of every ten, and even then, I sometimes saw a label. The experts, too, have their disagreements. I had started the day by admiring superb clumps of the wild Greek *Galanthus gracilis*, whose leaves are distinctively narrow and twisted. At Colesbourne, however, some of the clumps called *gracilis* show no twisting at all. Fortunately, we have an authoritative botanical guide, Aaron P. Davis's *The Genus Galanthus*, a magnificent work of reference published by Kew Gardens and the Timber Press, but even Davis has his moments of uncertainty. Snowdrops have intermarried, bred and multiplied, often from ancestors which have been left in peace in country gardens since the nineteenth century. Near the end of his life, the great gardener Lewis Palmer found other people's names and identities confusing and used to complain that if only they were as distinct as snowdrops they would be easy to sort out. The rest of us will never pin all snowdrops to a family tree.

Nor can we pin them down to rigid rules. The standard practice nowadays is to dig up their clumps when still in leaf and split them for immediate replanting. Even the experts differ over the best timing, some recommending action just before the snowdrops are in full flower, some preferring to wait until the flowers have gone. In my experience, bulbs which are transplanted before the flowers open are even more likely to flower well in the following spring. My light soil is tolerated by snowdrops, but is not ideal for them. At Colesbourne, the garden director follows a third option: he plants snowdrop bulbs in autumn when no leaves show. So long as the bulbs have not dried out, they will move very well in autumn too. Drying out is their problem in the mass-market trade, but not in private gardens. At Colesbourne, thousands of clumps prove that autumn transplanting still works.

Gardening in Texan Adversity

Like snowdrops, many gardens have to grow in hard conditions. Nonetheless, gardening in adversity always encourages me, and when seen abroad it stops our complaints about local problems. What is a hot summer in England to gardeners who have had to cope with years of drought in Australia? What is a badger or two to gardeners in America who are invaded by urban deer? In February I widened my grasp of adverse gardening by research in that land of plenty, Texas.

One plant from this home of oil rigs and wildcat drillers is familiar to British readers: the Texas yellow rose. During the wars with Mexico in the 1830s, the Texan generals profited from a secret weapon who was active behind the Mexican lines. She was Emily, a young lady of mixed-race origin, a 'yellow' in Texan language of the time. Taken captive, she was assigned one of the least challenging missions in military history: to seduce a senior Mexican after lunch. She duly bagged the top general and sent a message to the Texans, who promptly attacked his leaderless troops. In her memory the yellow rose became a Texan icon. At home I grow *Rosa × harisonii* 'Harison's Yellow', the rose which that supreme gardener from the American south, Nancy Lancaster, always told me was the right Texan yellow. It flowers in late May on a prickly bush about three feet high and will grow anywhere.

Out in Houston the temperatures in early spring rival those of an English June and are hot enough to bring the Texan yellow rose into early flower. When I ventured out on to a highway running westwards from the city I felt less envious. In summer the Texan heat is debilitating and if rain ever comes, it falls in a brief deluge. When summer breaks, tempests are then a threat in the wake of tornadoes. In Houston itself, the soil is usually a heavy black clay which is unworkable when it dries out. The sunny spring skies are lovely, but the temperatures can drop to several degrees of sharp frost at night, enough to ruin many plants which would best survive the hot summer. Keen gardeners warned me of the worst hazard: freak bouts of very cold weather which blows down from the far north in a wind corridor. It is known as the Alberta Shuttle and was at its worst in 1983.

In late February, therefore, I did not expect too much when I called on a great rarity, a Texan garden supported by its own Foundation on ten acres of tough soil beside a busy road an hour's journey west of Houston. Further along the road middle-aged motorbikers meet for hamburgers at the Thirsty Parrot Café. Wild pigs live in the surrounding woodland and crawfish burrow up among the garden's plants wherever the soil is soft. I had not reckoned with the founder and owner of Peckerwood Garden, the softly spoken John Fairey, who is now in his late seventies. He started to garden on this patch of adversity in 1971, but has made it into a Texan treasure by a thoughtful reaction to its natural limitations. He has given it years of hard work and has applied the eye for beauty which has sustained his career as a teacher of design. His aim is to teach students how to see differently and in his garden he offers the lesson to us all. He is one of those calm optimists whose skills as a gardener I recognize from long experience. If I was a plant, I would grow for him.

Peckerwood Garden is a lesson in how to work with adversity. John Fairey has not spent a fortune in trying to change local conditions. In 1988, he began making expeditions into Mexico's mountains across the border in order to collect seed from hardy but drought-resistant flora which would survive in the difficult Texan conditions. By experiment, he learned the best ways of germinating these unusual plants, and before long he was supplying Kew Gardens and other botanical institutes with his collections. He was joined on his trips by various British plant-collectors, James Compton and Martyn Rix among them, many of whose foreign collections are important for gardeners too. Enhanced from Mexico, Peckerwood Garden is informally planned as a shrub and tree garden with a changing layer of bulbs and low planting. It contains more than 3,000 species, ranging from unfamiliar Japanese oaks to excellent magnolias and scented mahonias. It is a garden for close inspection by plant-lovers, although they will struggle to name many of the best sights of the moment.

I first realized that Fairey was special when we passed a climbing plant on a flimsy fence in his front gravel garden. I did not recognize it, but he told me it was a climbing philadelphus, or scented mock orange. I know this family well in British catalogues but I never knew that some members of it are natural climbers. We went on past unfamiliar Mexican yuccas and grey-green agaves, including a sharp-toothed one which Fairey has named Jaws. My notebook was already working overtime and we had not even reached the small-flowered camellias from Japan. I became truly lost among the mahonias. Admittedly, we had just seen the first single white flowers on a rare bloodroot under some fine shrubs, but I was not expecting to see the Mexican *Mahonia pallida* which has delicate heads of pale lemon-yellow flowers. Word had been reaching me of new, delicate members of this family, but I never expected to be enchanted by them within earshot of a highway in Texas. These Mexican forms of mahonia are hardy and are sure to become a mainstay of gardens as stocks in British nurseries build up.

I could make no more sense of Peckerwood's hardy magnolias, especially the evergreen forms from Mexico. The garden's superb oaks were no more familiar, least of all the hardy evergreen oaks from Japan. Even our own nursery experts, including Hillier's, have been importing seed from Peckerwood of these new collected forms. In a British garden I would be happy to look up through the branches of Peckerwood's ten-year-old *Quercus glauca*, the Japanese blue oak. The hardiest such oak is the most beautiful, *Quercus myrsinifolia*, the bamboo-leaf oak, with long, narrow leaves which are a shining green on top and slightly grey underneath.

Thankfully, I recognized some of the garden's white-flowering halesia trees and began to understand how the mature areas had been planted with an artist's eye for the trunks and bark of the tallest trees. They are set off by a recurring use of the softer grey tones in Mexican yuccas and rare hardy forms of palm. America has justly famous botanical gardens and arboretums but the most impressive private gardens tend to be backed by their owners' personal fortunes and to pay respect to established European or Japanese styles. Peckerwood is different, the work of a single owner during nearly forty years of his thoughtful collecting and planting. It has grown to need supporting staff and now needs to be assured of a long, public life by a benefactor

A corner of John Fairey's Peckerwood Gardens

with the intelligence to work with its creator in the later years of his life and guide the garden for the future.

John Fairey kept on impressing me by his resilience. Sure, a tornado took out some of his trees in 1983 but as a result new ones could be tried in their place. Sure, the crocuses die out after a year and the tulips fare no better, but you can then grow carpets of ipheion in their place. If the climate is difficult, think out of the box and go out and collect seed in an under-explored zone with similar natural problems. Even the local wild pigs are a fact of life, to be countered with a special sort of hog-trap, baited with corn. After taking notes in Texas, I will think twice about going into a decline at the first patter of a squirrel's feet. In Texas there are urban gardeners who wrap their early flowering camellias in fairy lights and illuminate them on chilly spring evenings. Perhaps I should wrap up my badgers in last year's lights off the Christmas tree and watch them make colour patterns as they excavate the lawns.

Weevils in Charge

Whether in Texas or chilly northern Tyneside, burn your old copies of *Spare Rib;* pulp *The Female Eunuch*; melt down your sorority pins. For more than thirty years, feminists have been declaring Gender War, but it looks out of date when seen from the level of the soil. No feminist author has ever realized it, but while they have been telling women to burn their bras and take over the show, a population within feet of their armchairs has long done exactly that. Even the great Aristophanes would have to run for cover. It is not just a case of females running the state. Close to us all, females have been managing for centuries without any sign of a male at all.

In a research greenhouse near Dusseldorf, I became aware of this neglected dimension to issues of sexual politics. In order to understand the fellow inhabitants of our planet, we need to talk to the people whose living depends on combating the pests in its population. Under the glass roofs of Germany's chemical Bayer Group, I inspected a sickly pelargonium in a flowerpot and learned that it was the consequence of Females In Charge. It was a barely living answer to the question with which every couple have tormented themselves: would things go better if women took over? Within walking distance of Germaine Greer, a female population has been teeming in pot plants, compost and many of the plantings which she buys in containers from garden shops.

For years, I have dreaded the very name of Vine Weevil, believing that it is one of the few menaces which have not yet invaded my garden. It attacks roots, slaughters fuchsias and punches the margins of healthy leaves. The expert Helen Dillon tells us to check our bergenias if we want to know if we have vine weevils. If the edge of a bergenia leaf has been clipped as if by a ticket collector, then vine weevils are in the garden. Holes in the middle of the leaf are due to slugs, not weevils. So far, I only have slugs.

After visiting Dusseldorf, I am even more thankful that vine weevils have not yet discovered me. The truth may be familiar to entomologists, but is ignored by social theorists and harassed gardeners: the population of the vine weevil is exclusively female. Nobody is sure what happened to the last of the males. On one view he did not survive the Ice Age. In my view, the females bit him to death in the locker room. They had discovered how to cope very well without him because they had learned a hideous truth: how to reproduce without sex.

The implications are extremely suggestive. Theologically, I do not think that the vine weevil has yet been taken into account. For tens of thousands of years the females have been reproducing prolifically by virgin birth. They are thought to produce up to 1,200 eggs in a month and their children hatch into a single-sex family which keeps the weevil sisterhood strictly to its orientation. In the 1970s we briefly lost control of this all-female world. Until then, male gardeners had dealt with it in a masculine way. They had sprayed it to death with DDT and stopped females getting the upper hand. When DDT was banned, females started to proliferate. What sort of society have they decided to run?

For a start, they dispensed with the traditional barriers of colour. Manifestly, they have decided that the polarization between blacks and whites is masculine and unacceptable; their grubs are creamy white and mature to a dull shade of black. I need hardly add that the entire female adult population is thick-skinned and completely unsquashable. The little lady weevils, according to expert informants, 'are said to resemble space creatures'. To show that they will be fit to join a hen night, they grow up legless. Most of their activity occurs by night, including virgin-birthing. They hate the winter with a truly feminine hatred. Not until May and June do they dust off their space-age suits and set about building a new society.

The result is parasitic and extraordinarily aggressive. They begin life as if up a pole, hiding in the leaves of plants on which they punch a ticket-collector's imprint. They then come down, burrow into the base of a plant, and disappear below ground. They are extremely hard to catch when misbehaving and their main aim is to ruin the roots of anything which grows. If they feel threatened, they hide under a central bulb or corm. This habit makes them a menace in pots full of cyclamen. Their entire attitude to life is blinkered, focused and obsessive. All they want to do is to ruin as many of the surrounding roots and plants as possible and to eat lunch and dinner without becoming fat. They are much happier indoors where it is warm than outdoors where the weather will spoil their complexions. They revel in a soft, squishy compost, especially peat. As a result, they have been multiplying alarmingly since the introduction of black polythene containers and spongy peat compost. Every weekend, when gardeners drive down to the garden centre for a pot-bound shrub, they risk bringing back with it a microcosm of a virgin female society. The shrub's compost is likely to be riddled with vine weevils, invisible to most human eyes.

Life's major question thus seems to be answered. If there were nothing but females in the world, they would start by making short work of the curtains, then savage the soft furnishings and go and hide under the sofa. Other questions are more awkward. What would they do if they saw a man and how can we exterminate these virgin creepers in our post-DDT age? The possibility of introducing a man and answering the first of these questions is tantalizing. You may remember Basil Ransom in Henry James' novel *The Bostonians*. 'The masculine character, the ability to dare and endure, to know and not to fear reality, to look the world in the face and take it for what it is . . . this is what I want to preserve.' I propose that our ingenious scientists use their genome knowledge, build a male vine weevil, instil Basil Ransom's qualities and let him loose on the female population. Imagine the poor little virgins when they see him coming. Will they think of him as fit only for speculation and parasitic trading? Will they cluster, and charge him out of the compost? I like to think that deep down in their post-glacial consciousness, they will feel a mysterious, buried dimension stirring. They will go round in south-westerly circles and suddenly find that they have fallen in love. The effect on a potted poinsettia will be shattering, but we ought to send this feminist enclave the only Valentine it will appreciate.

Lady-Killing Progress

For thoughtful gardeners, the question remains: how can we exterminate these all-female vine weevils in an era when DDT is banned? There is no effective 'organic' answer and without chemical weaponry, gardening and farming would degenerate into chaos. Fortunately chemists have come up with a compound to kill the ladies off. It was discovered by males and is marketed as Provado in garden centres, where it is labelled 'The Ultimate Bug Killer'. I repent of my occasional complaints that gardeners are sold less effective chemicals than those available to farmers. The hard commercial fact is that without farming, gardeners would never be treated to new chemical allies in the first place. Provado is based on an active compound which was developed by chemists at Bayer in 1985 from research which began in 1972. It cost Bayer more than $100 million to develop the compound and bring it through ever more stringent tests for licensing. By itself the gardening market cannot sustain the risks and costs of developing a new product. New chemicals which we buy as gardeners have been widely available to farmers for ten years already.

The chemical breakthrough became known as Imidacloprid and worked wonders in the years before gardeners could buy it openly. The 'green movement' needs to recognize that Imidacloprid is one of the saviours of the cotton crops in Turkey, the citrus crops from the Aegean eastwards and acres of those 'farm-fresh' tomatoes which we buy because they have been grown within sight of open country. In Italy, Imidacloprid is being used to prevent the yellowing of leaves on the plane trees which line roads. Imidacloprid kills whitefly, blackfly, greenfly and the proliferating lily beetle. It destroys an all-female invasion by vine weevils and protects plants against them for at least six months. When you next buy an unwaxed lemon in a wholefood shop and congratulate yourself on your organic custom, remember that citrus crops were at risk to the citrus leaf miner in 1990 and that without

Imidacloprid there would be no lemons to wax or unwax anyway.

Nonetheless, Imidacloprid is a chemical. Before 'green' gardeners protest, it degrades very quickly in sunlight. It does not wash out into the water supply because it binds itself loosely, but unshakeably, to particles in the soil. Provado Pest Free is the brand recommended for amateur gardeners. In Britain, packets carry the statutory warning 'high risk to bees', but it applies only to bees who are wrongly targeted with this compound head-on. Provado Pest Free should be used to drench the soil, not to spray straight on to bees or insects in the air. It can be sprayed on to plants in leaf, but should be kept away from plants in flower. It will then not affect pollinators and is harmless to bees unless they are sprayed with it directly in the face. Professional brands with Imidacloprid have been stringently tested and licensed for use on such fundamental crops as sugar beet, hops and lettuces. It is so safe for mammals that it is used to kill fleas on pets. It could also be used to kill nits in children's hair.

Imidacloprid does not deter insects from feeding on a plant which has been treated with it. This effect is crucial, because other chemicals simply drive bugs away to another type of plant. It is taken up by root hairs into the plant's general system and acts systemically, killing only the bugs which eat it. Its method of killing is extremely ingenious. All-female weevils and other insects have nervous systems which transmit impulses from 'releasers' to specific receptors. Most of the previous chemical killers attacked the 'releasers', but Imidacloprid blocks the receptors. As the experience is a new one, the population has no resistance. Brands of Imidacloprid are a godsend against the termites which ruin house-timbers and buildings in Japan and America. No longer is it a case of Termites On Top. I wonder how organic enthusiasts expect to protect their decking in such climates if they refuse the use of all chemicals.

I know how I protect my fragile bedding-plants. I now water the Provado range on to all bedding plants and pricked-out seedlings before they leave their boxes and go into open ground. They are then defended against bugs and weevils throughout the season, having taken up the chemical into their system. In my potting shed, there are two non-negotiable allies. Brands based on glyphosate kill couch grass and most of the broad-leaved weeds without any sign of poisoning the soil. Provado reverses the war against lily beetles and teeming female vine weevils.

It was charming to read recently of the writer Candace Bushnell that she likes the country and tells her visitors, 'Honey, we live here and the bugs live here too', so as to stop them complaining about rural infestations of insects. Down my way, honey, the bugs no longer have a chance and it makes no difference if every single one of them is female like yourself. When I drench them, they are dead.

Early Flowering Cherries

Before vine weevils are wriggling in our new spring pot-plants there are weeks when the contrast between town and country gardens is acute. It shows in mid-March when gardens outside the extra warmth of a town are decidedly retarded. They still have crocuses in flower, caught as if in a fridge, whereas southern cities already have flowers on their magnolias and bushes of yellow forsythia.

I would therefore urge anyone with a chilly new country garden to make a strong commitment to prunus. In southern British cities, the first clouds of prunus blossom now open in mid-March, but in the rural mud, country gardeners can enjoy the second flowering on the winter varieties at that time. These flowers are hardly a second best, as the winter cherry, *Prunus* × *subhirtella* 'Autumnalis', is exceptionally pretty. Nearly thirty years ago I picked on it as the finest tree for a flower garden and I see no reason to change my choice. The pinkish-white flowers first open in mid-November and are magnificent when cut and arranged indoors. We expect to see hothouse plants at that time of year, so the simple elegance of this blossom is a charming surprise in a drawing room. It grows anywhere and can sometimes be bought as a bush, not a tree, if space is scarce. The plain form is better than the pink one, which flowers marginally later.

If frost hits the early winter flowers, they re-form on the terminal shoots and then flower in spring all over again. As they eventually fade in mid-March, my next favourite is the neglected *Prunus* 'Okame' with acid pink flowers. This fine tree is wonderfully untroubled by cold weather and flowers strongly even in exposed countryside. 'Okame' has a more vivid rival, *Prunus* 'Kursar', which is less easy to buy but, if anything, is even better. It originated in Central Turkey where it was spotted by the great cherry expert Captain Collingwood Ingram. In later months, the strong pink of its flowers would seem harsh, but it is a bright opening for the rural season and appears to be untroubled by foul weather. Both 'Okame' and 'Kursar' are small trees, the latter reaching no more than twelve feet in height with a modest width. Many country gardens have room for one or both, and they deserve wider recognition. So does the excellent *Prunus* 'Hally Jolivette'. It makes a medium- to large-sized shrub with thin, graceful stems which are covered with semi-double pink-white flowers in late March. It is easy and very pretty, but few gardeners make it a first choice in a new plan, probably because they have never met it. I hope to reverse its neglect, because it is weather-proof, disease-proof and extremely easy to grow.

On dry banks or at the top of a low stone wall, late March then becomes the season for that other vivid shrub, *Prunus tenella*. The common name of this straggly, low bush is dwarf Russian almond. The one snag is that bits of it will sometimes die out, but even so the whole plant is seldom killed and soon covers over its gaps. It likes to fall forwards and cover quite a wide span of ground. The masses of red-pink flowers in the common form called 'Fire Hill' are very heartening during late March and early April. I have learned to grow vigorous forms of alpine clematis at a distance of less than five feet from it and let their stems wind horizontally through the prunus's untidy branches. The blue forms in this group of the clematis family, especially 'Frances Rivis', make a splendid accompaniment. In the wild, these alpine clematises grow flat over low shrubs more often than they try to climb vertically. It is only we who class them as climbers for walls.

As the first blush of hard and reddish-pink flowers on these prunus trees fades, the next wave of blossom needs more thought. Few of us want double-flowered varieties which verge in colour towards black-currant ice cream, but I can recommend the semi-double pink flowers of *Prunus* 'Accolade'. It deserves its Award of Merit from the Royal Horticultural Society, as the shade of pink is charming and the trees seem well able to function on poor soil. I have one growing well at a distance of only three yards from a high hedge of the vile Leyland cypress.

By mid-April, the single-flowered 'Umineko' takes over, an upright tree which is good in an avenue and is followed by the arching and spreading white *Prunus × yedoensis*. White cherry blossom then comes thick and fast until the final, distinctive flush in mid-May on the excellent *Prunus* 'Shimizu-zakura', popularly known as *longipes*, botanically renamed 'Shagetsu' in recent lists. These whites are a fine threesome, but there are no British festivals of cherry blossom to celebrate them. We do not go out on a public holiday to view the flowers on these cherries or even to become mildly drunk beneath them on picnic rugs. For cherry fiestas we have to go to the Far East. I have longed to see such a festival in action since I first became a cherry-lover at the age of twelve, and used to practise the names of the famous Japanese beauties, 'Shirotae', 'Yoshino', 'Shimizu-zakura', and many others. Recently I saw the flowers in their festival season in the ultimate home of so many wild cherries, Korea.

In Korea the holiday crowds do not set out to become drunk under falling cherry blossom. They turn out in thousands and even take special trains to outlying towns where the flowering cherries are especially good. I chose to avoid a cherry-blossom choo-choo and centred my researches on the capital city Seoul itself. The city scores poorly for green space, but there are magnificent cherries in its expanding perimeter as it leads away to a distant prospect of hills. They surround the city like a ring and tend to escape visitors on business who remain caught in Seoul's stupendous traffic.

I began my historical cherry-trail in the city's Cultural Monument Number One. Changdeokgung is the best restored of the palaces of the Choson dynasty which ruled for five centuries until 1910, the year of Korea's annexation by the Japanese. Cherry blossoms are much in evidence along its outer courtyards, among trees of *Magnolia kobus* with upright flowers of pure white against their bare branches. In earlier times Choson princesses aimed at having a 'garden in every gulley' so as to imitate the mountains around their city. Big trees of *Magnolia kobus* and wild white cherries evoked the mountains and welcomed visiting scholars, as they still do, to the palace's library garden beside a landscaped pond.

From the palace I moved on to two of Seoul's universities and checked for cherries on their campuses. As spring broke on the main avenues of Seoul National and Korea Universities, I walked down long pathways of the fine white cherry, *Prunus × yedoensis*. Justly named the King Cherry, it is a wide-spreading tree which is a superb choice for bigger British gardens too. In Korea, cherry planners do not mix colours or choose varieties with heavy flowers of raspberry-red.

Prunus 'Tai Haku' by Arabella Lennox Boyd's lake at Gresgarth, Lancashire

The dominant flowers in springtime are white, and two young Korean graduates guided me down their long avenues.

Discreetly, they proposed a final outing to Seoul National Park, and with hindsight, I am ashamed to have feared that they might not know what English visitors expect of a worthwhile garden. With their usual uplifting practicality, Koreans have divided Seoul's National Park into numbered Beautiful Places, and while fearing the worst I was guided to Beautiful Place Number Ten. Among the funfairs and the garden-railway, the world then smiled on us all. Far into the distance, double lines of mature King Cherries exhaled a haze of white blossom onwards and upwards to the blue-grey peaks of the mountains beyond. Korean ladies strolled along cherry avenues wearing eyeshades of green and pink and carrying parasols in matching colours, while a nearby office bus decanted members of the Tax

Inspecting Association of Korea for a visit to enjoy the view. For once I wished their profession well, feeling that they, too, had come to be uplifted by the natural world.

Among the publicans and sinners one of my guides then brought me down to earth. 'Cherries mean Japan to us,' she remarked wistfully. Big public plantings of King Cherries were a Japanese initiative during their years of power in Korea, but the results have been so widely imitated that I cannot believe that Koreans look on them all as foreign symbols. So much in their style of gardening was already shared with their temporary Japanese conquerors. These King Cherries are not simply statements of past historical rule. They are among the loveliest avenues in the world.

Let Them Eat Squirrel

From Christmas onwards, while winter cherries brave the winter months, there is a sound of scuttling in the evergreen *Magnolia grandiflora* which has finally reached the top storey of my house. It terrifies overnight visitors, but the noise is caused by squirrels under the gutter: grey, prehensile little nuisances who have stripped the upper branches of the shrub and will be taught a smart lesson if they continue their capers lower down.

While Parliament wastes its time on human ASBOs, daylight robbery by squirrels is allowed to run riot. Up on the roof they sharpen their teeth on the lead and bite holes in it which then leak water through the ceilings of the house. They are a menace to crocus corms and in Chiswick they have developed provocative tendencies. My sister has watched them remove individual bulbs one by one, roll them away for uncertain purposes and replace them with a peanut, impudently pinched from a bird-table, which they drop into each empty hole.

For two decades I have watched the increasing tide of squirrel violence in my Oxford college's garden. In defence we had to fit fine-meshed netting over each window box and nail it into position. We even tried covering the plantings of tulips in open borders with unsightly stretches of green netting until the bulbs' growth showed through. In reply, the squirrels outdid the students by vandalizing the tulips when in bud and leaving fragments as proof of their trespass. It is no use arguing that squirrels should be treated as honourably as people because they share so much of our DNA. If people came into my garden, barked the young beech trees and devastated the tulips, the police would put the offenders in handcuffs.

Self-defence is called for, but culture is an obstacle. We think so fondly of those red squirrels which grey squirrels have now slaughtered as a lesson in unmanaged 'wild life'. We have all been brainwashed by dear Beatrix Potter and her seminal tale of Squirrel Nutkin. How can we punish anything with a brother called Twinkleberry? Here, I am grateful for the front-line experience of a primary schoolteacher in the days when primary schools still taught French. You may remember the seductive picture in Nutkin's story of those squirrels who 'made little rafts out of twigs' and paddled away with their tails held high to visit their ruthless co-predator, Owl. My friend tried teaching French to a primary class from copies of *Noisette L'écureuil*. When she asked a young pupil to translate the passage in which Nutkin's squirrels paddle over the water '*pour ramasser les noix*', the child hesitated and looked at the colour picture. He then went on, 'they paddled away to ram the island'. Try thinking of squirrels as ram-raiders and you will be less sentimental about their habits in flowerbeds.

Trained by politicians, I justify the war as necessary defence. One way of trapping squirrels is to put grain in a squirrel-trap, examples of which are sold in market towns for £29.50 each. Another way is to let a greyhound after them when they are more than fifty yards away from a tree trunk. In country settings I recommend prudent use of the gun. More is at issue than pest control. There is also the chance to enrich the larder.

Here we come to one of our culture's paradoxes. Squirrels are eaten freely in the southern United States but I cannot find a recipe for squirrel stew in my copy of *What Shall We Have Today?* by the great Marcel Boulestin. The artist Toulouse-Lautrec would often eat squirrel in Paris and described the flesh as refreshingly nutty. I have just followed suit, guided by *Classic Game Cookery*, an indispensable book by Julia Drysdale. She knows exactly what she is talking about, and is guided by advice from the Game Conservancy Council. She is accurate on how best to choose a dead rabbit: 'a good young rabbit should have soft ears which are easily torn, and sharp teeth and claws.' She is a practical guide to squirrel cuisine. Think of squirrels as organic, fed on nothing but natural produce and reared within sight of open country. There are no E-numbers in nature's furry tulip-killer. Drysdale's suggestions include an excellent Squirrel in Cider which combines chunks of three squirrels, bits of ham, cream, cider and seasoned flour. Lautrec would love it. It should be put on the national school menu with an accompanying lesson in facts about wildlife in gardens.

In France, they still eat horses. In Italy the best restaurant for horsemeat is in Mantua, within sight of the former stables of the

Organic squirrel

Dukes of Mantua. It is we who draw boundaries around what we will eat and what we will protect. Realistic readers of the *Financial Times* draw realistic boundaries and one of them sent me a variant on Drysdale's Squirrel in Cider from a wartime recipe which was published to ease the problem of rationing in Britain in 1941.

Kill three squirrels, grey being preferred. Cut off the tails, skin the rest and cut into pieces, soaking them in cold, salted water for 20 minutes. Wipe them dry and dust them with seasoned flour. In a heavy saucepan, brown 100g of diced fat ham. Add the squirrel and brown the pieces in the ham fat. Just cover them with cider and simmer with a lid on until most of the cider has boiled off and the meat is soft. Add two tablespoons of unsalted butter; turn up the heat and brown the pieces again. Transfer them to a warm serving dish; pour 200ml of warmed cream into the remaining juices and stir in the brown bits off the pan. Mix half a tablespoon of plain flour and one tablespoon of butter into a paste. Stir it gradually into the cream and juices. Season with salt and pepper and strain the sauce over the browned nutkins. Display on the centre of your table with the tails arranged around the dish in a neat triangle.

Readers testify that the meat is superior to rabbit and is preferable to the supermarkets' apology for steak. It costs nothing. I presume the tails should retain their fur when displayed.

Spring view in the rhododendron wood, Bowood, Wiltshire

Spring

Some people like daisies in their turf; others don't. Jean-Jacques
Rousseau ascribed pinky eyelashes to the daisy, thought it a general
favourite, and called it the robin of flowers. To John Skelton it was
'daisie delectable', Beaumont and Fletcher thought it 'Smell-less and
most quaint', incorrectly, for a bunch of daisies has a peculiarly earthy
smell, especially when it comes as a hot little gift in the hand of a child.
Wordsworth, peering closely, noticed that it cast a shadow 'to protect
the lingering dewdrop from the sun'. Tennyson, who was usually
extremely accurate about such matters, went very wrong when he
claimed for Maud that

> '. . . her feet have touched the meadows
> And left the daisies rosy,'

for this is simply not true. Enchanted by this idea, I wasted many
youthful summer hours stamping on daisies, in fact I still do, but
never a daisy has so far blushed beneath my tread.

Fortunately for those who like their turf green and not speckled,
it is very easy for them to reverse the old song and give their answer to
Daisy. A selective weed-killer will do the trick economically and with
a great saving of labour, though it may be necessary to go twice with
the lethal watering-can over the ground.

Vita Sackville-West, in *The Observer*, 11 March 1956

Spring begins at an indeterminate moment which even the great pre-war gardener E. A. Bowles took several pages to try to pin down. In Northumberland, spring stirs only in a compressed few weeks from April onwards. In Cornwall camellias give hints of it as early as February. Outside warm London, spring dawns for me when *Magnolia* × *soulangeana* begins to flower, an event which has often come forwards to mid-March in the weather's warmer phase.

Magnolias are the necessary first initiative for any new garden. The work which they repay takes place before they are planted, a time when enthusiasm is running high and no effort seems too much to improve on the garden's previous owners. The planting-hole for a new magnolia should be deeply and widely dug and well manured to improve the soil's texture. A basic fertilizer should be mixed in below the new plant's root-ball to give it the chemicals it will need for swift progress. The plant should not be mulched deeply when it is planted because some of the finer magnolias have been grafted in infancy and a deep mulching may cover over the point of grafting with fatal results. During a new plant's first summers I drench its roots fortnightly with half a watering can of diluted Miracle-Gro. This treatment is not prescribed in other gardening books, but on my quick-draining, poor soil it works wonders. The young plants grow away strongly, leaving others, undrenched, far behind them. With young magnolias, preparation and fertilizing are crucial.

Varieties continue to proliferate and we are now spoilt for choice. Gardens on acid soils are most spoilt, but others have plenty to enjoy too. My top ten include the superb, all-white *Magnolia* × *soulangeana* 'Alba Superba', the loveliest of choices as a shrub against a tall west- or south-facing wall. Two recent forms have flowers of an unusual shape, *Magnolia* 'Manchu Fan' and 'Star Wars'. 'Manchu Fan' is a fan-shaped white flowerer of distinction and 'Star Wars' has the

The supreme classical scholar, E. R. Dodds, uprooting an anemone in Greece in spring

biggest flowers of all, huge rose-pink flushed cups which open to more than a foot in width. Both will grow on lime and 'Star Wars', especially, is vigorous and free-flowering from an early age. Its flowers are so showy.

Gardeners on acid soils are blessed with the option of magnolias whose flowers hang downwards like white lids. *Magnolia wilsonii* is one of the easiest and is sometimes recommended for gardens on lime soils too. It will grow there, but it is usually not happy, and in neutral or acid soils it is three times as good. By contrast all of us can enjoy elegant forms of the excellent *Magnolia* × *loebneri*, with narrow strap-shaped petals which open just before the leaves. I first saw × *loebneri*

'Leonard Messel' thirty years ago as a small tree in the Hillier Gardens in Hampshire, an excellent place for gardeners in the Home Counties to visit in order to view magnolias. It looked far too elegant for my sort of soil, but ten years later I planted one, drenched it with Miracle-Gro as it crawled along and now marvel at it in spring. The flowers have a heavenly pink-rose flush. Its cousin, 'Merrill', is a pure white which impatient gardeners and regular house-movers may prefer. 'Merrill' flowers very freely from a young age and takes the waiting out of wanting.

Once planted, magnolias are no problem. They need no pruning, no training, no weeding. They just develop and improve yearly. They anchor a spring garden which otherwise becomes such a rush for gardeners. Everything is accelerating, and there is so much to sow, plant and weed before the great surge of green growth in May. Before then there is time for just one quick glimpse of spring in the Mediterranean in March or early April and at least one trip to a great collection of old, established rhododendrons in early May. I have, therefore, let my thoughts wander here to two such outings, but Spring is above all the section for activity, in which initiatives multiply and advice could go on forever.

Two observations guide me, one practical, one aesthetic. The practical one concerns the planting of those shrubs and border plants which tempt us every spring in black pots of spongy, dark compost. Many of them have become too dry in the centre or lower half of their root-ball and need forcible watering before they go into their final hole outdoors. If their so-called 'soil' looks anything other than dark black-brown or if the root-ball feels light in the hand, take a hose and ram the tip of it up into the root-ball's underside and let it run until the ball becomes heavy and water is running freely out of its sides. As the weight of the soil increases, so do the plant's chances of surviving hard life outdoors. Its roots will probably be matted and twisted round and round its central ball too. If so, it is worth teasing them out sideways, or scoring them with the upper blade of a pair of secateurs so as to cut into their coiling and twisting and coax them to spread outwards into garden soil. The transition from light, drugged compost to genuine garden earth will often prove difficult. These plants have been pushed along in artificial compost on artificial food so as to

top: *Magnolia wilsonii*   above: My *Magnolia × loebneri* 'Leonard Messel'

reach a big pot-size quickly and sell at a higher price. They may also have sat for a month or more in a nursery, waiting for a buyer, so that their roots have coiled round their container's circle. When planting, I try to put a light coating of compost round the root-ball to persuade the roots to creep through it and meet the reality of Cotswold soil at one remove. If they are faced with such soil at once, they recoil and continue to twist around in their comfort-zone, their growers' apology for earth. Thoughtful gardeners even isolate newly bought convalescents and pot them on in a mixture of compost and local soil for another three months before planting.

Visually, spring gives us an array of fresh, invigorating colours, backed by the vivid green of new leaves and grass. So much is written about matching one flower's colour with another and placing plants with care, but in spring, under a clear pale light, this advice seems irrelevant. Everything goes together, set off by vibrant green. I smile wryly when 'guides to gardening' continue to recycle the old 'colour wheel' which the chemical engineer M. E. Chevreul devised in France in the 1860s. It set out the colours of the rainbow in a circle and was used as an argument for placing 'neighbouring' shades side by side in the garden or for combining pairs of colours which were directly opposite each other on the wheel, blue with orange perhaps, or red with green. Such pairing and matching were even believed to have a special stimulation for the 'rods' of vision connected to the human eye. The science of these 'rods' has moved on nowadays and although this wheel suggests one way of matching colours together, there is no reason to consider it the only authoritative way. I am more impressed by art than pseudo-science. When van Gogh looked at the spring flowers in the strong sunlight of Arles in southern France in the 1880s, he was delighted by combinations which the 'wheel' of a previous generation had excluded. He painted orange marigolds with dark maroon scabious or nasturtiums. He liked to use silver, a colour absent from Chevreul's wheel. He loved blue and pink as a pair, and when he found a garden to the north of Paris belonging to the artist Daubigny's widow, he wrote in the last months of his life how he would paint it with green and pink grass, a beech tree with violet leaves, and yellow lime trees, a lilac-coloured bush and 'sky pale green'. The painting still survives, a marvel which ignores the colour wheel's rules. Van Gogh

A spring view in Le Jardin Plume

thought carefully about 'entwining colours' and 'colours which cause each other to shine brightly', as he once wrote to his sister, 'which form a *couple*, which complement each other like man and woman'. He found them in pairs which ignored Chevreul's wheel. Increasingly, he looked back to Delacroix for examples of bold colour combinations.

Like van Gogh, the master of colour, gardeners need not be governed by the colour-wheel's rules. They are only one way of combining differently coloured flowers. Even their enthusiasts refer less to them in the bright mêlée of spring. In multicoloured April the wheel seems mysteriously to stop turning.

A Goat Island Garden

The first taste of spring is the sweetest and is usually tasted outside Britain. It is particularly evocative on the isle of Capri, in Italy. In the summer season, Capri is no longer a jewel near the top of informed travellers' wish lists. Too much has been built on it for expatriates in the early twentieth century and too many groups are now shipped across and told to shop and enjoy it. Out of season the island is not exactly a gardener's destination, but in late March I came to Capri on the tracks of a Roman emperor, Augustus' notorious successor, Tiberius. Unexpectedly, the island's flowers took over from its ancient history.

For ten years, between AD 27 and 37, the elderly Tiberius withdrew to Capri and continued to rule the empire from its rocky peaks without going anywhere near Rome. He is said to have owned twelve properties on the island and I wanted to see for myself where he resided, in a big house on the edge of the island. His years of retreat became the subject of gossip so salacious that even two thousand years later it was not translated from its original Latin in texts intended for general readers and schoolchildren. Only recently have editions of Suetonius' *Lives of the Caesars* and Tacitus' *Annals* made the allegations available. They are still strong stuff, of which compulsory sex with babies is only one of the disagreeable items.

I tried to forget the Latin words for swinging threesomes as I took the long uphill track to Tiberius' ultimate refuge, the so-called Villa Jovis, or Villa of Jupiter, on the far western tip of the island. Actually its plan is the plan of a palace, not a villa, at a time when the emperors did not yet have a proper palace in the heart of Rome. There were no signs of orgies, not even when a trio of goats appeared on cue at the path to what the text of the best ancient manuscript of Suetonius calls '*villa Ionis*', not '*villa Iovis*'. Contemporaries called its grounds the 'old goat's garden', referring to Tiberius' goat-like behaviour with boys and girls in its bushes. I did not follow the goats into the undergrowth.

My thoughts, rather, were historical. How ever did the Roman empire continue to function while the managing director was away for ten years on an island, enjoying the most spectacular view in the Mediterranean without anything so elementary as a phone? Tacitus artfully tells us that some people said the emperor had retired in his sixties because he looked so repulsive: his face was pockmarked and covered in bits of healing plaster. It is as if a British prime minister were to decide to withdraw to Lundy island, off the coast of Devon, for the rest of his term in office. It is interesting to wonder which modern states would function no worse if their leaders pulled out and kept quiet.

Pondering the question, I was not prepared for the exceptional view from the ruined floor of the emperor's residence. Who would ever prefer Rome to this sweeping panorama across the Bay of Naples and its unsurpassable coast? I then looked down, not out, and was even less prepared for the proofs of spring beyond my feet. Whatever may once have happened in the palace and its gardens has done nothing to deter the wild flowers. Down the cliffs and the goat-garden's sea face, flowers tumbled with a message for us all. Small pale-lavender irises were already flowering among the aromatic cistus. There were tufts of good blue flowers on bushes of wild rosemary beside the louche old emperor's bedroom. Above all, single, starry mauve-pink flowers showed by the hundred down cliffs where no goat, old or young, could reach them. Beside them on the crests of the rocks there were bushes of a blue more brilliant than any British forget-me-not. I had hit on the villa's unreported survivors, anemones and lithospermums, in their finest spring flush.

The mauve-pink anemones are the peacock anemones, which are better known in reds and purples on the slopes of stony Greece. I have grown them in Britain but they are best in the related coronaria form, which has flowers in brilliant scarlet, ringed centrally with white. The coloured anemones we use most often in gardens are the heavenly sky blue of *Anemone blanda* and the related pink and white. I began with about a hundred of them some ten years ago but now have ten times more. They have the merit of being unpalatable to British wildlife. In shade, the best choices are the woodland forms of *Anemone nemorosa*, the most delicate member of the family. It is worth paying extra for the best-named forms, including the pale yellow × *lipsiensis*. They are all easy plants, but life on a cliff in Capri is too hot for them.

What is the identity of the palace's deep blue lithospermum? The name is based on the Greek words for 'stone' and 'seed', a pointer to the plant's preferences in the wild. The Capri form is a relation of *Lithospermum diffusum* 'Heavenly Blue', a tempting deep-blue-flowered alpine for pots and low beds. 'Heavenly Blue' needs a lime-free soil and would never colonize arid, limestone cliffs. The modern name of the plant on Capri is *Lithodora rosmarinifolia*, the name by which botanists now call it, as they have dropped the well-known *Lithospermum* from their listings.

On my return home I checked my memories of this plant in one of my older bibles, the manual of the king of alpine plants, W. E. Ingwersen. The manual was published as a book, although it simply reprints the catalogues of Ingwersen's famous Sussex nursery between hard covers. On alkaline soil I have grown the lithospermum's lovely Spanish relation, *Lithodora oleifolia*, without any problems for twenty years. I recommend it, but the rosmarinifolia variety is more brilliant. However, it will not tolerate a chilly British winter.

To my delight, Ingwersen's manual comments simply that rosmarinifolia is 'spectacular on Capri'. Did the great alpine expert once see it there as I have? As I retraced my tracks through the imperial goat-garden, the goats were celebrating spring in a way that Tiberius would have appreciated. They had no interest in flowers which are even more blue than their island's famous Blue Grotto. Tiberius' palace is now a flattened, baffling ruin, better known as the object of ancient gossip, whose twitter makes other societies' tweets seem very tame. Nobody mentions wild flowers among the reasons for the old goat Tiberius' puzzling retreat from Rome. I would like to believe that the anemones diverted him, but somehow I doubt it. As for the blue lithodora, there was never even a word for it in Latin.

Special Spring Shrubs

Back in Britain, early spring shrubs are best in gardens with acid soil which are sheltered from the cold, exposed weather. Warming winters suit them, like their winter-flowering predecessors, but some of the best are still missed by gardeners. When winter's witch hazels have begun to fade, the limelight falls on the family of corylopsis, the witch hazels' botanical relation. If you have acid, leafy ground suitable for camellias, you have an excellent chance of a haze of yellow flowers on corylopsis in mid-March.

Corylopsis is happy in North America and is nowhere better than in the Brooklyn Botanic Garden in New York where it thrives on acid soil. The most impressive variety is a Chinese one, *Corylopsis sinensis*. In Britain sinensis likes light shade and a damp soil with light leaf mould. It grows into a shrub up to eight feet high and covers itself with hanging clusters of yellow, scented flowers on bare branches. In full flush, it is a spectacular sight, the flowers being heavier and more significant than those on its more widely seen relation, *Corylopsis pauciflora*. This one is Japanese and is pretty in lightly shaded acid soil too. Its flowers are a paler yellow in a more delicate shape than those on sinensis, but they have a similar sweet scent. Pauciflora grows about four feet high and when happy spreads outwards into a wider girth.

I covet it but it detests life on my lime soil. A better hope is *Corylopsis glabrescens*, whose flowers hang in heavier bunches. The problem is that it is markedly less hardy, although warmer winters now make it worth a risk. Altogether easier is its fellow Japanese *Stachyurus praecox*, a remarkably obliging shrub with hanging flowers in shades of yellow, this time tending to green-yellow. Its bushes grow taller, up to ten feet eventually, but their hardiness is not in question and I have had happy specimens growing in an exposed north-facing site. Stachyurus is a reliable shrub when competing with rough grass, so long as the underlying soil is damp. It is an easy shrub there and will need no further attention.

Corylopsis pauciflora

Far easier on all soils are the indestructible forms of flowering currant, in the family of ribes. Indoors, they can be enjoyed in very early flower if you pick branches of them in February and bring them directly into a room so that the buds will open early. Outdoors, their great virtue is that they will grow in difficult dry shade, provided that there is sunlight through the canopy early in the year. Their impact is so pleasant, including the currant scent of the leaves and the range of available colours. The best-known forms are red, and I like the deeper shades best, including the later-flowering *Ribes sanguineum* 'King Edward VII'. The good news is there is now an extra-good white form, *Ribes sanguineum* 'White Icicle', which is much brighter than previous white forms and is one to track down. These varieties of ribes are excellent choices for difficult corners along the boundary of a garden where they are tolerant of dry and difficult conditions.

Camellias, by contrast, are not for everyone. Acid soil is their pre-requisite, but the easiest group for outdoor gardeners contains the

Camellia × *williamsii* 'Debbie'

× *williamsii* hybrids, in which there are two excellent varieties from the same breeder in New Zealand. One is a particularly good yellow-centred variety, 'Jury's Yellow', which is compact but upright in growth. It makes an excellent plant in a large pot and, in spring, shows the most beautiful flowers with an outer ring of white petals and a central yellow cluster for contrast. The pair to it, raised by the same Mr Jury, is the unusually weather-proof pink *Camellia* × *williamsii* 'Debbie'. This mid pink form has several virtues. It starts to flower early and will be fully open in London in mid-January. It stands up relatively well to rain and a touch of frost and, above all, it drops its faded flowers when they are finished. The dying flowers on other camellias have a habit of hanging around for too long, especially on forms of *Camellia japonica*. 'Debbie' is a good choice for a large pot, but like 'Jury's Yellow' must have acid compost only and be kept away from lime, even when watered with tap water.

Denied camellias by my lime soil, I have the early spring varieties

of prunus instead and am hoping to see a return from the double pink
Prunus triloba from China against a wall. Its flowers look almost
artificial from a distance and although I had no luck with this plant in
open ground, on a wall it is said to be easier. It needs to be pruned hard
after flowering and is enchanting if given this minimal attention. The
omens look good for *Prunus triloba* 'Multiplex' in only its third year.
In pots, meanwhile, there is an excellent new possibility, the single-
flowered *Prunus incisa* 'Kojo-no-mai', which is now commonly offered
in garden centres. Early March is the time to select plants because they
are in delicate flower along their small branches and you can see what
you are buying. They have such charm to their flowers and make
excellent shrubs for pots in a front garden, where they mark the beginning of longer days and garden-friendly weather. After their spring
flowering, you can take the twiggy small bushes away and put them
somewhere less prominent. This treatment does not worry them in
the least. 'Kojo-no-mai' needs no pruning but has been overlooked
until recent years. When we start to think about active gardening
again, this early-flowering plant urges us to get out and get on with it.

Harassed by Perpetual Bother

By mid-April, the shrub which many of us still call 'japonica' is starting to flower in gardens from Boston across to Rome. To many, it is no more than an admirable shrub for a wall in spring, best grown in a strong red-flowered hybrid form, of which the spreading 'Rowallane' or the flaming red 'Knap Hill Scarlet' are two of the best. They will flower facing north, east, or in tangled clumps if planted as thickets in rougher parts of the garden in order to suppress weeds. The botanists make us call the japonica *Chaenomeles* and even a semi-gardener finds it a difficult plant to kill. There the matter may rest for you, as you bask in hopes of sunshine on a day near Easter. For me, it is the beginning of a deeper story. The red japonica evokes letters, people and a predicament which has changed what I see in its yearly display.

Nobody has been a more straightforward spokesman for the beleaguered British countryside than the nineteenth-century poet John Clare. In his early life in Northamptonshire he would 'watch for hours the little insects climbing up and down the tall stems of wood grass'. He later remarked how 'in my boyhood, Solitude was the most talkative vision I met with'. Two hundred years ago, in Northamptonshire, cowslips were still known as paigles and John Clare observed them without botanical training. He loved and knew them nonetheless. Part of Clare's life was spent in the village of Helpston near the stately home of Lord Milton and his head gardener, Joseph Henderson. In 1836, the following exchange of letters took place between these admirable men. 'Will you have the kindness,' asked Clare, 'to give me a few shrubs and flowers, a few woodbines (honeysuckles) and something my wife likes she calls everlasting; have you got a drooping willow and a double blossomed furze? My wife also wants a red japonica . . .'

Joseph Henderson was just the man to cope with this request. He was not a head gardener of the type which colleges produce nowadays, trained in the use of chopped bark and rules about health and safety. He corrected the grammar in one of Clare's most famous poems and hunted down books for him in his employer's antique library. One of the female servants in Lord Milton's big house turned out to know a ballad called 'The Song of All the Birds in the Air'. On Clare's behalf, Henderson promised to copy it from her singing. He duly sent the poet the words.

Henderson was also a dealer in antiquities. Whenever Roman coins were found on Lord Milton's estate, they were brought to Henderson who would pay up to sixpence for 'such as he thinks good' and sell them on to educated collectors. If you wanted a denarius Henderson would see you right. He was well able to meet Clare's request for the red 'japonica', which I assume to have been a variety of *Chaenomeles speciosa*, already known in England for some years before 1836, although its home is in central China. Henderson wrote back to Clare confirming the order and promising to send a man to plant them in. He would be 'including some chrysanthemums, the plants I believe Mrs Clare calls everlasting'.

In mid-April I take cuttings off my chrysanthemums and you may think that this idyllic exchange of letters between two self-taught thoughtful gardeners makes a happy mental accompaniment to the job. It was not, however, as idyllic as it first seems. Clare ended his letter by saying: 'I am hardly able to say more.' The japonica arrived and flowered, but the participants went in different directions. Henderson, the gardener, moved to service in Surrey, but poor Clare was afflicted by mental disorder. It took him first to the asylum in Northampton and then to intensive care, well meant but misguided, at High Beech in Epping Forest. He arrived there about a year after Henderson's gift of the japonica and wrote that he had 'arrived in the land of Sodom where all the people's brains are turned the wrong way . . .' Some of you may recognize your school days, others may think of those nowadays who are still in prisons or in care.

Five years later, Clare was still hoping for news of the drooping willow and the flowers in his abandoned cottage. He then sent the most heart-rending letter which has ever been carried in the post. It went to his wife, whom he pictured in charge of the garden, and told her in simple capital letters: 'My sojourn here has been even from the

A 'red japonica' in spring

beginning more than irksome but I shake hands with misfortune and wear through the storm – the spring smiles and so shall I, but not while I am here . . .' With the clarity of long confinement, he then told her: 'It was my lot to seem as living without friends until I met with you and though we are now parted, my affection is unaltered . . . Essex is a very pleasant county. Yet to me "there is no place like home" . . .' The letter cannot have been easy reading for her among her husband's everlasting flowers. It became even more direct. 'For what reason they keep me here I cannot tell, for I have been no other-ways than well a couple of years at the least and I never was very ill, only harassed by perpetual bother . . .'

Out in the country which he loved so well, many of us are 'harassed by perpetual bother' in smaller ways. It is not a bad description of gardening life. I like to think that his wife received the letter, read it by the red japonica and remembered how their life had once been lived before his stability deserted him. 'I would sooner be packed in a slave ship for Affrica than belong to the destiny of mock friends and real enemies . . .' In mid-April *Chaenomeles japonica* comes into flower and as Clare wrote earlier in his life: 'We see a flower not only in its form and colour. Our imagination, too, brings a world of associations adding beauty and interest to the object actually before our eyes.'

Put Them on Prozac

Mid-April ought to be the height of the season for flowering bulbs, but their range in my garden is restricted by uninvited residents. Badgers remain a subject of public debate. Should we cull them or should we cuddle them? Officially, the question is whether or not they spread TB round cattle. During winter and most of the early spring, my garden is battered by badgers who dig holes in the lawn, uproot every tulip and destroy my small-flowered crocuses, planted devotedly over many years. As usual, the government is advancing towards the problem on too narrow a front. We need urgent research not only on badgers' role among cattle but on the crocus-locating facility of the adult badger, which is one of the miracles of the animal kingdom. It might prove to be a discovery as useful as radar. Armed with it, a badger can sense bulbs where they have been sleeping for decades.

Beset by badgers, I have come up with a new solution: put them on Prozac. Why Prozac? I regard it as proof of the lateral thinking for which an Oxford education is famous. In the bathroom I have one of those cupboards which fill up with pills prescribed in emergencies but never consumed over time. Their owners have come and gone in my life and when spring arrives, the urge to clean is in the air. Why not give the pills of absent women to the badgers on the lawn? Here is the logic behind my thinking, based on scraps of badger literature which have explained what may be wrong.

Those of you who work in the public sector will not be surprised to hear that the problem is social. It is not the badger's fault. It is not even that a well-off, middle-class badger would want to eat a crocus out of choice. The problem is the badger's age. When a male badger becomes old, he becomes the most dreadful bore. The rest of the group cannot put up with him and so they expel him from their social circle. A boring badger has to go on the wander and ends up in our gardens, taking disgruntled revenge on the tulips. I recognize this problem because it sometimes afflicts elderly academics of distinction. The years pass and they never fully retire. When they come in for the day from the academic woods they cause younger colleagues to go into hiding at lunchtime. Gone are the days when a king of potential boredom used to send his academic colleagues a courteous postcard, giving details of the days when he would be in Oxford. On it he would write, 'in case you wish to absent yourself'.

Prozac is supposed to cure gloom and isolation, especially as the years pass. If an ageing badger is socially miserable, why not cheer him up? At dead of night I did it. I crushed Prozac in the food mixer and spooned it into lumps of crushed peanut butter which fellow sufferers tell me is the supreme badger-attractor. I put sixteen heaps of the mixture at intervals around the lawn. The next morning they were all gone.

I feel half ashamed and half proud about what happened next. Two days later I returned late at night from work and, with due astonishment, found a badger trotting down the road off which my drive runs. I caught him in the headlights and, obligingly, he swung right up my drive. How fast can a badger run on Prozac? I am sure we were doing twenty miles an hour, but I lack the callous blood-lust of the anti-hunting classes. Every day I pass the road-cull of these liberal opponents of blood-sports who have squashed cock pheasants, rammed a few rabbits and usually left a badger somewhere in their wake. My reason kept telling me that I had a free gift in the headlights, the supreme enemy of the winter garden who was on the run before me. For a hundred yards I could not bear to accelerate but when I finally put on speed, the old boar dodged sideways through the lime trees and vanished from view. I think the Prozac saved him. Full of goodwill and optimistic about the world, he had broken the previous record for a badger sprint.

Many of you may be feeling sympathetic to badgers, but you have been misled by propaganda and those stories that badgers are wise old throwbacks to the pre-Roman era in Britain. A badger in the wrong place is a Class A menace. Why are people sentimental about the species? The Royal Horticultural Society has even teamed up with the Wildlife Trust for a joint initiative for 'wildlife gardens'. What will trusting wildlife gardeners do when a badger cuts loose among the thousands of crocuses recently planted along the Broad Walk in Kew Gardens?

A happy badger – on medication?

Since the tranquillized peanut butter, there has been a remarkable quiet on my lawn. It is just as well because I am now considering an alternative: the sleeping pill Temazepam. If it was strong enough for Marilyn Monroe, it ought to be strong enough for Mr Brock.

Sow and Scatter

While my badgers bask in a new happiness, the combination of rain, cool temperatures and sun on mid-April days is ideal for sowing hardy annual seeds directly into the ground. Seize the moment and join those who reckon that the results are what make them happy gardeners. Every variety I mention is available from the tireless Chiltern Seeds at Bortree Stile, Ulverston, Cumbria, or from Thompson & Morgan at Poplar Lane, Ipswich, Suffolk.

I will refer only to hardy annuals for which no greenhouse is needed. To sow them you need to have a proper rake, as you will need to smooth over the soil in the beds where you wish to sow. Break the soil up first with a fork of manageable size. Bash any remaining lumps to dissolve them and then rake the surface over to establish a tilth. A tilth is soil with a fine consistency, the sort of consistency which you would get if you put a packet of digestive biscuits into a food processor and scrunched them into crumbs. Water the tilth, if necessary, and leave it to drain for an hour or two. Then with the back of the rake, press a shallow seed-drill in a straight line into the tilth, aiming at a depth of about a quarter of an inch. Into this drill, scatter the contents of the seed packet and then rake the tilth back over it and pat it lightly down with the head of the rake held flat, not at an angle. If the weather turns dry, you will need to water regularly from a can with a fine rose. After three weeks, seedlings should be showing, probably in dense clusters unless you are more deft at sowing pinches of seed than I am. You can thin them out either by discarding the surplus or by transplanting them into the empty spaces which you left between the lines of the seed-drills.

The fun comes in the choice which is available. There is no way that you will be able to buy pre-grown scented mignonette from shops in late May. To enjoy its scent, you have to sow it for yourself, finding it under the name reseda in catalogues. It is extremely easy to grow. So

White-flowered
Silybum marianum

is another of my favourites, the good old pot marigold or calendula. I like all the varieties, including the short, double 'Candyman Yellow', but I recommend a taller double mixture called 'Prince' because it is especially good for picking. These easy flowers give a lift to the garden from July onwards and will often self-seed from year to year. They flourish in all weathers and I recommend them.

I also recommend a prickly little number called silybum. The one to find in the family is the St Mary's thistle, whose leaves are beautifully cut and marked with white spots, attributed to that globally abundant substance, the Virgin's excess milk, flowing freely since her time at Bethlehem. The seeds are very easy to handle and I like to fit a few plants into gravel or the corners of buildings, where their conspicuous spotted leaves become very pretty. The flowers are not interesting, although there is now a white form. Again, St Mary's thistle will not be seen in supermarkets. Nor will the excellent forms of annual sunflower. The name 'helianthus' hides the best available, which grow up to four or five feet and flower in rich colours. They are not as gigantic as the commercial sunflower of Mediterranean farming, and instead of its sunny yellow I recommend the dark crimson-chocolate 'Velvet Queen'. Its flowers enliven the back row of a herbaceous border from late July onwards.

Most gardeners are unaware of two lovely low-growing blue annuals, the rich deep blue *Phacelia campanularia*, which prefers sun, and the sky-blue, white-centred *Nemophila menziesii*, which prefers shade and water. They are easy, charming and too seldom grown, as is the annual blue pimpernel, blue anagallis, which will usually succeed if sown directly outdoors. It, too, is a fine plant for the front row of a flowerbed where its blue flowers continue into the autumn.

Cornflowers are much more familiar in our mind's eye but it will soon be hard to find the colour we really want. Packets of cornflower seed are drifting away into mixtures of blue, off-pink and so forth, whereas the classic blue is the winner and is much better if it has not been miniaturized to a height of six inches. Keep up demand and perhaps we will keep the separated colour of 'Blue Diadem' in the trade. It is the easiest of annuals to sow as its small seeds are like little shaving brushes. It looks so pretty when dotted through flowerbeds of supposedly more distinguished company, or alternatively it can be segregated into a pot and treated as a treasure. It performs very well when pot-grown and catches visitors by surprise for being so straight-forward in a special place. I also grow some of the tall varieties for cut flowers and enjoy them in glasses of water indoors.

Even if you are not good at making a tilth, you will succeed with the common forms of annual poppy. Most of the easy ones are forms of *Papaver somniferum*, which have been selected for particular colours and shapes to their petals. I much like the vivid one called 'Red Bombast' which I saw last summer in the garden of an owner who justified the plant's name. There is no missing it as it is such a strong colour. I also like the striped and spotted colouring of the selection called 'Flemish Antique'. They have the look of fine poppies in a Dutch painting and if you thin out the germinated seedlings, the plants will develop strongly, even in dry years. They are obliging as fillers and we do not yet make enough use of them.

We also ignore something so easy and elegant that it ought to be everywhere but never is. The popular name of agrostemma is corn cockle and my favourite is still the one called 'Milas', named after a corner of south-west Turkey where it must have been found as a wild flower. The tall, elegant plants take up very little room and reach about two-and-a-half feet, producing lilac-pink flowers for most of the summer, or a deeper red-pink if you choose 'Milas'. I never tire of them and even in dry summers they will succeed as they succeed in Turkey.

Mixed annual poppies in Le Jardin Plume

To enjoy these self-raised plants, there is no need for a greenhouse or a cold frame or particular skill. There are dozens more annuals to choose from, all of which give a garden the look of a thoughtfully chosen patchwork which has not been bought ready-grown. They attach us to the process of gardening and make us feel responsible for their generous success.

Harmonious Rhododendrons

When it is warm, green and heavenly in an English spring there is no lovelier time in a landscape. It is particularly lovely if you live on lime-free soil and can grow the great May-flowering trees and shrubs from the Far East. Supreme among such shrubs are rhododendrons, but do they fit into the green nature of Britain when they are at their best? Rhododendrons have their opponents, many of whom do not know the family's full range. They seem to think that all rhododendrons have mauve or purple flowers and are as rampageous as the rampant ponticum form in Sunningdale or Scotland. They also bring up the controversial placing of rhododendrons in natural parks and landscapes, especially Stourhead in Wiltshire, where they gleam around the historic lake in the eighteenth-century garden.

Recently, I went to a lunch for the rhododendron's friends and experts and saw a setting which refuted the contention about rhododendrons' incompatibility. In Wiltshire, rhododendrons have been sharing another famous landscape with a great design from the eighteenth century and have not detracted from it at all. At Bowood, home of the Lansdowne family, rhododendrons have had a happy history for more than 150 years. About 200,000 visitors now enjoy Bowood every year, but are slow to hunt out the entrance to its great woodland garden. This separate area of the park can still be enjoyed in fitting tranquillity. It owes its beauty to the family's long involvement with rhododendrons, a relationship whose continuity is unique.

At Bowood the two great elements of the garden are kept separate. From the house, the high point of the landscape is one of the greatest of all lakes by Capability Brown. In the 1760s, the landscape designer was at the height of his powers and his original plan for Bowood's park survives, a tribute to the confidence of the designer and his patron. On it, curving belts of trees are marked in detail for the park's far horizons and a lake is sketched out, placed so as to draw on five natural springs.

Rhododendron augustinii in a haze of bluebells at Bowood

These springs have never failed, not even in the long drought of 1976. To make room for the lake, a shabby village had to be destroyed and re-sited in a less intrusive position, and its inhabitants had to be transplanted to new homes. In 2007 the foundations of their former village were rediscovered on the floor of Capability Brown's lake, found by members of a sub-aqua diving club from the nearby town of Calne. It was as well that the villagers had moved out. As I walked to this lake past a fine fern-leaved beech tree, I thought how unfair the wits of the eighteenth century had been to Brown. One of them told him that he was fervently hoping to die before him. When Brown asked why, he replied that he was so wanting to see heaven before Brown improved its 'capabilities'. By the lake at Bowood, visitors can feel grateful that if ever they see heaven, they will be seeing it when the lake's designer has had time to reshape it.

Where, then, are the rhododendrons? Their first home, during my visit, was on the tables during lunch. The present Marquis of Lansdowne, the family's ninth, had picked a selection of varieties only a few hours before the party and had put them in vases on his guests' tables. Even the expert Roy Lancaster struggles to identify rare yellow-flowered varieties from Bowood's past. After lunch, we set off in a motor-convoy to a far corner of the park, where Bowood's rhododendrons have been developing since the 1850s. They are not the oldest rhododendrons in Britain, some of which are now classed as 'heritage hybrids' and live on at Highclere Castle near Newbury, where they date back to about 1815. Bowood's plantings are slightly younger but they have had an exceptional continuity in the care of one and the same family. The Lansdownes are still planting new varieties, and their beautifully planted wood should be a first stop in May for the thousands who enjoy the rest of Bowood's magnificent park. It is worth a special trip along the M4 in order to see how rhododendrons will cohabit under a tall canopy of oaks and parkland trees above the most beautiful carpets of English bluebells.

At a rhododendron lunch, always try to sit near an expert so as to keep up with the questions and answers. In a rhododendron plantation, allow the experts to go into a huddle with their breeding books and dispute the inmates' identities. They will even debate the parentage of the pale brown fur, which they call 'indumentum', on the undersides of old varieties, and they debate it especially keenly if the plants have not been labelled since 1854. Bowood has great old specimens which stretch experts to the limit, while the rest of us happily admire the spacing and the colour planning, and recognize old friends like Rhododendron 'Loder's White'.

It is important that these shrubs are generously spaced. Big rhododendrons in banks of flower are easy to accommodate, but they look so much better if sweeps of grass intervene between them and set off their colours. A rhodo-wood is not difficult to maintain if the nettles and other weeds are sprayed from a backpack during their growing season. It is also easier if the soil stays as damp as Bowood's with the help of natural springs. The blue haze of Bowood's mature *Rhododendron augustinii* is a marvel, and even an opponent of rhododendrons would soften before the subtle pale yellow of 'Cool Haven'. When you learn the difference between 'Beauty of Littleworth' and the yellow markings on evergreen 'Glory of Littleworth', you want to grow them both. Dazzled by the colours, I asked the experts which of the strong, clear red varieties they would recommend for amateur gardeners. Their choice was the intense 'May Day', an excellent flowerer which is late enough to miss spring frosts. Their insider knowledge also recommends the later-flowering varieties which carry the season on into July. If you think that rhododendrons are over by mid-June, look out in future for varieties which have been bred in Liverpool and are named after parts of the city. They will flower long after the usual bushes have finished.

Nothing stands safely still in gardens, not even in a mature woodland which has remained in one family's care. In 1990 a storm destroyed one side of the upper canopy in Bowood's rhododendron wood and ruined the shrubs beneath the trees. The line of the damage is still clearly visible, but Bowood's owners continued to replant, adding to the evolution of their great woodland garden. Capability Brown may have gone to heaven and improved it but he died before seeing the rhododendrons whose capabilities have improved his own.

Reappearing Poppies

By late May, gardens are dominated by the colour green, the vibrant green of young leaves on the trees or the fresh green of grass as it accelerates its growth. In his 'green shade' this green seemed 'lovely' and 'amorous' to the poet Andrew Marvell. Thoughtful gardeners consider it overpowering. The classic correction is to send for bright scarlets and reds, a vivid counterweight. Gardeners are no longer so afraid of strong colours in May and early June, and the highest value has come to be set on particular forms of red oriental poppy. These poppies used to be prefaced with apologies. Gardeners had to be warned that their colours could be strong and hard to place and that after flowering they would quickly disappear, leaving unwanted gaps. Nowadays, these vices are seen as virtues. The vibrant reds of the best oriental poppies are an antidote to the excessive green of early summer. Gaps are now seen as a blessing because they allow yet more ingenuity and tightly packed planting which will prolong the season after the early flowerers' disappearance.

Poppies have also prospered mightily on the new wave of garden photography. Perfect colour pictures set the standard for gullible gardeners and few look better than a photo of a poppy, caught in the early morning or late evening without a hint of blackfly or rain damage on its petals. Photographs catch only a brief moment, and the short flowering period of the best poppies is not the photographer's business. Photos of fancy-coloured poppies are deceptive, too, because their shades of grey, brown-maroon or peach-salmon look so much better on film than they do in a living garden. Not long ago a flattering photograph of a poppy called 'Patty's Plum' sent collectors scurrying to south-west England to find stock of this damson-coloured beauty. The price soared upwards and I was grateful to the reader in Taunton who sent me a small plant with her compliments. Two years later I can see why she was willing to be generous. 'Patty's

Plum' is an immediate seller at the plant fairs which are organized so nobly in private gardens for charity, but when it flowers off film, it is disappointing, the colour of a muddy tea cloth.

The varieties which deserve acclaim are the ones which used to be avoided because they were too vivid. They have flowers of a blinding scarlet or a deeper red, held on tall stems and opening to a size which makes an impact. I have learned to dot them around the garden at intervals and rely on them to lift it out of excessive greenness in the weeks between the irises and the main showers of roses. Red poppies are also spectacular companions for stretches of roughly mown grass. Here they will compete with a new season's growth among the decaying leaves of daffodils. If the grass is left uncut until late June, the poppies' dying leaves can be cut down at the same time, and year after year the strongest varieties will survive this meadow treatment. By contrast the classic red poppies of cornfields and Impressionist paintings are only annuals. They will not last from year to year unless they happen to seed themselves successfully.

Scarlet-flowered perennial poppies are the ones to work into the setting of a garden. My particular favourites are the strong pink *Papaver orientale* 'Raspberry Queen', the self-supporting 'Brilliant', the tall, deep red 'Goliath', and its upright form 'Beauty of Livermere', whose deep red flowers are wonderfully marked with black. These varieties are extremely easy to grow on dry soil in sunshine, where other late developers can be planted close to them so as to make a tangle from July onwards and cover their decay and disappearance. They are plants to be used individually but they also allow two separate seasons in the same patch of ground. Since Livermere discovered its Beauty, important poppy-breeding has been going on in Europe, as a recent trial of the family at Wisley gardens established. Varieties like pale pink 'Karine' and red-and-black 'Spätzünder' have now proved to be stunning too. Poppies of this quality will not come true from seed and cannot be divided. They put down a long taproot and cannot be split from above, although the clumps of leaves seem to invite an assault in late April. The way to increase them is to take root cuttings, an easy and enjoyable task which is best delayed until late autumn. Root cuttings turn one plant into half a dozen within two years and their method is extremely simple, though it risks being forgotten in this age of supermarket shopping. Dig deeply round an established poppy in autumn and try to lift it from the ground with as much of the taproot as possible. Cut the taproot into pieces about two inches long, laying them out carefully so that you know which end of the cutting came from the upper part of the root when you dissected it. Transfer the cuttings to pots of sandy soil, plant them with the upper part uppermost, water them and put the pots under the staging in a cold greenhouse or on a sheltered area of paving outdoors. If you muddle the ends of the cuttings, you can simply lay them lengthways on a well-watered seedtray of good compost and then scatter another half-inch of well-watered compost on top of them. The miracle then takes place and new shoots will sprout through the soil by the end of the following spring. It is all so easy, but I feel proud when it works. The young plants should be potted on in good, nursery soil and then moved into a permanent place in late summer. They will flower in the following spring, about eighteen months after the start of the operation.

When Connie Met Oliver

Up in Derbyshire, off exit 30 on the M1, a very short drive leads to the gardens at Renishaw Hall, home of the famous Sitwell family for hundreds of years. Their roses are remarkable and in chilly Derbyshire the brilliant blue *Ceanothus* 'Italian Skies' is as prolific as elegant *Magnolia wilsonii* with its hanging flowers. The resident Sitwells still tend and improve the garden with taste and understanding, but the reason for a visit is its history. Renishaw combines two extremes: the formal classical and the seditiously romantic.

The classical extreme connects to a most unusual book, *On the Making of Gardens*, which appeared in 1909, written by the present owner's grandfather, Sir George Sitwell. Its text was the result of painstaking observation and stylistic effort but it was a flop when it first appeared. Even now it is impenetrable, but it has acquired the fascination of a distant time and taste. The book is the literary pair to the backbone of the garden which we now see at Renishaw and it has become an unusual chapter in the history of looking at nature. In the 1890s, Sir George had already been attracted by the green architectural style of the great gardens of Italy. Basically, he had no taste for flowers, thinking them a common distraction. In 1900 his obsessively practical and antiquarian mind had a brief breakdown, after which he travelled, no less obsessively, in Italy, taking careful notes on more than 200 half-neglected formal gardens of the distant Italian past. You might think that he then returned home and laid out his garden on the new principles which this travel had taught him. Not at all. Even before leaving, he had begun the formal design of green yew hedges and geometric patterns which is still one of Renishaw's distinctions. By November 1900, Sir George's garden was already being commended for its 'architectural fitness'. The nervous breakdown, the Italian travel and the book elaborated a taste which he already had. Nine years later, in 1909, the book never mentioned Renishaw, his home. Instead, Sir George tried to establish 'principles of design' and to explain the causes of our pleasure when we look at gardens. His theories are a gold-mine of intellectual debris from the Edwardian past. They link up with a fashion of the time, the Italian style of formal gardening which was being described simultaneously by the novelist Edith Wharton. Another component was the bundle of popularized theories through which Sir George absorbed amateur psychology, evolution and the principles of popular science. He then tried to explain our pleasure in viewing a garden as if it is an echo of our evolutionary history. At the same time, he thought, it exploits more recent elements of our psychology and vision, and more flexible elements of our mental power. His own theory is appealing rubbish and is written in an extraordinary style. His son, the famous Osbert Sitwell, described how Sir George would go to endless pains when trying to research and construct a single sentence. His prose is an unintended tribute to the contrary value of spontaneity.

One of his other sons, Sachie, wrote that 'to have been alive and sentient is the grand experience'. It is, therefore, intriguing to find that Renishaw is not just a classicizing monument. It has had an impact on the literature of life and feeling whose 'grand experiences' are known across the world. Beyond doubt, Renishaw is the model for the great house, Wragby Hall, in D. H. Lawrence's *Lady Chatterley's Lover*. The name 'Wragby' was borrowed from a Lincolnshire village, but Renishaw's house and grounds were the basis for those scenes of sentient life between her ladyship and the gamekeeper at his cottage in the woods.

Walking down Renishaw's fine vistas in search of the cottage, I found myself turning back to Lawrence's erotic masterpiece. Perhaps Lawrence visited Renishaw in September 1926, and certainly he talked with Osbert Sitwell in Italy in the summer of 1927. The disabled Sir Clifford Chatterley owes a debt to Lawrence's impressions of Osbert Sitwell, who was also a baronet's son. Chatterley's house is deliberately described as 'a dreary old house in a defaced countryside, with a rather inadequate income'. It was there that Lady Chatterley found herself dreaming of wild horses and craving the rough kiss of male flesh in the garden grounds.

Lawrence's text survives in several versions, beginning with ones in which Mellors the gamekeeper is called Parkin and there is a greater presence of flowers. After hours of passion in the keeper's hut, Lady Chatterley steadies herself by gardening. She settles down to work with Wragby's housekeeper in a garden which has double lines of auriculas, called 'recklesses', significantly, in Derbyshire dialect. 'For some reason she felt drawn to Mrs Bolton as if she had something in common with her.' Together, the two women 'peg down carnations', a forgotten aspect of modern bedding-out. They also put in 'small plants of flowers for the summer' which turn out to be 'columbines', a most unlikely flower for the summer season as they are aquilegias and would have finished flowering by mid-June. Nonetheless, 'Connie felt a delight in softly putting in the roots into the soft black earth of the borders'. It is one which I am unable to confirm: 'She felt her womb quiver with pleasure, as if something were taking root there, in the same way.'

Floral bedding-out took on a new meaning for her because of her previous bedding-out in the woods. 'Four miles' away from the house, according to Lawrence, lay the gamekeeper's cottage where Connie met Oliver, at least in the book's first version. In his arms, she felt 'like a volcano' at those moments when she 'surged with desire, with passion like a stream of white hot lava'. Flowers, even so, came into the affair. The gamekeeper's cottage was distinguished by the only wild daffodils in the area. When the inmate made love to her on a heap of dry wood, she had the 'grand experience' of 'wonderful rippling thrills and peels of bells'. The steady, silent gamekeeper then admired her ladyship's breasts, 'longish' breasts, according to Lawrence, while her naked skin looked 'faintly golden' like a 'Gloire de Dijon' rose. Nowadays, *Rosa* 'Gloire de Dijon' is somewhat prone to mildew. Afterwards, her ladyship went out naked into the garden and in the first version wreathed those longish breasts with honeysuckle. In the second version of the book, Parkin did it for her and even tucked some 'sprays of fluffy young oak' underneath them. I did not see honeysuckle at Renishaw in early June and I wonder how those oak-sprays stayed in place.

Both of the men in Connie's life were readers, albeit in different ways. Sir Clifford, master of Renishaw, was fascinated by the ancient Greeks, especially by Plato, at least in the novel's first versions. He thought the Greeks were 'sometimes like little boys who have just discovered they can think, and are beside themselves about it'. Thinking, however, was not what his wife wanted. Eventually, Sir Clifford matured from the thoughtful Greeks to material business and started to invest in the local mines. He threw his disabled energy into making them profitable, but his wife, like Lawrence, was horrified. 'A great portion of his consciousness seems to have lapsed, like a flower blown out. And what remained of him was this idolatrous ecstasy to the shrine of Money.' This mania for business struck Lawrence as 'the danger of the Greeks . . . They too had this mad egoism and the insane love of money.' It is not how the famous ancient Greek poets and orators present themselves, but they certainly knew how to make passionate love.

Igniting such passion in a lady was not the gamekeeper's only talent, either. He, too, was a man of unexpected range. As Connie looked round his 'bare little bedroom' in the morning light, at least in the text's later versions, her eye lit on a 'shelf with some books, and some from a circulating library. She looked. There were books about bolshevist Russia, books of travel, a volume about the atom and the electron, another about the composition of the earth's core and the causes of earthquakes: then a few novels: then three books on India. So! he was a reader after all.' When the thoughtful keeper moved away, he became a Communist in a factory.

When ladies say they are 'passionate gardeners', I think of Connie their patron saint planting those columbines in May, a fortnight before they would flower. There were pleasures evoked by Renishaw's gardens for which Sir George's 'evolutionary echo' was much more apt than he realized. As for the patron of thoughtful gardeners, he is not a lecturer in a college of landscape design. He is Parkin the gamekeeper carrying honeysuckle and 'fluffy' oak. 'If only she could stay,' her ladyship yearned, 'if only there weren't the other ghastly world of smoke and iron. If only *he* would make her a world.'

Peonies

What are gardeners gaining from the commercial openness of China?
The great plant-hunters of the early twentieth century brought back
trees, shrubs and bulbs from east Asia which transformed our plantings in the West. In the 1960s, while a thousand flowers bloomed
under the pickaxes of the Revolutionary Guard, the gains for
gardeners ceased. Since the 1980s matters have improved, as botanists
returned to China and began to discover how much more remained to
be introduced to gardens. The first collectors had focused on rhododendrons and other big shrubs, and as smaller plants were less popular
with their patrons, these awaited a second wave of discovery. The risk
to them is no longer revolutionary. It is the risk of industrialization
which diverts water and then dynamites their mountains for stone
and metals.

One natural Chinese family has long been known, but has been
elusive for Western gardeners who want to acquire and cherish it. The
tree peony has had the highest status in Chinese art and culture but
until recently it has been difficult to find historic varieties in European
nurseries. The most sought-after plant for connoisseurs has been a
lovely white form with a dark central blotch on its big, ruffled flowers.
Paeonia rockii was discovered in the northern mountains of China
by the collector Joseph Rock, and its first growers emphasized how
unusually tough it was in cold weather, drought and bug-infested
gardens. Nonetheless, it almost disappeared from the trade. Ten years
ago, my hands shook with excitement when I found two young plants
of it in a cold frame in the middle of nowhere. The proprietor quickly
took them away and hid them, insisting they would never be for sale.
I hope they are setting buds, unscathed each spring.

Back in Imperial China, great peonies had had a restricted circula-
tion too. Essentially, they gravitated to the Emperor's gardens where
they were planted in special beds edged with polished stone, the sort

of edging which is used in the West round graves in wonderfully vulgar cemeteries. In China, this polished edging was not the kiss of death. Civilized courtiers competed to grow peonies of their own and exhibit them in vast shows which were held in the capital at Luoyang. Spectators would sigh over the richness of the peonies as thousands bloomed in these shows and caused ordinary viewers to envy them as the privilege of the rich and good. Peonies were supporting items of class-superiority before history became a class struggle. As a result, they acquired a touching poetic symbolism. Most of us know classic Chinese poetry only through the romantic veil of Arthur Waley's translations, and I have to take his word for some of the great peony poems of the past. In the Tang era, about AD 890, while Britain was somewhat barbaric, a poet in China was comparing peonies with his lady love. 'My lover is like the tree peony of Luoyang', is how Waley renders his verse. 'And I, like the common willow. Both like the spring wind.'

The poets were not thinking of double-flowered herbaceous peonies, the forms of *Paeonia lactiflora* with names like 'Kelway's Glorious' which are such a stunning sight in late May for gardeners who take the trouble to stake them. Those forms have a different history which traces back to central Asia and the researches of a doctor at the Russian court. Instead, the great Chinese forms are Moutan peonies which grow into woody shrubs about four feet high. They should never be pruned like herbaceous varieties, but they are no more difficult to grow. They can be very long-lived, although in the trade they are grafted so as to give them an accelerated rate of growth. Sometimes, the graft breaks and the main Moutan dies but the fault is its initial grower's, not its own nature.

Where can we buy peonies with such a venerable bloodline? It is a splendid sign of changing times that several British nurseries now import young plants and list them in the *RHS Plant Finder*. Kelways at Langport in Somerset are traditional experts, joined by Binny Plants on the Binny Estate near Broxbourn in Scotland's West Lothian and a good list from Peony Passions at The Old School House, Bracknagh, Rathangan, Co. Kildare in Ireland. All of them cater for orders by post and even the seedsmen Thompson & Morgan offer a range of young tree peonies by mail. We can rush to book plants of the classic *Paeonia*

The Delores Defina Hope Tree Peony Collection at the New York Botanical Garden

rockii, three- to four-year-old specimens at only £14.99 each. The finest range of all is offered by Phedar Nursery, Bunkers Hill, Romiley, Stockport, Cheshire, who supply some of the best Chinese forms from Gansu province, offering them by mail order. Ultimately, the Chinese peonies still derive from trade sources in Luoyang where they have had such a history for more than 1,500 years, or from Heze in Shandong province which is still crucial for the export trade to Hong Kong and, eventually, to the West. More than 500 tree varieties are kept on sale in these Chinese centres, but only a handful of them have yet come the way of Western gardeners. The annual April peony festivals in these places are spectacular, although nowadays they are a trade fair, not a show of superiority by the upper class.

Chinese tree peonies have had a special relationship with British collectors but they grow very well in the gardens of Britain's European neighbours. On the Continent, an experienced source of the classic tree varieties is Pivoines Rivière at Drôme in south-west France. This nursery now lists up to a hundred different tree peonies, many of which grow well in the hotter climates of French and Mediterranean settings. In dry heat I fondly remember a fine show of tree peonies which I viewed imperiously from horseback in the gardens of the main public square in Ronda in southern Spain. They were lightly shaded by a canopy of tall trees, a reminder that they appreciate shelter in such hot settings and will then grow readily there too.

China's fine peonies also migrated rapidly to Japan, where they found another appreciative audience, this time two-legged. Japanese gardeners called them *bo-tan*, which sounds like Hollywood's version of suncream. The Japanese varieties are excellent garden plants, many of which have the most delicate flowers and again, they are now available from British suppliers in colours which range from shell-pink to the prized, but less subtle, yellows. As a general rule, a *bo-tan* with the letters 'ji' in its name tends to have ruffled double flowers, like the lion which the Japanese word for them signifies. They survive cold winters and ought to outlive us all.

Is there a blue peony out there somewhere? Like Luoyang peonies the thought has haunted Chinese collectors and lovers of women. I am not sure what to make of the idea. Sometimes I drift off to sleep, thinking of that 'last blue mountain barred with snow' which haunts all earthly pilgrims and ought to have blue peonies on its lower slopes. Then, I try to picture one and feel happy that we have found the blotched white rockii instead.

Corona's Imprint

Do owners imprint themselves on their gardens? In their lifetimes, of course they do, as gardening is an art and gardeners are artists who express themselves by what they place and plant. What happens when they die? Sometimes we visit locations which are still marked by the feeling of an absent personality. Their gardener seems to live on. What lies behind this feeling and where does it confront us? It is not ghostly or otherworldly. Gardening is a personal art and for a while it persists, even when its organizing mind is gone. At its best it leaves a sense of its creator, fading as time passes but recoverable for some time after a death. A garden does not acquire a new calm or peace when its owner is recently dead. Instead, there is a period of time when it is deserted and therefore quieter, impressing us all the more with its stillness.

An absentee's post-mortem imprint is best caught soon for reasons which are natural, not supernatural. Fine though the gardens still are at Sissinghurst in Kent, I do not think that they now give us an impression of the lingering presence of their makers, Vita Sackville-West and Harold Nicolson. Too much has had to change and adapt to the ever-increasing numbers of visitors. Gardeners who were most admired for their plants vanish even more quickly. I do not catch the recent presence of Margery Fish or E. A. Bowles in their gardens in Somerset or Middlesex. Too much has died out, although a charming white-flowered sorrel called *Oxalis* 'Bowles's White' still carries its planter's standard in his garden near Enfield.

Instead, I have a strong feeling of an absent presence in an Irish garden in County Carlow to the south-east of Dublin. For about 100 years the gardens at Altamont were fortunate in their family owners. Across two long generations the remarkable sequence of a father and daughter gave this exceptional site the planting and planning it deserved. Since 1999 there has been no heir but the gardens are kept up by four gardeners from Ireland's Office of Public Works. There have been deaths, inevitably, but the main features are so far intact.

By origin, Altamont is a very old garden. Its avenue of beech trees commemorates a community of nuns who once lived on the site and is as fine as only Ireland's beeches can be. In 1923 the owner, Fielding Lecky Watson, began to plant the grounds with shrubs and rhododendrons newly found in the Far East. He made a three-acre lake and surrounded it with ever finer camellias. He was a passionate expert and when his daughter was born he did not name a new rhododendron after her. Instead, he named her after his favourite rhododendron, 'Corona'. In due course Corona married Garry North, but Altamont remained her life-long devotion. Her father had had his big lake dug out by hand in order to give local employment during Ireland's years of depression. In wartime, Corona worked to save his legacy from encroaching weeds and lilies. She would row slowly across her father's lake while cutting away the jungle of weeds, helped by one elderly assistant.

I know her only through others' memories. Tall and blue-eyed, she was a lady with a genius for nature and I like to read that 'when her mother died aged 102, Corona finally moved into the big house'. Herself a widow, she was by then a legendary gardener, working for an apparently free effect which conceals her great skill as a sensitive planter. *Rhododendron* 'Corona' can still be seen in flower in her garden beside a variety which also does her justice, 'White Pearl'. She is remembered as a strong, exceptionally kind and talented lady. It was not only that she mowed her own acres of grass, milked the cows, lived on her own vegetables and dismayed Ireland by 'dying when she was only seventy-seven'. She had begun gardening in her early twenties and continued wholeheartedly until her death, leaving an imprint and an example of sensitive interaction with a place and its context.

Along the main view from its house, the garden at Altamont still has a long central avenue of clipped box with archways of yew whose shapes Corona restored and maintained while adding dense planting on either side. There are still the big, rare rhododendrons around the enchanting lake. Many of the best old roses still flourish, and against the grey stone walls of the house she planted pale pink-white species of rhododendron, including the lovely *triflorum*. The climate is mild enough to allow such Chilean treasures as *Olearia phlogopappa* 'Comber's Pink', and at lower levels she grew excellent scented daphnes, including

The historic lake at Altamont, County Wicklow

simple *Daphne collina*. Without ever being too formal, she grouped the white-flowered *Primula pulverulenta* artlessly beside a path but if peri-winkles in white and blue ran freely too, she did not interrupt them. She went on planting trees for years, including excellent varieties of oak and an entire meadow of mixed sorbus. Her choice of rhododen-drons befitted a lady christened in their honour. She had the right soil for the best flowering cornuses, but it is a joy to meet them in informal clearings where the wild bluebells run beneath a light canopy of trees. The garden is enormous, and a bracing walk round it takes well over an hour, including a climb up a flight of a hundred steps, laid out by Lecky Watson with advice from William Robinson. Its boundary is the magical River Slaney, still a clear-flowing home for migrating salmon. Eventually, the walk circles round and branches off to Corona's most formal feature, a free-standing temple in the green landscape.

Her garden was her universe and she never planted at cross-purposes with it. Away from the house, the two long box-borders on the main axis are planted with sympathetic roses. Her favourite rose was the soft pink 'Celestial' with its grey-green leaves, a choice which helps engage me with her eye. Above all, the setting is Ireland. When she began, one of the only nurseries was Daisy Hill in County Down, which described itself as 'the only nursery in Ireland worth a button and the most interesting nursery probably in the world'. In her later years she and her garden owed much to their sensitive and dedicated neighbour, Assumpta Broomfield. Under Altamont's new Heritage Committee, there is a good nursery now in Corona's own garden, beside two densely planted borders in her memory, though they are not entirely in her style. Despite the divided command, the legacy of the garden's two creators seems unusually strong. From mid-May until mid-June, Altamont deserves a visit as a place with a special presence for thoughtful gardeners. It is given a singular wistfulness by the Irish quality of its gentlemanly house, seemingly left unoccupied in the ten years since Corona's death. I covet it in her wake. Undisturbed by visitors, I stood under a brick-orange *Rhododendron cinnabarinum*, a species brought newly to the garden by Lecky Watson in the 1920s. I then looked past his old camellias to the lake where lily leaves, reflecting the light, were being skated on by a family of ducklings. I thought of Corona, who saved this lake, and of her father and the workers who dug it and how, in a still magical garden, a deeply considered imprint survives its creators.

Digging In

The dead may imprint themselves on gardens, but so do living animals. I am about to apply for a licence to cull. I want to kill a new neighbour who has trespassed and wrecked the garden. He never gets up in the morning and he has amassed an unsolicited heap of rubbish. He is living only fifteen yards from my front door. I can hardly believe what I have to report. After two years of mutual warfare, a badger has built an extension to my house and is living with me.

Throughout the spring, chunks of the lawn went missing, as if somebody had been taking shovelfuls of twigs and rotting leaves. I was slow to realize that they had been piled up between my two prefabricated garages by a badger who had gone to ground. I can smell him but I cannot see him. When I leave for work he is snoozing and when I return to snore, he goes out on the prowl, digging pits in the lawn and rooting round the white-flowered viburnums. Recently, a lady author was interviewed in the *Financial Times* magazine and described herself as 'living alone with the sound of badgers'. I do not believe her. Badgers make no noise at night and only in my dreams do they snarl when disturbed. Scientific teams continue to report to parliamentary committees on whether to consider a cull on badgers because of the risks which they pose to cows. Once again, I beg them to consider the risk to gardeners. I am not bovine and I am not at risk from tuberculosis. My call for a cull is high-minded and horticultural. Badgers have destroyed my spring garden. They have dug up all the crocuses and have chewed up all the tulips. My bulbs now have to be grown in pots which are too high for their paws.

Naturally, I have asked experts at the Chelsea Flower Show but none of them has a clue what to do. One spokesman for wildlife even told me that I must strike immediately because badgers will undermine the foundations of a house and will cause a garden on a hillside to collapse. My badger will have its work cut out. To destabilize me he will have to dig down between two garages whose floors are solid concrete, laid by the village's former GP.

Here the moral menagerie makes its presence felt. My badger is impudent but is it not rather touching that he has had the nerve to choose to live with me? It is even more touching when you remember a badger's stripy habits. In spring, as I have explained, the younger members of a sett become restive and turn on the old boars. I presume they are tired of their conversation. They are fed up with being told to deliver 'teaching outcomes' and 'targeted care' by old boars who have done neither. My badger and I may be boars of a similar kind. The really penetrating question was put by a member of my family who asked if I had given my badger a name. I have, sort of. I tried 'Wedgwood' and 'Benn' and, for a while, 'Boycott' nearly sounded right. His present name is Howard because it suits his pattern of activity. Like Michael Howard, as described by a fellow Conservative MP, he has something of the night about him.

The tale of his arrival may not be quite so heart-warming. I have described how in spring I cleaned out the family medicine cupboard and as I had read that badgers in gardens are unhappy, I hid Prozac in lumps of peanut butter and put the lumps out on the lawn. Is my new friend an addict, hanging around the back door in the hope of another dose? Those to the left of centre refuse to believe this diagnosis. They are adamant that he has come from a failed sett and the only answer is to invade it. The trouble is that I am scared of the inhabitants. If my licence is approved by Defra it will have to be a licence for dogs, spades and a quick cull.

It may be relevant that I live in an old vicarage. Until recently I would simply have turned to Crockford's, that annual bible of ministers of the Anglican faith. You could find anything you wanted among the old-style clergy of the Church of England, except for a bishop who had officially come out. On Sundays, country vicars used to receive the skins of classified vermin from their parishioners and reward them according to a tariff published in the church porch. Badgers were rewarded six times more highly than rabbits. The tariff has gone nowadays, but I live just beside the church and I am sure the congregation would sing a specially adapted hymn for me. 'Brock of Ages . . .' ought to soothe a badger into benignity. In the past I could simply have turned to Parson Russell, a fellow student from Oxford who studied for the Church there in the 1820s. He bought a fine little dog called Trump from the local milkman and bred the badger-hunting terriers which still bear his name. We have one in the family but she has been reared within sight of London's parks and if it comes to an official cull, I will have to shut her in the car and let her watch until Howard is a carcass. I will then turn his skin into a bath mat, his bristles into shaving brushes and I will even consider roasting his haunches, because a reader in Somerset tells me that he used to eat roast badger at his village's annual badger-supper. It tastes like smoked ham, a chance for a Howard's End sandwich.

Am I being heartless? Again the moral menagerie thickens. Young thrusting badgers will never follow an old boar whom they have driven out to live on his own. At his age he has little hope of finding a mate, and as nobody seems interested in stripy partners in our newspapers' sections on Affairs of the Heart, I think I am safe from a disastrous mid-life litter. By keeping the old boar alive I am protecting myself from invasion by his previous partners in horticultural crime. While my garden is his bachelor territory, he will scare off the badgers who expelled him in the first place. I hate to admit it, but I feel I may have to leave him alone. I must be the only man in Britain who is still holding on to Howard for fear of something even worse.

Valerie Finnis

What makes a real gardener? It is certainly not soppiness about badgers. Is it patience or a strong back? Is it firmness of touch, precision and an even temper? An acceptance of the year's rhythms is important, as is a capacity for solitude at short notice. There are many elements but I think they should include a fondness for dogs and an amazing taste in hats.

These two qualities are confirmed for posterity in *Garden People: Valerie Finnis and the Golden Age of Gardening*, by Ursula Buchan, a classic record of great gardeners. Published in 2007, it remains an unmissable book, because it shows photographs taken by the late Valerie Finnis, one of the great gardeners of the past half-century. She was a superb photographer and her pictures have a humanity and eloquence which make them classics. Histories of gardening tend to focus only on the names who wrote most, spent most and made the most fuss, but Valerie Finnis's photographs are the defining record of sixty years of English gardening and the people who really knew what they were doing.

Valerie knew where to aim the camera because she understood the subject so deeply and recognized its true geniuses. She was also exceptionally helpful and generous to younger enthusiasts, as I know from my own experience. In 1964, aged eighteen, I wrote to her when I found her listed as the secretary of my local Alpine Garden Society. My request was not entirely normal. I wished to be appointed to the staff of the alpine section of the Munich botanical garden, which is recognized as the supreme alpine garden in Europe. We had never met, but Valerie wrote back at once and gave me the address of the garden's director, Wilhelm Schacht, a giant of a gardener who had even laid out a big alpine garden for the last-ever king of Bulgaria. She also wrote to him, so when an unsuspecting Schacht received his first-ever request for a job from a pupil at Eton College, he agreed. One reason,

Valerie Finnis in Waterperry's potting shed

he later told me, was a mistake. He mistook the address 'Middleton House' on my family's writing paper for 'Myddleton House', the address of the famous plantsman and gardener E. A. Bowles. He also knew better than to say no to Finnis. A classic photograph in *Garden People* shows Schacht in typically sturdy stockings while focusing his camera tripod on one of the supreme rarities of the Dolomites. Beside him a picture shows the flower in close-up: the sky-blue *Eritrichium nanum* which has been called the king of all mountain plants. By taking these photos at high altitude, Valerie has immortalized the best of plants and the best of men.

Valerie Finnis was born in 1924 and died in October 2006. She loved plants from an early age, a fact which she always relished when she found it shared by other people. Her plant-loving mother, Constance, was a fundamental influence on her but it was in wartime that the young Finnis's future changed. She was sent to Downe House School near Newbury where she befriended one of the gardeners, who had trained at a ladies' college. On leaving school in 1942 she enrolled at her friend's former training ground, the Waterperry Horticultural School for Women near Oxford, under the direction of the inimitable Beatrix Havergal. I have met some unusual women in my life, from Ingrid Bergman to Iris Murdoch, but Miss Havergal is the most extraordinary. At Waterperry she founded, directed and dominated an amazing school for girls, the land girls and female gardeners of the future. Men were excluded. Miss Havergal would stand to command in her trilby hat, while a big stomach-girth held in her dark clothing. When she asked me as a boy to show her if I knew how to hold a trowel, she was wearing green woolly stockings and a green blazer. Fortunately I knew, and so I was treated to a plant in one of the clay pots which were deployed by the thousand in the garden's frames.

Miss Havergal maintained her school by selling the fruit and vegetables which her squadron of digging girls cultivated as part of their practicals. Lessons would stop when the weekly lorry arrived to pick up a load of produce for sale in Oxford and Covent Garden. Much of it grew in the Waterperry greenhouses which were heated and were the girls' responsibility to maintain, whereas the big school-house was left unimaginably cold. In its dormitories, the young Pamela Schwerdt met the young Sybille Kreutzberger, beginning a relationship which has lasted for a lifetime. It was a crucial meeting for the history of British gardening. The two of them went on to work at Sissinghurst in Vita Sackville-West's lifetime and then took on the garden for the National Trust, raising it to the highest standards, so that it was admired by ever more visitors, who thought they were still seeing Vita's own plantings.

Through the Waterperry school Valerie Finnis began to meet the unsung heroes of gardening and, as her eye and skill became known, experts engaged with her on equal terms. Year after year she photographed them: men with their pipes and fox terriers and women with

Wilhelm and Frau Schacht inspect an alpine sink at Waterperry

hats so unfashionable that they ought to be donated to *Vogue* magazine. A great lady grower of small bulbs was even photographed with her white Maltese dog sitting happily on the bulb-bed behind her. Such dogs seem to go quite often with gardening genius. So does a sharp, firm tongue but I disagree with Valerie's obituarist that she had 'a knack for engineering and enjoying spectacular fallings-out with people'. I would rather say that they were dramas which she vividly maintained. Her photographs include pictures of the strong-willed Miriam Rothschild, famous scientist, apostle of wild flowers and wearer of white Wellington boots even in her drawing room. In a memoir Valerie describes her as 'the greatest of all human beings, the kindest and the most courageous'. I confess to laughing, because I remember how in my presence she once compared Miriam to a 'bulldozer with a habit of pushing its front bucket into one's face'.

Oddly, the publishers of *Garden People* opted for a picture of the stylish Nancy Lancaster for the cover. She and Valerie were respectful friends, but as I used to garden with Nancy and enjoy her endless wit and sharpness, I asked her about Valerie and heard her describe her as 'all of a tizz'. There was a constant drama but it was Nancy who remarked of Valerie, then unmarried, 'I prefer my whippets to be mated.'

To her surprise, Valerie learned the whippets' lesson and suddenly married, aged forty-six, choosing another supreme gardener, Sir David Scott, who was already in his late seventies. Their friends look on their marriage as the greatest tribute to true love. David had had a sharp eye since boyhood for trees and shrubs, and to his excellent garden beside Boughton House in Northamptonshire Valerie brought an invasion of several thousand small hardy plants. He treasured them all just as he treasured her. Eventually he became confined to the armchair in his sitting-room where he sat, warmed by a blanket, with his copy of the supreme historian, Thucydides the Athenian, on the side table beside his right arm. We would discuss the events of the contemporary world and David would speculate how Thucydides would have analysed their course. Valerie, meanwhile, would set out into the garden, equipped with a long-range mobile radio whose volume, eventually, she learned to control. While David paused to consider Thucydides' view of the Falklands War, a second radio beside him would crackle into action and Valerie's voice would be on it, talking him through the sights of the day in the flowerbeds which they had planted together. 'Have the flowerheads faded yet on the xanthoceras?' he would ask her down the wire, and there would be a lull while she walked up to report on this fine, white-flowered shrub's progress on a south-facing wall. 'Of the gods, we believe, and of men, we know,' David would quote from Thucydides, 'that they rule wherever they can.'

'Twenty-eight flowers on the xanthoceras,' Valerie would report, 'with eleven more buds to come,' and images of the shrub they had

top: How to use a trowel: Miss Havergal, her dog and a student at work
above: Miss Havergal in uniform leaflets a visitor to Waterperry

Sir David Scott and his bride Valerie, an hour after their wedding

planted would soften his bleak thoughts on world affairs, just as Valerie's photos of plants and gardens still soften the edges of a hurried world.

Taking Cuttings

Gardens are idealized, but as Valerie Finnis exemplified, basic gardening is in need of champions. Nothing is more basic than the propagation of garden plants and no champion has been more distinguished over the ages than Augustine, the Christian bishop and thinker. In one of his most civilized moments he wrote: 'Is there any more wonderful sight, any moment when man's reason is nearer to some sort of contact with the nature of the world, than the sowing of seeds and the planting of cuttings? It is as if you could question the vital force in each root or bud on what it can do, what it cannot and why.'

May to July is an excellent time to put Augustine's observations to the test. You may enjoy buying plants in a garden centre, but you are not a gardener who enjoys the full pleasure of the art until you have grown a new generation from your own stock plants. Cuttings are all around us, waiting to be taken and grown at no cost. Here are my six rules for easy entry into this useful skill. The first rule is never to buy a gadget unless you have to. The simplest accessory for the taking of cuttings is an array of empty plastic bottles which once held lemonade, cola and so forth. Cut off their bottoms and gather up some plastic flower pots over which the bottles can be placed like plastic hats. At no cost, you then have your own mini-propagator. When the plants root, you can take off the bottle cap and introduce them gently to fresh air and ventilation.

The second rule is to spend money on a suitable compost. There are endless possibilities here but for easy rooting I have come to trust the widely available J. Arthur Bower's pre-mixed compost for seeds and cuttings, to which I add white perlite to make up as much as 50 per cent of the total mixture's volume. Cuttings prefer an open compost which retains water and the perlite keeps the right texture. It does not decompose when the rooted cuttings are first planted into open soil, but this minor disadvantage does not outweigh its value as a retainer of water, lightness and openness in the soil mixture. I then water my mixture of soil and perlite and put it into small plastic pots. Square pots will sit closely together under a specially bought plastic hat, whereas round pots are best under plastic bottles. It is important to soak the dry perlite and compost thoroughly in advance and leave them to absorb water until the mixture remains slightly damp when squeezed. Do not put cuttings into a dry mixture and then try to water it afterwards, as the watering will dislodge the cuttings.

The third principle is to take a polythene bag whenever you go out on your prowls. You may be prowling at a lunch party with a keen gardening friend or abroad on a sunny holiday. Freezer bags are ideal companions, so I try to travel with a few in the car or my pocket. When you see a plant worth propagating, you can then cut pieces off, with permission if necessary, and put them at once into your personalized plastic holder, adding a few drops of water and sealing the bag. If sealed with water, the cuttings will stay fresh and firm for several days.

Many experts would say that the next rule should be the carrying of a very sharp razor blade or Stanley knife. Perhaps it should, but I have never armed myself as a horticultural teddy boy. A penknife or secateurs usually suffice for taking a strong young shoot off a healthy parent plant where it attaches to older wood. If you pull such a shoot downwards quite sharply, it will come away with a little strip or heel of older wood attached to it and this extra heel will often help it to root. If you are taking soft-stemmed cuttings off plants like dianthus, cut them just below a joint in the stem. Always take unflowered stems and cut as cleanly and sharply as possible so that you do not end up with an outer tube of stem, empty inside. When applied to smaller soft plants, secateurs tend to mash the stem on their lower 'anvil' blade. I see the point of carrying a razor blade for this job, but I am not deft or reliable with one.

The fourth rule is to put the cuttings into a plastic bag at once. Never let them sit in open air or sun, and seal the bag up as soon as possible to keep the maximum freshness. Eventually the bag is taken over to the pots of damp compost and perlite and the plastic bottles, bottom-free, which are waiting to cover them. Use a pencil to poke a hole in the compost which is deep enough to take about 40 per cent of your cutting's length. Take the cutting out of the bag and with a knife or other sharp weaponry, trim off all leaves along the length of stem which will be under or on the soil. Then put the cutting into the hole you have bored, making sure that it rests firmly on the bottom of the hole without an air pocket beneath. If possible, put the cuttings round the edge of the pot, close to the plastic walls, where they will root more easily. Make sure that the soil is very firm around them, adding more soil from a reserve heap of mixture if necessary: pull on the cuttings to test that they are sitting tightly and if they move, firm them in again. Surface the pot with some perlite for appearance and drainage and set a bottom-free bottle over the top of the pot, leaving its plastic cap screwed on. Stand the cuttings in a light, airy place in semi-shade where they will sweat and put a mist over the sides of the bottle. After a week or so you can lift off the bottle, wipe its walls and check that the soil is still damp. If not, add water very gently from a can with a fine rose on it and afterwards check that each cutting is still firmly in the soil. If the water is delivered too hastily it will dislodge the soil-mix and the cuttings. When you see signs of new growth from the tips or joints of a cutting, it is rooted. Unscrew the bottle-top to let a little air in and a few days later you can pot it on to an individual pot of Bower's compost without further perlite. It will grow away and fill its small pot with roots, soon reaching a size for which a nursery would be charging you £2 a plant.

The fifth rule is to begin by taking plants which root easily. Successes do wonders for morale and some of them will be unexpected. In July, hopes of success run high for rooting dianthus, or garden pinks, especially the old laced and striped varieties which make such elegant edgings. However, varieties vary widely in their willingness to root easily. After long experiment my own star is one which I used to name *Dianthus* 'Robin Lane Fox'. I thought it had come from crosses I had tried in the 1970s, but I now find that it originates from a plant whose label I had lost and its real name is *Dianthus* 'Farnham Rose'. It has rose and white mottled flowers and is extraordinarily vigorous and willing to root. As the *RHS Plant Finder* now lists only two suppliers, it is worth buying a parent plant in the sure knowledge that anyone can turn a single plant into twenty more.

Other worthwhile snippets in late July come off all forms of lavender. If rooted in August, they will make good pot plants for planting out next spring. So, too, will the many varieties of mock orange, or *Philadelphus*, which have just finished flowering. Old plants are covered then in excellent new shoots for rooting, especially the lovely smaller variety 'Sybille' or the large and handsome *calvescens*, which is harder to find in the trade. Other June-flowering shrubs like weigela or kolkwitzia are also apt for cuttings at this same time.

The sixth rule, therefore, is not to be scared of trying cuttings from any shrub or herbaceous plant which sends out soft shoots from a hard central stem. I was surprised to discover that the golden-leaved scented *Daphne odora* will root quickly from cuttings taken in July at points where its growing tips connect to the previous year's growth on the stem. Ever since, I have had plants of this daphne at no expense while the index-cost of daphnes has far outperformed inflation. Young plants now cost as much as £18 in garden centres and even then are prone to virus. Instead, you can root half a dozen cuttings very easily from a disease-free parent in your own keeping.

The Prince of Wales thinks we should talk to our plants, Wittgenstein implies they 'say' things and Augustine wishes we could question them. Mundanely, I recommend being firm with them and keeping their cuttings away from fresh air and strong sunlight. If the good bishop had known about plastic bottles and freezer bags, he might have been even more impressed with the latent power of the natural world.

Mansfield Poke

Have gardening columnists ever been crucial to great literature or art? You would surely think not, unless you have watched one of the BBC's cultural showcases, its film of Jane Austen's *Mansfield Park* which is shown quite often in holiday seasons. It is so hard for fans of Jane Austen to be sure that they remember exact details of her work when the television tests their memory. At a crucial moment in this televised version, a gardening journalist arrives from London and causes great excitement by expressing a wish to write about recent changes to the owner's country garden. His visit precipitates a fine turn in the film's plot. Inside the mansion, the doors are opened upstairs and efforts are made to find the owners to tell them of this unexpected interest in their landscape plans. In one of the bedrooms, the searchers find something altogether more startling. The newly married lady of the house is caught in bed with the visiting bounder Henry Crawford, a suave young gentleman with a Cambridge education who has already been trifling with hearts on screen for more than an hour. Or so the television would have millions of viewers believe. Is it correct?

   In the film version of *Mansfield Park* a gardening columnist unwittingly diverts the plot. In the novel whose title the BBC film so proudly bears there is no gardening columnist, no capture of a couple in the act. As always, Jane Austen proceeded more obliquely. Henry Crawford's bad behaviour was announced to the heroine only by letter and was reported as an elopement. Where, then, do the televised inventions stop? What about the startling TV scene in which the owner of Mansfield Park is shown throwing into the fire his sketchbook of black slaves? They are shown suffering tortures and dangling from ropes, but how many of us have read anything about that in the novel? Jane Austen's owner of Mansfield Park had estates in Antigua and in real life her father, a clergyman, was trustee of one such enterprise. In a fine scene in the book, the eighteen-year-old heroine Fanny Price complains that when she raised the topic of the slave trade after dinner on one occasion, the rest of the family was silent. Modern voices have been led by the indiscriminate Edward Said to pounce on this 'silence' about slavery. They even consider it to be political and insist it is a sign of embarrassment. In the text of *Mansfield Park*, it is nothing of the sort. The point there is that the rest of the family dislike serious conversation, although their father, Sir Thomas Bertram, would have liked to talk on the subject, awkward or not.

I have several objections to such televised travesties. The first is entirely ironic. Should we now allow for unmentioned activities by gardening columnists to explain undisclosed items in the plots of other great books we think we know? Did a gardening columnist from the *Petersburg News* first catch Vronsky in the act with Anna Karenin? Did a gardening columnist first warm up the French governess in old Prince Bolkonsky's garden in *War and Peace*? Is that why she fell into the arms of the suitor who had come for the hapless Maria? There is not only the matter of what film-makers put in: there is the important matter of what they leave out. How would viewers ever guess that the text of *Mansfield Park* contains a brilliant interplay of observations on that eternal question, the merits and stupidities of landscape gardening? The issues are still familiar: superfluous improvement at vast expense, designers' egocentricity, and the charms of an existing landscape. Typically, the smooth Henry Crawford claims to have designed his own park while still at school at Westminster and to have added a few touches while at Cambridge before he reached the age of twenty-one. The pretensions of such lavish 'improvements' and the hiring of designer-improvers have never been more sharply punctured than in Chapter six of Jane Austen's novel. She adds an outburst of petty jealousy, touched off in onlookers by the grandiose plans of would-be landscapers. Such rivalry is still with us, but Jane Austen attaches competitive cattiness to the merits of a variety of apricot called 'Moor Park'. Throughout, she implies much sympathy for leaving a well-settled house in the setting which it already has. 'I should not put myself into the hands of an improver,' says the Etonian Edmund Bertram, 'I would rather have an inferior degree of beauty of my own choice, and acquired progressively. I would rather abide by my own blunders than by his.' Competitive gardeners still have their 'Moor Parks' and their social rivalries about plants. Extracts from Chapter six should be printed in red and displayed on the banners at next year's Chelsea Flower Show.

Televisual outrage is also done to the sensibility of Fanny. What TV viewer would guess that Fanny is the first person in literature to realize that by 'passing March and April in a town' she had missed all the pleasures of spring? She lost what we all recognize, 'the earliest flowers in the warmest divisions of her aunt's garden, the opening of leaves on her uncle's plantations and the glory of his woods'. She admires the evergreens in the little wilderness which contains a walk around Mansfield's nearby parsonage. She is a cardinal character in the history of the enjoyment of gardens and it is gruesome that the BBC edited out this aspect of her. Predictably, the fox-hunting in the text is also suppressed. There is not a hint that Henry Crawford liked the sport (he was reduced, however, to three days a week) and that he earned affection by lending Fanny's brother one of his horses for a day with hounds.

The real *Mansfield Park* is a sharp observation of social diversity and its heroine retains a wise judgement and a stillness which many critics have overlooked. Why, then, should we be invited to watch it being violated? In an inclusive age, we are otherwise brainwashed to do verbal justice to any minority of the BBC's choosing. What, then, about the minority of single women who are obliged, like Jane Austen, to live with their brothers and sisters but who happen to give a large part of their life and energy to writing a masterpiece? We do not need a government minister to defend the good name of gardening columnists. We need a minister for authors. Thousands more people are studying English literature than ever before, and among reasons for allowing them to do so, I used to tell myself that a good reason is that their increased knowledge will be good for the future of literature and even for Britain's economy. As practised readers, these graduates will surely understand and do justice to our greatest national assets, the English books which are known and loved more widely across the world than anything produced from British schools of business. Instead, we have ended up with self-willed narcissists who rape the very books they feebly claim to be 'adapting'. Anyone is free to base their own fictions on a masterpiece of the past, but if so they must rename it. *Bridget Jones's Diary* claims to be based in part on *Pride and Prejudice*, but it has never thought of stealing that famous name. Gardeners need to compensate for this televised distortion by reading *Mansfield Park* for themselves. When the BBC screen their film in future, they should be more honest and change the title to *Mansfield Poke*.

Animal Mischief

Gardening in England in late spring is not only unpredictable for the half-hardy bedding. We never know what the weather will do to us. We also do not know what our furred and feathered friends will do next, those busy little sharers of our natural environment. I have had my fill of sprinting and shovelling badgers, but at least in summer there are no snowfalls to reveal the tracks of their animal bloodshed by night. In late May the only tracks are the ones which animals dig so deeply that they last through the night.

On the evidence of these tracks there is continuing mischief in my garden, but the latest round seemed to have begun as an untidy game. Eighty years ago, my long flat lawn was laid out for the noble sport of archery, in the days when its resident vicar took spiritual exercise in hitting a harmless target. On this green and pleasant land, he loosed his arrows of desire and so far as I know, he never hit a parishioner on the church path in the background. At three separate points on the archery-lawn which he laid out for sport, signs appeared recently of someone playing a different game: golf by night. I assume it was golf, because the players forgot to replace the divots. They left plantains and lumps of grass in heaps at three separate points, as if they had taken three separate shots at holing in one into the lilacs. Benignly, I replaced the divots and assumed that it was a round of animal putting. Animals, I believe, play golf like businessmen, except that they play off higher handicaps and make even more of a mess.

After two more nights of animal golf the divots became deeper and thicker and their replacement began to become a bore. At Chelsea Flower Show, I put the problem to experts but once again they were explicit and unhelpful. They told me that the holes were the work of blackbirds, who were digging for worms in the early morning dew. Perhaps there are super blackbirds in those experts' gardens, but they could never have dug holes so deep and round as those in mine. The digging then took on a clear pattern. At each of the three scuffle-points, a small area of scuffling on the surface was accompanied by two deep holes, dug about two feet behind the scuffle and spaced about a foot apart. The holes were becoming deeper, as if the digger was enjoying itself. It was not, I now realized, a game of golf: the answer was much more animal. The scuffle marks and holes were animal signifiers and made sense if gendered by the human eye. The scuffling was plainly the work of a female, mildly enjoying her activity. The spaced-out holes behind her were the foot-holes of a male who was plainly enjoying himself very much indeed. Not long ago, a famous female fund manager told me that her particular talent was anticipation. I asked her if she had anticipated anything special when she first met her husband. 'Yes,' she replied, 'I knew it was really animal.' Since mid-May it has been really animal on my lawn by the light of the moon. The female has scuffled patiently, while the male has discovered that if he digs his hind legs in deeply, he can greatly improve his leverage. Highly leveraged rabbits are not mentioned in my RHS dictionary of pests and diseases. One theory is that there are three pairs of them out there and nightly they take up position at the same three points on the lawn. My personal belief is more economical: there are only two rabbits at work, a heroic young buck and a consenting doe of his choice. He leverages himself up once, recharges while she patters over the next twenty yards and then leverages himself up twice more.

Whatever you may feel about his stamina, the leveraging has to stop. I have tried looking out at 6 a.m., but by then the animal activity is over. I cannot face waking up earlier to throw bricks at the couple while the garden is still dark. Garden centres offer a prevention, but it is beneath my dignity. It is a ferally-correct compound called Renadine, which is said to smell like a fox and to divert unwanted wildlife from its sphere. Unless I Renadine the entire lawn, I will merely displace the partners and encourage them to try their leverage elsewhere. Those of us who have spent winters chasing the real animal cannot sink to putting artificial fox-scent onto lawns in summer.

Rapid action is needed for an obvious reason. One highly leveraged rabbit will soon lead to many little rabbits, each of whom will be taught that leverage is the route to their future happiness. No doubt they will come and repeat the lesson on my lawn. One Saturday, I resorted to the obvious answer: saucers of sugared milk, heavily laced with weedkiller. I considered using lettuce instead of milk, remembering how lettuce made Beatrix Potter's Flopsy Bunnies feel so soporific. The problem, I reckoned, was that the weedkilling glyphosate would scorch the lettuce leaves before anything could come and eat them. Unfortunately, it rained very heavily on the Saturday night of my initiative. Nonetheless the saucers of laced milk disappeared and Sunday evening was such an animal occasion that it suggested that even rain-diluted poison has a kick. Where there had previously been two foot-holes for a proper grip, there were now four, as if the female was digging in too. In one case I am sure that I counted six. It is wonderful what a cocktail of house poison will do for the nightlife of those who drink it.

I remember a correspondence with a dutiful civil servant in the 1980s when I complained in a gardening column that weedkillers are unnecessarily weak in garden stores and that agricultural chemicals are so much more effective. He defended the labelling and diluting of garden weedkillers on the grounds that the ordinary gardener could not be trusted with strong poison. You never knew, he said, what such a man might do: he might even give it to his wife. On the evidence of last weekend, I can see why a civil servant might be worried. After one saucerful of poison-enhanced milk, Mrs Rabbit starts digging in for better leverage, too.

Where do I go from here? A visitor scared me rigid by suggesting that the players are not rabbits: they are yet more badgers. Has Howard, my back-door badger, invited some young friends in for a stripy pyjama-party? It is no use telling me to set the alarm and use the shotgun. I will never wake up in time and I am much too worried about hitting my best delphiniums on the rebound.

Separate Beds on the Bay

To take the edge off this animal leverage I started to think about grand holiday gardening. It is not an extravagance which began only in the Hamptons. It did not even start on the French Riviera, let alone in Sottogrande. Its roots lie in the unsurpassed landscape of the Bay of Naples, where I went for a walk on the cliffs and found myself thinking about the past and ourselves, about nature and culture and how our ideas of a garden have changed.

The great gardeners on the Bay were ancient Romans, especially the rich and grand contemporaries of the aspiring Cicero in the first century BC. It is no use looking for their gardens along the shores of the modern bay. From the few ruins which remain, you would never guess the scale of their achievement. The best place to begin is in the National Archaeological Museum of Naples, where wall paintings from the region give a better idea of the Romans' capacity for elegant fancy. At first sight, they seem much like the leaders of our age of landscape excess. They undertook gigantic assaults on nature. They built into cliffs and founded densely pillared houses on man-made jetties or on flat promontories levelled from the rocks. Their houses were open to the sun and wind and, at their best, had curved and angled façades. Their designs would still set a fashion on island resorts in the Mediterranean.

I enjoy looking at pictures of these houses in the Museum, but in order to enter their world, we have to read and use our imagination. Our knowledge of Roman gardens depends above all on the letters and poems which were written about them. As I looked across the bay I chose as my couple of the moment a married pair of well-off Romans who were celebrated in florid Latin poems. The poems' author was the admired Statius, who was himself a resident of the Bay of Naples in the latter part of the first century AD. In flattering language he praised the gardens of a couple who had no doubt paid him to praise them,

Pollius Felix and his wife Polla. I suspect that Polla paid for the poems because Statius praises her for her youthful grace. At the time she was aged about forty, so some of our aspirations never change.

We can still enjoy a little adventure to find the site where the couple seem to have lived. Their garden is gone but local Italian place names preserve its memory on the road beyond modern Sorrento. The best directions are given in my personal bible, the *Blue Guide: Southern Italy*. Take the road towards Massa Lubrense and head out towards the tip of the Bay of Naples which points in the direction of nearby Capri. There is a marina there whose Italian name derives from Pollius' name, and from there on, you need the *Blue Guide*'s route.

If you read between the lines of Statius' poem, the couple seem like ideal readers of a modern weekend newspaper. Pollius is not short of money. He has had an active life on the council of his local town and is now retired, though the reasons for his retirement are unspecified and may not be entirely of his own choosing. He has taken up poetry, much as retired persons nowadays take to courses in creative writing. He likes to be thought of as a philosopher but not in a strenuous way. He would enjoy the modern books by Alain de Botton. Pollius was an undemanding Epicurean who tried to rise above the ebb and flow of life, and perhaps he succeeded. He did not believe in hell, and he would not take papal edicts on the subject too seriously nowadays. He certainly made a suitable second marriage, because Polla shared his literary interests and appears to have been the daughter of a man who had made a fortune in banking. A rather crude translation of her second name, Argentaria, would be 'Moneypenny'. She is even praised, intriguingly, for keeping a portrait of her first husband over her bed. Pollius was not bothered by it, no more than are those good second husbands who put up with photographs of their predecessor nowadays. It even seems that Polla's first husband was much more famous than Pollius, her second one. First time round, she had married the admired Roman poet Lucan, but he died at the age of twenty-six. It is fun to imagine Pollius and Polla's bedroom, but behind all Statius' flattery I think I catch a hint that in older age they had called a truce and opted for separate beds.

Instead, their energies went into the house and garden on a shel-tered sea-cove. From afar, their house looked as if it had a thousand roofs and as if it had been drilled into the face of a resistant cliff. Up to it ran a colonnade which 'creeps zig-zag through the heights, a city's work, mastering the rugged rocks with its lengthy spine'. There were rare marbles all over the house which they had shipped in from Greece and let into the floors or left to glitter as columns. They had even built a vineyard where the cliff met the sea, and in it sea-nymphs were said to enjoy picking the grapes in autumn. How little we change, you might be thinking, but I am not so sure. Visitors to this seaside home were most impressed by the pair of heated bath-houses whose steam rose in clouds on the beach. These houses needed a heavy diet of brushwood and fuel which was cut and supplied by household slaves. The slaves would shock us and ecological gardeners would scowl nowadays too, because the time has passed when saunas were some-how thought 'natural'. Curiously, too, there is no praise in Statius' poems for any of the surrounding flowers. Nor is there emphasis on the natural flora of the local landscape. Instead, Statius' verses con-gratulate the couple on turning a dry and thirsty cliff into an exotic villa. To correct the picture, I walked down a neighbouring cliff and thought how much they had missed.

On an hour's walk downhill to yet another ancient villa on the bay I found the items which no Roman poet mentions: the last of the blue-flowered grape hyacinths, the first of the wild orchids and several good clumps of local white *Allium neapolitanum*, an easy-growing white-flowered bulb which enjoys a light soil in English gardens. Off-white irises were happy among the rocks and there were dozens of yellow-flowered broom bushes. Between the stones of a shaded wall, there were wild lessons for English gardeners. Hundreds of plants of the little *Cyclamen repandum* were showing their rose-pink flowers and the heart-shaped leaves which are so attractive. The lesson is that this particular variety is happiest out of direct sun and will flower very well in a sheltered wall. Of course there was dark-blue rosemary, yellow sun roses and plenty of myrtle and cistus. In such company, I decided that the owners of the ancient Roman villas were sadly unappreciative of their micro-landscape.

Nowadays we keep a more open mind and carefully cultivate wild flowers. Our bath-houses are not heated with trees from the hillsides and we do not buy and sell slaves. Across the centuries Pollius and

Polla seem close to us but from a modern point of view, they have their blind spots. I admire them for that picture of a former husband above their bedsteads, but I doubt if Pollius ever picked a bunch of wild irises and put them on the table beside his wife's bed.

Ways With Wisteria

The end of May sees the end of a clear phase in each English season. From now on, it is time to change the bedding, stake where applicable and try to do battle with ever-present weeds. There are compensations as the season turns: azaleas and rhododendrons on acid soils and wisterias on soils of every type. If you have failed to do the wisteria justice in your garden, you need the first-class guide *Wisterias* by Peter Valder. It was first published in 1995 by Timber Press in America and quickly reached its fourth reprinting. It deserves to be widely read in Britain.

Valder and I disagree on one cardinal principle which he states very clearly: 'Wisterias are almost impossible to kill.' In 2002 I planted eight grafted wisterias, four of which have died. Nobody knows why, as they are all in a similar type of soil. I would blame their grafting, except that they died with the grafts apparently intact. There is no sign of disease, no coral spot or fungus. Vigorous Chinese varieties survived, but others like 'Caroline' and *floribunda* 'Black Dragon' died after only four good years.

In British gardens, the American wisteria tends to be written off as inferior. Thereafter, tastes divide: do we want a Chinese form or a Japanese one? Anyone who looks at an amazing black-and-white photograph from Japan which Valder reproduces will vote for the Japanese. On 6 May 1914 the great plant-hunter E. H. Wilson photographed a forest of poles on which long bunches of Japanese wisteria were flowering as if on pleached trees about eight feet above the ground. This sort of canopy has not been widely imitated in Britain where gardeners think of wisteria tunnels and arches. In Japan, families used to build special terraces for wisteria-viewing, and associated themselves with the exceptional beauty of the flower. Japanese artists represented the long bunches of flower with exquisite skill on early painted scrolls. In China, by contrast, there seems to have been less enthusiasm for the wisteria in early poetry or in art. Recent

Wisteria sinensis 'Prolific' at Iford Manor

travellers to China, however, have found spectacular specimens of
wisteria growing through the mature trees in temple gardens or
spreading sideways over bare ground on lightly cultivated hillsides.

Despite E. H. Wilson's photography, my vote goes to the Chinese
varieties. When I planted climbers for four distinctive metal arches,
made to resemble gigantic tiaras, I put Chinese wisterias on either side.
They rapidly met in the middle, touched tendrils and flowered their
heads off, justifying their name of *Wisteria sinensis* 'Prolific'. By
contrast, Japanese varieties have very long trusses of flower and
although they are recommended as the glory of an average pergola,
the flowers on many forms sold in Britain are pale and washy and lack

the density and vivid colour which make the Chinese varieties so good. Many gardeners have been saddled with inferior wisterias, raised from seed and distributed round the trade, so it pays to buy a named and guaranteed variety. Valder's book discusses all sorts of named varieties and, in the Chinese section, recommends the darker colour of 'Amethyst' and the wonderful strength of flower on 'Prolific' (which he calls 'Consequa'). The latter, he rightly remarks, is one of the 'great garden plants of all time' when firmly controlled in the space available. Proper control of Chinese wisterias involves the removal of long, weak shoots throughout the growing season and the cutting back of each new shoot to two or three leaves at its base, instead of cutting it out altogether. The weeks after flowering are the best time to attack a Chinese wisteria and keep it within bounds. Bad pruning is a main reason why it may refuse to flower well.

On the Japanese side of the family, the most sensational form is *Wisteria floribunda* 'Macrobotrys' (or 'Multijuga', its latest botanical name). The length of its bunches of flower differs according to season, site and the age of the plant. At its best it is unforgettable. It is highly vigorous and Valder would rate beside it the exquisite white-flowered 'Shiro-noda', which has the particular merit of flowering late. In Britain, therefore, this white wisteria is at less risk from spring frosts. It is one of the four wisterias which have survived life on my tiara-arches, but botanists now name it *Wisteria floribunda* 'Alba', grouping several white-flowerers under this name. These Japanese varieties should be pruned hard, too, when they have finished flowering. A further tidying is then needed in autumn. If you do not already have a wisteria, you might try to imitate a lovely effect which is best seen in south-east Asia. Plant one near an established tree or informal hedge and let it climb to the top without regulation. On the sunny side, it will flower very freely and give years of pleasure. A hedge of feathery Leyland cypress will never look better than in a mantle of vigorous wisteria.

View to a clipped hornbeam walk at Brécy

Summer

Half an hour later Nikolay Petrovich went into the garden to his favourite arbour. His thoughts were gloomy. For the first time he recognized how far he and his son had grown apart [. . .]. 'My brother says, We are right,' he thought, 'and setting all vanity aside, I do myself think they are further from the truth than we are, but at the same time I feel they have something which we don't, some advantage over us . . . Youth? No, not just youth. Doesn't their advantage lie in their being less marked by class than we are?' Nikolay Petrovich sunk his head and rubbed his face with his hand. 'But to reject poetry?' he thought again. 'Not to have a feeling for art, for nature . . . ?'

And he looked around him as if trying to understand how it was possible not to have a feeling for nature. Evening was now coming on. The sun had gone behind a small aspen wood which lay a quarter of a mile from his garden and cast its seemingly unending shadow over the motionless fields [. . .] Swallows were flying high; the wind had dropped; lingering bees lazily, sleepily buzzed on the lilac blooms; a column of moths danced above a single protruding branch. 'My God, how beautiful it is,' thought Nikolay and some favourite lines of poetry were about to spring to his lips when he remembered his son Arkady, the book Stoff und Kraft [which the boys had praised], and fell silent. He continued to sit there and continued to indulge in the pleasurable, melancholy sport of solitary reverie. He liked to dream – living in the country had developed that propensity in him.

Ivan Turgenev, *Fathers and Sons*, translated by Peter Carson

In his unsurpassed guide to gardening, *Your Garden Week By Week* (first published in 1936, last published 1992), the expert Arthur Hellyer began 'General Work For June' with the instruction, 'Spray Against Pests'. The battle persists and even more pests are arrayed against us, including the recent leaf miner on horse chestnuts which I discuss in this section and badgers and highly leveraged rabbits in the wrong place, on both of which I have expressed new views. Even so, spraying is the least of amateur gardeners' worries. Nowadays summer begins with bedding-out, slides into dead-heading and looks best in August if thoughtful choices prolong the garden's season. June and early July are the easy summer months because roses fall everywhere and love the British climate. I can only select a few of the best here, but I profit from the longer season which well-chosen climbing roses allow, beginning with the fine mauve-pink 'May Queen' and running on into late July with the usefully late 'Paul's Scarlet Climber', worth a place for its delayed season of flower. The art nowadays is keeping up a garden's momentum from mid-July until October, months in which many of the gardens in Britain which open to the public are revealingly closed.

Well-established bedding plants remain colourful until the frosts, but the trick is to establish them smoothly when they first go out. Gardeners with automatic irrigation are not bothered by dry Junes, but the rest of us expect to be watering the new bedding during its first weeks outdoors. From the start I include a dash of artificial fertilizer in the water, beginning with the seaweed-concentrate Maxicrop at half strength. Many annuals grow on poor soils in nature, but they are twice as good in cultivation if they are fertilized every ten days or so. Plants in big pots are especially responsive to this treatment, for which I use the simple diluter from Phostrogen which fits on to the end of a hosepipe, takes in powdered fertilizer and releases it, diluted, as the water passes through its receptacle on the way to water the plants. Watering and fertilizing are thus easily combined.

If dead-headed, the bedding repeats and persists for months. I have devoted one chapter to dead-heading here because it is the essential job in mid-July when other, thoughtless gardens start to go over. Gardeners now have a superb new pair of hardy geraniums, 'Rozanne' and the spreading 'Jolly Bee', which are two necessary plants for every garden, large or small. They flower all summer in a fine combination of mid blue and white and are incomparably the best hardy varieties on the market. They need dead-heading, but not as acutely as all their sprawling relations which are so often recommended as the busy gardener's best friends. Geraniums like pink *endressii*, tall *psilostemon* and all the blue forms of × *magnificum* need to be ruthlessly cut back after flowering, so as to reduce them to their central crown of roots and young leaves. I take barrowloads of debris out of the borders in mid-July and notice how many other gardeners do not.

With the debris out of sight, the eye fastens on clearly coloured perennials from mid-July until autumn. I emphasize in this section the important progress made with agapanthus, but I could say the same of crocosmias in reds, yellows and oranges and even the lovely monardas which used to be sadly short-lived. Crocosmias have turned out to be hardier than expected from their South African origins and many, but not all, will come safely through a frosty winter in open ground. The yellow × *crocosmiiflora* 'Norwich Canary' flowers freely in an excellent shade of clear yellow and the tall, dark red 'Emberglow' is also generous with its striking flowers. There are many intermediate shades, of which red-yellow 'Severn Sunrise' and the fine × *crocosmiiflora* 'Debutante' are particularly good. Crocosmias like full sun, but they also like plenty of water in their growing season, even when they are planted in quick-draining soil.

The improvement of the monarda is excellent news. For years I have wistfully remembered them, not because their native name is bergamot but because they looked so good in gardens in the cooler north of England which I remember from my youth. They always flowered well in their first season and spread into a mat of roots. They brought a fine range of pink, purple-red and deep red flowers to the centre of planned borders at a height of about three feet. The problem was that they lasted for only two or three years. Their weakness was caused by mildew, which attacked the leaves after flowering and was so debilitating that I gave up on the family. Recently, new mildew-resistant forms have been bred and proved their worth in wet summers. 'Squaw' is an excellent strong red and 'Violet Queen' is self-explanatory. These new monardas are robust plants and change the colours with which we can safely play.

These colours, I think, should be restricted to a few, clear tones in particular parts of a border. One-colour beds are boring and there is no need in summer, either, to be bound by the dogma of that 'colour wheel'. Remember Nancy Lancaster and her remark that 'in time, you'll begin to like anything with anything'. I like white, blues and pale yellows in one bed or scarlet-red and white in another ('blood-and-bandages' to fussy flower-arrangers), or in another, shades of burnt orange and yellow shading into each other with occasional spikes of purple-blue *Salvia* × *superba*. In a long border, it is worth repeating a striking patch of colour at intervals down the bed so as to draw a spectator's eye down the full length of it. In a smaller garden or section of a garden it is worth dotting around individual plants of one and the same bold colour so as to give the whole picture a similar highlight. Personally, I exclude rose-carmines and muddy rose-purples, but otherwise I ban nothing, merely limiting particular groups to particular shades, if possible. Too much precision in colour-planning goes wrong nowadays because the weather is so unpredict-able. If you try to follow Miss Jekyll's principles of 'colour grading', in which strong colours are carefully approached through paler related shades, the chances are that an early, sunny season will cause all the wrong flowers to open at the wrong times. The academic colleague who asked me if 'all the flowers had been the right colour' was addressing a subject on which I have learned that firm rules merely break down.

Irises on Drugs

Fifty years ago, the thinker and novelist Aldous Huxley stared at a bunch of flowers on his desk and described them in words which many a middle-aged corporate financier would prefer to deny having read in his youth. A purple iris seemed to him to be shimmering with the beauty of eternal life. In his essay *The Doors of Perception*, Huxley described his experience. He had seen 'what Adam had seen on the morning of his first Creation, the miracle moment, the moment of naked creation'. Huxley was out of his mind, having swallowed pills of mescaline, the hallucinatory drug.

Thanks to this class A substance, Chemical Aldous believed that even old Plato had been wrong. Plato, he said, had separated Being from Becoming and had reduced it to an abstract mathematical Idea. In Huxley's view, 'Plato could never, poor fellow, have seen a bunch of flowers shining with this light, all but quivering under the pressure of the significance with which they were charged.' An ordinary purple iris struck him as a 'scroll of sentient amethyst'. Actually, Huxley was the one who was wrong. He was wrong about Plato. He was wrong about the rest of us who look at irises without the help of pills. He is refuted every year in the grounds of my Oxford college garden. He is also refuted by a significant moment which occurred to me in the open air in Paris.

To take Plato first. It is far from clear that Plato would have denied the help of intoxication in order to ascend towards his ideas of higher being. Ideas, however, were divinely beautiful, certainly more beautiful than Chemical Aldous's perception of an iris. On reading his book Plato would have wondered whether Huxley had really approached the ideal Form of an iris, and he would have been sane enough to tell him that he was under distorting influences. So far from seeing more truly, Huxley was out to lunch.

My college garden contains a different lesson. In late May tall

Iris 'Lyons Blue' on the
French balcony of
Isabelle Brunetière

bearded irises shimmer down its long borders. It has taken years to
build them up, the vibrant yellow *Iris* 'Starshine' which I first saw at
Chelsea in 1963, the superb violet-black 'Sable Night', which I owe to
the former owner of Scotts Nursery in Somerset, and a fine blue called
'Big Day' which flowers with extraordinary freedom. I doubt if
Huxley had ever concentrated on a garden plant before he took his
pills. Those who take time to contemplate flowers and plants see as
much vibrant beauty as was induced by drugs in his unpractised eyes.
It is one thing to see an iris and quite another to contemplate it. Try
looking long and hard and spare yourself Huxley's flourish about
Adam and Creation. Without it you can apprehend the exceptional
beauty and changing grace in these lovely flowers.

In Oxford, we give the drugs to the irises and we like to think that
we keep them away from their spectators. On sunny afternoons, those
spectators are undergraduates on the lawn, furtively throwing frisbees
against a backdrop of iris-beauty. You may wonder if this audience is
chemically neutral, but the beauty of the irises exists independently of
them. In Oxford, irises owe their beauty to chemical maintenance, not
to the chemical enhancement of their viewers.

At the height of the iris season, I verified this point in the great collection of irises in the Parisian garden at Bagatelle on the edge of the Bois de Boulogne. In the mid-May of the fiftieth anniversary year of Huxley's drugged enlightenment, I found myself on a Sunday morning in a garden of pure irises with a beauty which his pills had not been needed to simulate. Behind a hedge and a high wall, Bagatelle's display garden shows a superb collection of modern irises which flower at their best through careful cultivation. While I visited, elderly French couples in grey suits and dark skirts were walking critically between the beds, dressed as if they themselves would never touch a sprinkling of garden compost, let alone a hallucinogenic pill. Together, we wondered at the beauty of the collection, noted down the best varieties and quietly contemplated the display. In Paris, the winners are not irises with French names. 'Rive Gauche' is too fluffy, the one called 'Paris, Paris' is too orange and 'Vin Nouveau' is not the best of dark purples. The winners come from other breeders, most of whom are active in America. 'Dardanus' is an exquisite shade of lemon-yellow, and there cannot be a better sky-blue than 'Proud Fortune' with tall stems. Primeval beauty was all around us, whereupon it began to rain.

At the first drops, the urban French viewers headed for a distant shelter. The rain became a heavy storm, but I continued contemplating in lone contentment until I saw a small group who were doing likewise at the far end of the garden. The irises glowed, Huxley-like, in the rain, and their only other spectators turned out to be English visitors led by the property manager from England's finest garden, Sissinghurst. Ignoring the rain, we compared notes and impressions. How, I asked her, did she bring the best out of the irises at Sissinghurst, many of which are old varieties but which light up the garden in June?

Mescaline does not come into it. Down at Sissinghurst, they put the irises on Dolo Dust every four or five years. This class D substance is powdered limestone from pure Dolomite rock, and is generally available through horticultural wholesalers. On the heavy soil in Kent, they find that irises respond to this extra dressing of grit and lime. Some of the best varieties at Sissinghurst were planted in the very spring when Huxley was playing with drugs, but their beauty has outlasted his perceptions.

In Oxford, we turn on the irises with a well-known dust called Growmore, applied in spring and readily available in garden stores. Huxley, by contrast, described his pills as 'objects of unique distinction', a phrase which government rhetoric now applies to my university colleagues before driving the best of them abroad. Fifty years on, the moral of these observations is simple. Take time, contemplate an iris as bold and beautiful as 'Starshine', and anyone can see a glowing beauty which suspends time and enhances their idea of the natural world. Huxley had his priorities in reverse. The student-spectators are the ones to be kept off chemicals. The irises should be given the drugs instead. Give Dolo Dust to the irises and a wake-up call to the young. Then, stand together and contemplate the consequences of chemical action in the flowerbed.

Six of the Best

After the irises, the high season begins for roses, brought forward by warmer seasons. Perish the thought, but suppose that you only had room for six roses, with another two or three on the walls of a moderate house. At least the restriction would stop you from massing all your roses into one long border, which is never the easiest way to display them. A rose border becomes a tangle and looks wretched in the off-season. It is better to space out a few varieties, stake them carefully and show them off in their profusion.

Which roses would you choose? I am thinking only of older varieties or varieties with an old-fashioned shape to their flowers and a more generous style as shrubs. My two personal winners have remained in the lead for years against all comers. One is the silver-pink 'Fantin Latour', which is a superb rose for spacing down the middle of a mixed border. It can be pruned hard so that it stays relatively upright and it can be clothed with a viticella clematis to give a second season of flower from August onwards. It has no connection with the great French painter of roses, except that his name was given to it in the 1930s by a great English lover of old roses, Nancy Lindsay. We still do not know how or where this miraculous rose originated.

Among the whites, its equal is the equally mysterious 'Madame Hardy'. Its thickly petalled white flowers are folded towards an enchanting central eye of green and the whole flower is scented. Perhaps 'Madame Hardy' is slightly more vigorous than 'Fantin Latour', but it, too, can be fitted in anywhere. It was first recorded back in 1832, and its pedigree is unknown. It has wonderfully fresh green leaves, better than so many old roses', and it has unusual strength on poor, dry soil.

It is a mistake to think that old roses are all big bushes, an idea that encourages those unfortunate borders of roses and nothing else. One of the best for strength and a second season in autumn is the pink-flowered 'Jacques Cartier', which can be pruned and kept to an easy height of about three feet. It grows equally well in dry conditions and its second season of flowers in autumn makes it a first choice for any restricted collection. Its close relation, 'Comte de Chambord', has even fuller and larger flowers, but is slightly less abundant and less willing to flower freely again in autumn.

Stripes and spotting on rose petals are particular fascinations among older varieties, although some of the most vividly striped forms are not easy to keep in good health. The most reliable remains the proven old 'Ferdinand Pichard', which is usually capable of a second crop of flowers in September. Most of its dark rose-red flowers are heavily marked with white and the leaves are a good dark green which stays relatively healthy. 'Ferdinand Pichard' will reach about five feet and is particularly good if supported on three or four strong stakes, pushed well into the ground around it. The long shoots can then be propped or tied on to them to encourage the flowers to stand well clear of the ground.

The most beautiful deep reds among the older varieties are seldom the easiest to keep in good health, and here I would look sideways to *Rosa* 'Geranium'. This hybrid rose (a cross with *R. moyesii*) turned up in Britain in the late 1930s and shows a clear shade of red on its single flowers. Their shape looks as if it has come from an old tapestry and they are followed by brilliant red hips in autumn, which are as bright as a second flowering. 'Geranium' has pretty, light green leaves and a rather upright style of growth to a height of about eight feet. It is a good shrub for a site on its own, perhaps beside the edge of a drive or in isolation against a dark evergreen background.

Shades of pink span a wide range in older roses. I have become fond of the lilac-pink flowers on 'Vick's Caprice', a rose which originated in the 1890s in America and remains an easily managed bush of about three feet with a long season of flower. For the middle-to-front of a big mixed border, a bush or two of the exquisite pinkish-white 'Juno' would also be a classic choice. 'Juno' arches naturally and reaches a height and spread of about four feet, whether or not it is supported on canes. It combines well with almost any border plants in June and is extremely easy to grow.

Perhaps you know and grow these roses already and want one which is less familiar at an odd season. The drier and poorer the

top left: Rose 'Ferdinand Pichard'   top right: Rose 'Fantin Latour'
above left: Rose 'Climbing Lady Hillingdon'   above right: Rose 'Princesse de Nassau'

conditions, the more I appreciate the pedigree and stamina of particular roses which were bred in America in the 1930s or earlier. The breeders knew that their roses had to survive a tougher life than those in more favoured parts of Europe. Back in 1843, one of them bred a healthy small-flowered climber with clusters of pale and very double cream-pink flowers and called it 'Baltimore Belle'. It is one of those excellent climbers which reaches its best when other roses have faded. It is extremely strong and obliging, but it is seldom seen now, after 150 years on the market. Perhaps there are still a few 'Belles' down in Baltimore, but this child of the 1840s is outstanding up a wall to a height of twelve feet or more.

Lastly, the long-running companion of my life with climbing roses: the heavy-scented 'Climbing Lady Hillingdon,' which has a purple flush to her stems. The flowers are a strong apricot-yellow, the scent is a strong scent of tea, and I have learnt to forgive her ladyship's one failing. In hot weather, 'Lady Hillingdon' does not hold her head up but allows her flowers to droop as they age. Only recently have I discovered her excuse. It was Lady Hillingdon, nearly a century ago, who remarked that she 'shut her eyes and thought of England' whenever Lord Hillingdon began to make love to her. Maybe we will discover a robust red rose in honour of his lordship but meanwhile her ladyship bows her head with her back to the wall in grateful gardens up and down the land.

Head for Herterton

As the old-fashioned roses fade in early July, the north of England is still behind the south. It is there that I have found a haven after the roses, a heavenly English garden which is not unduly big. There are no gardeners except its devoted owners, whose vision it is, their long-pursued aim for more than thirty years. It has not cost a fortune. While other gardeners have been rushing between Chelsea Flower Show and the latest garden centre, Frank and Margery Lawley have been selling home-grown plants to their garden visitors and keeping the weeds off their paths of sand and grit. The *RHS Garden Finder* calls their work a 'modern masterpiece'. I have had the honour of a descriptive tour with the masterminds themselves and as a result I understand so much more than has been written about their work.

Herterton House is a small farmhouse in Northumberland, leased from the National Trust, about twenty-five miles north of Newcastle upon Tyne. The neighbouring village is Cambo, birthplace of the great eighteenth-century landscape gardener Capability Brown. Frank Lawley remarked to me that Capability Brown's descendants are still nearby, but nowadays they are growing leeks. Meanwhile, the Lawleys have been drawing, planting and working their hearts out. Their garden is scarcely an acre big but it falls into four well-proportioned sections. It has no grass area to be mown but it is patterned with harmonious paths which make one forget about lawns. The surfaces are not hard or brutal, as many modern designers would have made them. They have been built up from about a foot's depth of farmers' hardcore, laid by hand and recorded in the photos of the garden's early creation which are preserved in its hand-built gazebo. This core was topped with a mix of dark reddish sand and fine grit from a nearby river and then packed hard and flat. The mixture avoids the mistake of the paths at the National Trust's nearby property Wallington, where yellowish shingle glares at visitors down some of the views. 'How do you manage to poison the weeds?' I asked, as ever inorganic.

'We don't,' Frank replied. 'We never let them start.'

I did not see a start-up weed during my attentive visit.

The first section of the garden is the nursery, where stock plants are grown in long, narrow beds. Reserve stock is dug up from the rich river-soil and sold too when the pick of the day has sold out in the main garden hut. The soil is a lesson to us all. The Lawleys inherited no garden, only a bare farmyard. They laid out their masterplan on paper and waited four years before planting anything. Meanwhile they improved their soil, using rich loam from the nearby rivers, including the poignantly named River Hartburn. To one side of the house, they then laid out a physic garden with small formal beds and herby planting. Its central feature is a formally clipped silver pear and the low edging to each bed is a small form of pink-flowered London pride, probably *Saxifraga* 'Elliott's Variety'. This little garden is pretty and has a good pink Rose 'Great Maiden's Blush' beside it, but it is not the garden's tour de force. Nor is the separate section of garden which fills the space between the house and the small public road, although its main planting cleverly uses topiary yew and box, clipped in the shape of hens, using silver-variegated box to suggest speckled hens. There is something curiously satisfying about the greenery on the far bank of the road here. It, too, has been landscaped, using the unusual variegated woodrush as if it was a wild flower, broken up by architectural plants which are spaced at irregular intervals.

Throughout the flowering seasons, the section of the garden behind the house is the central masterpiece. There is something uplifting and satisfying about the tall greens and trees which frame it. The beds fall into four little bands, with a formal pattern of tall box which hedges them off. I found myself ticking off old favourites, many not seen since the 1960s: prunella, red *Sedum spurium* 'Dragon's Blood', the right sort of bright blue cornflower, smallish inulas and the pretty strain of self-sown Cedric Morris poppies. Frank Lawley traded in oriental carpets to make a livelihood during the garden's early years. I told him that carpet-patterns had surely influenced his design.

Yes, he corrected me: 'but you are looking in too literary a way'. Frank began by studying classics, my own literary subject, but aban-

Herterton in July

doned it at university for art and design. Later he organized and taught
a special course in garden appreciation at the adult education centre in
Newcastle. The Lawleys then explained why the planting of this
section of the garden is so peculiarly appealing. They had pre-planned
it so that its colours run through the varying colour-phases of the day.
Cream and pale pink evoke the early morning light, captured in old
friends like pale *Erigeron* 'Quakeress' and an unusual catmint which is
rose-pink and upright. The day colours then show in a central bed of
golden yellow and orange to suggest the sun, where they centre on an
orange lily which I misidentified. It is *Lilium croceum*, at home on the
dykes near the sea in the Netherlands. In each bed beside this flowery

sun, the deep blues of adenophora, cornflower, harebells, and so forth suggest the clear blue of a summery sky. Next to them come pearly and grey-shaded poppies, suggesting clouds in late afternoon. Then, dark rare poteriums, purple cirsium and double dark lychnis suggest the darkening light of evening. Carpet-design gave ideas for the planting at the edges, where some beautifully clipped yew and box and specimen golden hazels and elders suggest a sunny frame. They bring light to the average grey of a Northumberland day.

The fine plants here owe much to the Lawleys' years of collecting and selecting, often conducted in the 1960s during visits to the legendary cottage garden of Margery Fish at East Lambrook Manor in Somerset. The crucial influences behind the effect of this garden have been painters. The Lawleys cite the example of Mondrian for the shape and colour-separation and Monet for the pale colours of early day. I thought, too, of Corot for the pearly-greys.

Above a final section and its formal knot-garden, the Lawleys have built a tall gazebo which allows visitors to view this dream from above. On one side are the rising Northumberland fields, but then viewers turn round and look over the garden, a triumph of art over nature. It is heavenly in a way which I have not seen elsewhere in England. The National Trust ought to go and see it and plan to save it, a masterpiece of patience which sums up an artist-vision, the best of thoughtful gardening in the past thirty years.

Not-So-Hot Pokers

In summer gardens like Herterton, flowers of all colours are present but the colours are limited in separate beds for particular effects. In lesser gardens, flowering pokers are a divisive subject. When I first suggested a plan for a border to a young friend I included two groups of red-hot pokers and was nearly sacked. They were too much for rarefied taste. If you look them up in that excellent guide to gardening, *The Small Garden* by Brigadier Lucas Phillips, first published in 1952, you will find that even the old soldier was wary of their strong colour. 'All need careful placing,' he wrote, 'to abate their flamboyance.' He realized that they like a rich soil with good drainage and are not at their best in excessively dry conditions. He recommended them near the seaside, where they duly appear on councils' roundabouts.

A telling history of taste in English gardens could be written around this one unfortunate plant. Its botanical name gave it a bad start, as it was called Kniphofia after an important German professor of botany, Herr Kniphof. I doubt if any other plant name has been so seldom used. It quickly became known as the red-hot poker because of the vivid red colouring at the tips of its flower, and the name did no good to its reputation. By bad luck, the first form to be widely planted was the most flamboyant and the least easy to abate. It is still called *Kniphofia uvaria* and has the over-heated poker look. Meanwhile, dozens of others were being bred, selected and brought to the market, but until about twenty years ago, most of them had been forgotten. The red-hot forms condemned all others.

I can illustrate the change in fashion by my own pokers' progress. In the late 1960s civilized gardens were supposed to be pale, white and ghostly, and pokers were out of the question. I came back to them in 1991 in the excellent garden of a fine connoisseur, John Treasure of Burford House, near Tenbury Wells in Worcestershire, owner of a great collection of clematis. In his declining years, he showed me the most beautiful bed of cream-flowered pokers with toffee-brown tips. He even gave me one, telling me it was called 'Modesta' (it is now 'Toffee Nosed'). I was effusively grateful and then killed it in the next winter because it was one of many pokers which dislike winter wet. During the same visit I must have bought a greenish yellow one called 'Wrexham Buttercup'. It is still with me and is the one which first punctured my poker prejudice. It flowers very freely in August, sending up fat flowers which vary between green and yellow as they age. I bought it because the name was so odd and I recommend it to anyone.

My next adventure was due to my weakness for names with unpromising echoes of Germany. I already had that sparkling red rose, 'Parkdirektor Riggers', and what better to match with that busy little supervisor than a poker which I found labelled 'Star of Baden Baden' in a cold frame? At its best, it too should be green-yellow, but something had gone wrong with the label and I ended up with a fearsome red-tipped poker beneath the flowers of the obliging 'Riggers'. The German aunt of one of my pupils then invited herself to my garden, without warning. The most interesting fact about her visit was that she thought the blazing poker and the blazing rose went so well together. On a fine afternoon, they were the plants she photographed.

After 'Baden Baden', I continued to pussyfoot round the poker family by choosing only those forms which had respectable pale yellow flowers. I bought several called 'Little Maid' and put them along the edges of flowerbeds because they were so small. They were slow to grow there and I never had much luck with them. I learned more from the pale yellow-green 'Maid of Orleans', which still survives and starts flowering in early June. The lesson is that the poker season is far longer than many gardeners realize. Different varieties extend it from May until October and there is even a variety which flowers in winter.

By the mid 1990s I started to notice how gardens were using vivid yellow, orange or pure red pokers in forms which were infinitely better than mine. The National Collection had begun to be gathered at Barton Manor on the Isle of Wight, an excellent source of poker knowledge, and I began to observe how planting plans in old nursery catalogues had used single-coloured pokers with names like 'Bees' Sunset' and 'Johnathan', a very good red. At the same time the rhetoric of civilized gardening was swinging back to favouring strong colours and giving up on ghostliness. This change of tone was not an innovation, as strong colours had been popular before, especially in gardens between 1900 and 1935. In the 1990s we were going back to them after sixty years of pastel doubt. Even so, the true range of pokers fitted brilliantly into this change of fashion. Most pokers do not flower in a hard combination of red and yellow. They glow in a uniform orange, or subtle shades of pink-apricot or red.

Here, I have a cracking success, a famous poker called 'Samuel's Sensation'. It has long, thin spikes of flower which open to a shade of cream-white from orange buds, and if the occasional plant is placed at intervals down a border, the flowers light up the entire composition. This poker grows about three-and-a-half feet high and its flowers twist when they start to die. It is very vigorous and I rate it at the top of the family. It is not in the least red hot.

My other star is 'Tawny King', which is slightly taller. Its flowers stand out in a good shade of cream against brown stems and apricot buds, and although a few plants go a long way, they continue flowering until mid-autumn. They combine well with the earliest blue salvias and are one of the best among the scores of pokers which are now on sale, very few of which combine hard shades of yellow and scarlet. Never confuse the hot colour of a plant's flower with its liking for hot dry soil. Pokers like plenty of damp in summer, although they detest it in winter.

Roses in Dry Places

I like to think of thoughtful gardeners swathed in roses in mid-June and celebrating the magnificent generosity of these wonderful plants. Not too much is made of them in the garden plans of brutal minimalists and eco-planters but they remain the unsurpassed sight of British gardening, smothered in flower and not always ravaged by black spot on their leaves. Nonetheless, about fifteen years ago, fashionable voices started to complain about them, copying the late Christopher Lloyd who had thrown out his old rose garden at Great Dixter amid great publicity. In fact, his roses were old and not very exciting varieties. He was tempted, however, to complain about roses in general, giving a lead to susceptible beginners. I hope that each June he is repenting as he looks through a locked gate in heaven at St Peter's rose garden where there is no black spot and the dead-heading is done miraculously by angels.

So many of the best rose varieties are old, but roses are not standing still or ceasing to be better understood. I have high hopes for a pale yellowish double rose which I noticed only recently in the rococo garden at Painswick in Gloucestershire during a sunny August. Remarkably, Rose 'Princesse de Nassau' was still in full flower, showing fresh leaves and such stamina in late summer that I bought it and put it against a wall and am delighted to discover that its reappearance is owed to that great expert, the late Graham Thomas. The 'Princesse' turns out to be a form of the basic musk rose, *Rosa moschata*, which accounts for its late flowering season. The 'Princesse' will grow about eight feet high, and is thought to be a rediscovery of a lost old variety which was known in the 1820s. Like so many roses, she has been preserved by Peter Beales, one of the princes of rose growing, to whom Graham Thomas sent bits of his rediscovered stock.

Every year, I add new favourites, but I would like to speak up for the long season of the lovely 'Louise Odier'. She makes a bush about five feet high and has full pink-rose flowers in heavy clusters, with the most excellent scent. If she is well treated, she will flower on and off throughout the season after the first flush, refuting unfair critics who believe that old roses all fade within a fortnight. 'Louise Odier' was bred in 1851 and I hope we never lose her.

Roses like 'Louise Odier' flourish in rich, heavy soil, but this sort of soil spoils rose growers for choice. In the Cotswolds it is not mine. Where should you look for infallible shrub roses which remain disease-free even on dry, stony soil? Thoughtful reading of Peter Beales' excellent books gives some answers, including roses of such vigour on poor soil that the problem is how to prune them and keep them under control. The classic duo for dryness are the tall, scrambling 'Rose d'Amour' and the thorny, lower-growing 'Rose d'Orsay'. Again, a clear understanding of these two remarkable roses is owed to Graham Thomas. Both are of North American blood in spite of their French names. They have fresh pink flowers and green leaves which are never troubled by disease or black spot. Their parent is the wild *Rosa virginiana*, which puts up with a dry, light soil in its homeland and has the assets of excellent orange hips and yellow autumn colour. The one complication is that these two roses are very thorny, especially 'Rose d'Orsay'. I shirk the task of pruning them and after fifteen years I cannot say that they seem the worse for neglect. If you can track them down in a nursery list, they are ideal for gardeners on dry soil who want to plant roses and then forget about them, except when enjoying their flowers for no labour at all.

Climbing and rambling roses are more accustomed to dry places because the walls on which they grow are so often dry at their foot. They do not all like this fact of life. The high point of dryness is ground at the bottom of my necessary barriers, the hedges of Leyland cypress which I inherited with my garden's acreage. Here, I have tried several suggestions, all of which have survived, but two of which are outstandingly good.

On advice from an expert in the National Rose Society, I first planted *Rosa helenae*, a thorny single-flowered white climber with good clusters of hips. It has survived and grown quite well, but it has never surmounted a coniferous wall of feathery hedging twenty feet high. Rose 'Seagull' has fared better, but it too is happier when falling

left: Rose 'Long John Silver'   right: Rose 'Rose d'Amour'

forwards off the hedges and making a natural thicket as a reminder
that most climbing roses would rather not climb. Far the best has been
the natural candidate for life in an old vicarage garden. Rose 'Rambling Rector' is undeterred by the drought at the foot of a high screen of
conifers. Up the branches of Leyland cypress the 'Rector' rambles happily, turning the vicarage's hedges into a sheet of white flowers in late
June. If you have an old Leylandii in the garden, rector it and turn it
into a rose wall. *Rosa* 'Rambling Rector' is sometimes said to be
susceptible to frost, but in my garden it is sheltered sufficiently by a
supporting hedge and even on its north side, has survived all the cold
frosts of the past twenty years. It runs up to the top of a high hedge
but has none of the deadly vigour of *Rosa filipes* 'Kiftsgate', whose
weight and bulk will overpower any living host.

The one problem with a 'Rambling Rector' is its habit of throwing
off long, arching stems above a height at which it is easily pruned.
Great rose enthusiasts suggest that these shoots should be anchored
back on to the hedging and as they cannot be clipped to feathery
conifer-branches, one suggestion is that they should be weighted and
thrown back into place. The way to do it, I have been told, is to tie a
stone to the end of the outward-facing rose stem and then lob the

stone and the stem back into the bulk of the hedge. Weighted by this missile, the rose-stem, supposedly, will stay put. I count this advice to be the most ingenious and the most hopeless that I have received in any walk of life, including cooking. It is almost impossible to fix a stone on a sling to the end of a thorny, arching rose branch and it is impossible to lob it upwards into a twenty-foot hedge of Britain's most feathery conifer without losing the stone, risking the loss of an eye from rose-thorns, and encouraging the hedge's branches to wave around even more freely in contempt.

The 'Rector' is impervious to dry soil and good enough for gardeners to forgive its loose, upper habit. For a tidier effect its only equal on a desiccating Leylandii hedge is an even more beautifully shaped white rose, 'Long John Silver'. Peter Beales' rose catalogue has kept this one in the trade and although it lacks the 'Rector's' extreme vigour, it is a rose of the highest class. Its leaves stay green and fresh, its fully double white flowers appear usefully late in mid-July, and as it is another American-bred rose, it puts up with drought and never causes problems. I am thinking of planting it on every awkward wall in sight. There is a further advantage to it. When its heads of flower are cut and placed in a vase, the rounded white flowers look like a Latour rose-painting at its best. Between a 'Rector' and a 'Long John Silver', even the dreariest hedges and dry places can be given a month of shimmering white beauty.

On the Schynige Platte

In the mountains of southern Europe, mid-June until late August is the prime season for some adventurous and unusual gardens. They lie at high altitudes in the Alps and its outlying ranges and have close connections with nearby botanic gardens and with the surrounding flora of their own Alpine peaks. Munich's great Botanical Garden runs a famous out-station, the Schachengarten in the Bavarian Alps, which I knew as a garden employee more than forty years ago. Similar natural gardens have been laid out or restored in southern France, Austria and Switzerland. They are places for a summer pilgrimage.

On one such pilgrimage I found myself in central Switzerland with a choice of two destinations before me. 'The Top of Europe, please visit our Jungfrau', promised the railway signs in one direction. The Jungfrau is the celebrated ice-maiden of the high peaks above Wengen next to the Eiger. Who better to symbolize the top of modern Europe than a virginal Jungfrau who, by definition, has failed to meet the criteria for convergence? Signs in the other direction pointed to the railway station at Wilderswil. It must be the only station with the words 'Alpine Garden' on its platform's main sign. From Wilderswil, a heroic little train toils up a steep railway, built in 1893, and runs to the Schynige Platte above. Trains run at half-hour intervals throughout the day and move at a slow pace which equals the record set by Network SouthEast into London in those challenging days of 'leaves on the track'. The Wilderswil train can be forgiven its slow progress. It goes directly up a steep mountain to a height of nearly six thousand feet on a breathtaking route, flanked by swathes of wild geraniums, pink-purple campanulas and the bigger forms of gentians in the meadows.

The garden at the railway's end has now celebrated its eightieth anniversary. In 1928, this Alpengarten began to be laid out on the principle that it should display the differing styles of vegetation in the surrounding mountains. Anyone who thinks that ecological gardening

View across the Schynige Platte garden in July.

was invented by the modern green movement, or that wild gardening is the 'new wave', should study the achievement at Schynige Platte. Its garden was practising them long before modern apostles discovered these styles. A private society of friends of the Schynige Platte cares for it, assisted by the University of Berne which runs the site with sensitivity and science, a combination which often eludes botanic gardens at low levels. The garden is open from mid-June to autumn, although the second week in July is usually the best for alpine flowers.

In Britain, our most familiar wildflowers are nettles and rampant grass, mown by county councils with a budget for 'roadside tractoring'. In the Alps, the natural carpet of flowers is stronger than the local types of grass and the main mowers are the accompanying herds of cows. In Britain, so much is said nowadays about a 'native wildflower' style of gardening and the scope for reinstating the English meadow. Much less is said about the wild style of flowers on Swiss and German mountains, a 'wildflower' style which is wrongly neglected. Its flowers are more varied and beautiful than the limited English flora, and are far more diverse than sweeps of orange rudbeckias and pink poke-weed let loose in imitation of the Midwestern prairies. Alpine meadows and the carpets of flower on Alpine mountains are models for a style which has yet to have its day in England. At its best, it looks like the foreground of a great painting by Bellini, although Bellini never climbed as high as the Schynige Platte to see what nature could do in a foreground of her own.

Up on the Platte, the Alpengarten overlooks a snow-capped perimeter of distant mountains which surround it like icy guardians. The garden's main path runs on a round trip past natural hillsides, each of which is devoted to the ecology of a separate alpine landscape, running from the meadows upwards. The garden's general principle is to allow groups of plants to grow together naturally with the mini-mum of weeding during the 150 days when the site is not under snow. The labelling is excellent, the grouping is fascinating, and the result is an enchanting wild garden. Anyone who is based at Interlaken and waits for a sunny day to visit the garden by railway will have a day trip to remember. I returned with hundreds of ideas, revitalized by pale yellow-flowered *Hieracium intybaceum* or the white-flowered *Potentilla rupestris* which lingers on in a few British nurseries. A visit suggests a whole new way of gardening by working from botanical seed lists and growing these easy sub-alpine plants from seed at a fraction of the cost of a British nursery's alpine plants. In Britain they would make a small patch of 'meadow' when transplanted outdoors.

On a previous day's walk above Wengen, I had been bluffing to conceal my ignorance of a tall purple-blue flowered plant of the woodlands. It turned out to be the common *Cicerbita alpina*, which is seldom seen in English gardens. Under the trees I misidentified the purple-flowered *Adenostyles* as a *Petasites*, whereas it is a common and easy under-cover for woodland gardens, though never seen in Britain.

Spurred on by the Alpine garden, I now picture a garden 'meadow' of mauve thistle-flowered *Rhaponicum scariosum* and a tapestry of campanulas, mixed with rose-pink *Pimpinella major* which resembles a small cow parsley and the white Alpine marguerite, *Leucanthemum adustum*, which is totally hardy. I marvelled at the martagon lilies, coveted the gentians and desired the small, intense flowers of the higher alpines. At these altitudes their beauty is concentrated in the clear sunlight as if it has been reduced by rapid cooking.

The Schynige Platte garden flows beautifully over its natural setting. It is enjoyed by wiry Swiss in the know and botanical enthusiasts from further afield. It merges into meadows which occupy a pleasant day on foot. I think I may apply for a cowbell and go vegetarian during the summer season.

Dreamy Delphiniums

On calm, sunny days, delphiniums are the stars of late June and early July. I cannot imagine why they have become identified with laborious out-of-date gardening as they are one of the wonders of a gardener's world. They are far more spectacular than ornamental grasses and clumps of knotweed in prairie plantings. They are obliging in return for a few minutes of attention, and the effort makes me fonder and prouder of them.

It has taken a while to accept the truth about this family, that with delphiniums you only get what you pay for. If you buy unnamed seedlings or mixed hybrids with group-names like Galahad or King Arthur you will have respectable second-class results. The flower spikes will be relatively short and the flowers will fade quickly up the length of the stem. If you buy named prize-winning varieties like the cream 'Butterball' or the deep 'Blue Nile' you will pay twice as much but you will be rewarded many times over. The spikes are longer and better-furnished and the lower flowers will not have dropped before the upper flowers have even opened. Their colour and shape put the cheaper varieties to shame. The expensive ones are no more difficult to grow, but they cost more because they have to be raised from cuttings taken off a mature parent of the same name.

Long delphinium borders of these named varieties are still the summit of their experts' aspirations. At Godinton House, near Ashford in Kent, the British Delphinium Society has planted a magnificent example beside the local old brick walls. The garden is open to the public and in early July this border is as good of its kind as you can hope to see. There are a few late flowers as July advances and if the first crop is thoroughly dead-headed, there is a second showing in early autumn. The problem is that these long, exclusive borders look drab in the intervening weeks. I prefer to mix a few individual delphiniums as focal points in a varied border rather than in a border of their own.

Delphinium × 'Centurion Lilac Blue Bicolour' will flower in its first year from seed sown in January

In relatively small beds they can stand alone as individuals without having to go in the very back row in conventional groups of three or five. When they flower, they draw the eye but as soon as they fade, they are dead-headed and become lost once again in an emerging haze of asters and late summer daisies. Used in this way they do not become a mildewed and messy back row throughout most of July and August. A strong delphinium will tolerate neighbours in a border but it ought to have a circle of about three feet in diameter entirely to itself.

One of the happier sights at recent Chelsea Flower Shows has been the return to form of the traditional specialists in named delphiniums, Blackmore & Langdon of Stanton Nurseries, Pensford, Bristol. The company's season for sending out young plants ends in June but they can be pre-booked for next April, at a cost of about £7 for what will only be a rooted little plant in a three-inch pot. In the first year there might be a flower or two, but at only a fraction of the plant's eventual height. If possible, grow on the new arrivals in a well-manured bed and only transplant them later for their second, more glorious season. As recent cold winters have proved yet again, even the biggest and finest delphiniums are unaffected by frost. When they have died down in winter their enemy is not frost but the tireless slug. These hungry pests are still active below soil level where you cannot see them. Always leave slug bait around a delphinium from November to March.

Most of the named varieties will grow in dry conditions but they are far better in ground which does not harden like a hot brick. Trad-itionally, they were planted in soil that had been dug with animal manure and then topdressed with yet more rotted manure to keep in the dampness. The nutrients given by this manure can be given more effectively by adding a slow-release fertilizer to the planting-hole or to the soil around an established plant's neck. This fertilizer makes all the difference to named varieties, which have to put so much energy into their main season. Dampness can then be retained by a separate mulch of bark or compost around the plant. Many of the best results come from artificially fed delphiniums in beds with artificial irrigation systems. There is no special magic in growing them by 'organic' methods.

Here are some extra-special varieties, noted at the Chelsea shows and proven in my own borders. 'Celebration' is a lovely cream-white with a dark eye and 'Sandpiper' is a classic white with a black eye as a contrast. 'Blue Nile' has a charming white eye and 'Pandora' is a bright mid blue with a blue-and-black eye. All these fabulous forms are offered by Blackmore & Langdon, as is the softer blue 'Pericles' with its white eye. 'Pericles' appeals to me particularly because of its name-sake, the great political leader of classical Athens who dominated the people much as Pericles dominates a border in July. Amateur breeders have developed many other winners which are worth hunting down in the *RHS Plant Finder*. One of the best is 'Clifford Sky', a form with an intensely clear sky-blue flower on a very long spike, but a slug finally slaughtered my plants of it and I am consoling myself with the free-flowering 'Merlin', a clear blue, too, with a white eye.

What about the staking and tying? They were used as reasons for banishing delphiniums from 'labour-saving' gardens, as if we could never enjoy this brief, yearly task. Pressed for time, I leave it late, until the first buds are opening and the ground is usually hardened by a dry spell. Some of the necessary bamboo canes then break when they are poked into the surrounding soil, but even this regular setback has an anticipated rhythm. When a cane finally stands straight for every one or two flower spikes and the green twine is circling each stem, I feel pleased at the sight of orderliness achieved within an hour. If you place highly-priced delphiniums as individual focal points along a border, they will make a strong impact and develop strong stems which have less need to be tied up. When their flower spikes fade, the canes come out too as the second flowering, if any, is slighter, and is better able to support itself. The delphinium never deserved to become a symbol of laborious gardening. Its few needs are pleasant variations in the usual round of weeding and dead-heading. We have banished it for the wrong reasons.

The Etna Broom

My garden's best shrub in early to mid-July is yellow-flowered and minimally leaved. The family of broom bushes does not have many champions nowadays and the related family of gorse has even fewer. Nonetheless my winner looks like a broom and is classed in a family with gorse bushes in it. It has no thorns or prickles and it throws off a great shower of bright flower. It is *Genista aetnensis*, the Mount Etna broom, which is native to the hot, volcanic Sicilian mountain. No wonder it likes excessive sun and drought and is in its element in the days of debilitating heat in European gardens.

I first realized how good this tall shrub is when I saw it in the early 1990s in the once-famous Irish garden at Malahide, a short bus ride from the centre of Dublin. Emerald Ireland was suffering in one of the hot Augusts of the early 1990s, but the Etna broom was untroubled. In its heyday Malahide was celebrated for its collection of rare shrubs from Asia, Australia and New Zealand which had been amassed by its owner, Lord Talbot. They have dwindled over time, but *Genista aetnensis* remains a star in the diminished pack. Shortly afterwards I visited Mount Etna and understood why this plant is such a survivor. The lower slopes of the volcano are covered in fine black grit, the lapilli of previous eruptions. The conditions are dry but the genista's leaves need little water and are designed to retain it. The plants grow up to fifteen feet tall and erupt into a shower of yellow flowers when the Sicilian summers are starting to hit the heights of heat.

Back in Britain this genista was a favourite of Vita Sackville-West at Sissinghurst. She planted it cleverly in the back row of one of the narrow beds below her castle's old brick walls and recommended it to her many readers for its cascades of flower, describing it as an 'arrested fountain of molten gold'. Not many readers followed her enthusiasm, possibly because the flowers were yellow at a time when strong yellows were becoming unfashionable. Worse, some of the genistas

One of my
Etna Brooms

are prickly gorse bushes. By gardeners, gorse is thought to belong on down-at-heel hillsides in Ireland or on Britain's Celtic fringe. Such fashions in flowers are very restricting. Actually, gorse's orange-yellow flowers are extremely pretty there in early May. It has also been thought to belong with hunting, not gardening. 'There is never a story about fox-hunting,' remarks a sceptical lady in one of the best short stories by Saki, the master-artist of the genre, 'which does not have gorse bushes in it.' Foxes still shelter from the wind in gorse coverts, but a single bush in a garden is not enough to interest them.

When I first grew prickly forms of genista, I was delighted to read that the Swedish founder of botanical naming, Carl Linnaeus, went down on his hands and knees with delight when he landed on the English coastline and encountered their relations, gorse bushes. 'Swedes are always a bit odd,' said an American gardener to whom I told this story, but in this case the Swede had kept his wits. I learned only recently, in Linnaeus' centenary year, that the story of his thanks to God for prickly British gorse is a legend. The expert historian Brent Elliott of the Lindley Library in London pointed out that Linnaeus would have seen masses of gorse in flower all along his route through Germany before he ever took ship for England.

Some of this 'gorse' in Europe was *Ulex europaeus*, whereas spiny Spanish gorse and prickly English furze are genistas. The genista family does not need any help from a Swede on his knees. It includes the planta genista of the old Planta-genet kings of England. The seedpods of its flowers are wonderfully visible on the robes of the Plantagenet courtiers and angels in the National Gallery's great Wilton Diptych, the double painting of King Richard II and his earthly and heavenly attendants. My favourite genista, the Sicilian *aetnensis*, has no Spanish prickles, no strong orange in the golden yellow of its flowers and no special appeal for foxes, either. It is a great shrub, ideally suited to a warming world and extraordinarily free with its little yellow flowers. In a restricted space it can be pruned by taking out the central stem and letting the sideshoots spray sideways at a height of only five or six feet. If unpruned, it will eventually make a tall, widely branched tree, up to twenty feet tall but never so dense that it blocks out the light. The biggest and best in my experience used to belong to Howard Colvin, a former professor of English architectural history in Oxford. In hot summers we would sit beneath its wiry curtain of leaves and flowers, beside the bank of limestone tufa, his substitute for Sicilian lava, in which he grew alpines. Wind may eventually knock a branch or two off a big tree but the branches are light and thin and do no damage if they snap. An Etna broom would be an excellent choice for a large sunny back garden.

Perhaps this broom has suffered by being muddled with a lesser substitute. Similar pea-shaped flowers, bigger and brighter, are found on a shrubby Spanish plant, *Spartium junceum*, which is known as Spanish broom. This plant is only a shrub, never a tree, and has much more solid, pointed stems. It is good in its own right, especially in hotter summers and Mediterranean holiday gardens, but it is not so fine as the Etna genista. I was surprised to hear from a nurseryman that *Genista aetnensis* had suffered from recent cold winters. Outdoors it is totally hardy and I can only ascribe the losses of Etna broom in the trade to the plant's over-wintering in vulnerable plastic pots. For nearly twenty years I have failed to kill the Etna broom. I can give it no better recommendation.

Sickly Chestnuts

No pest or disease affects the Etna broom, but during its weeks in flower, all too visibly an epidemic is infecting one of our loveliest families of trees. It has a high chance of wiping out yet another mainstay of the British landscape. In the early 1970s, as Dutch Elm disease broke out, the one consolation was that elm trees were not the only trees in Britain's open countryside. The bark beetle was starting to destroy them, but the great stands of horse chestnut still stood foursquare in the face of danger and seemed to be indestructible. In May their huge branches were set with white flowers like candles. As children, we used to shred the green surfaces off the chestnuts' big leaves and leave the supporting ribs to look like fishbones. What could ever destroy such giants which have towered in England for more than 400 years?

This optimism was misplaced. Horse chestnuts have now begun to die at short notice, or to look sick and lose their green leaves by early July. Even their conkers fail to develop, and drop off the tree too soon. Few of the trees in distress are suffering from lack of water. The culprits are insects and bacteria, and although the effects of the bugs and the bacteria are distinct, it is hard to know what to do about either of them. The offending bug is a leaf miner called *Cameraria ohridella* which was first recognized in Britain in 2002. It is known in parts of the Balkans and has a toughness verified in Slovenia and active in parts of ancient Macedonia. It has the stamina of the army of Alexander the Great and is as difficult to destroy. Sometimes I wonder if I brought it in on my walking shoes after a trip looking for the elusive homes of his highland officers. The Balkans, however, may not be its homeland. No predator has yet proliferated by making a meal of it and the reason may be that the bug originated even further afield. Western China has been suggested, explaining why nothing in Europe yet eats it.

These leaf miners cluster in thousands and eat their way through the early summer leaves of juicy chestnuts. They cause pale blotches all over the leaves while their larvae wait to mature. The leaves then roll up like browned cigarettes and look extremely sick. There is also a leaf fungus, which attacks chestnuts and deposits brown-red smudges on the tips and edges of leaves, but it is easily distinguished from the leaf miner's action. At first, the insect's damage looks white and transparent and if the leaf is held up against the light, the larva's excreta will show through. The damage then becomes a dry brown patch, causing many leaves to drop off by early September. The only good point is that an attack is not fatal. It spoils the summer look of the tree and, after several years, it will surely weaken it. A few branches may then fall off, but the tree as a whole will not die. It is wretched if a tree has these insects but the only hope is to sit them out, waiting for a remedy or a predator to emerge.

Will a cold winter kill the insect? Unfortunately not, as the pest can survive 20 °C of frost. The best strategy is to remove all the leaves as they fall and to burn them or bag them up for destruction. An ordinary compost heap will not kill off any insects which are wintering in the leaves, as it does not generate enough heat. Instead, if you cover small piles of leaves with about three inches of earth you will prevent many of the larvae from emerging. However, the pest is not susceptible to a green offensive if you have a large quantity of leaves to collect. Piling up sufficient earth becomes too laborious and an adequate covering is hard to maintain.

This leaf miner is one more refutation of the dotty view that gardeners should simply 'work with nature'. Nature comes up with the most lethal pests. This one is able to produce more than 4,000 moths from one kilo of dead leaves, and in spring each one of these natural menaces then lays another 80,000 eggs. We need a chemical control, and quickly. One possibility is to inject the trunks of important trees with that great human invention, Imidacloprid, which already protects the tomatoes and lemons which we eat. It would be best applied when the tree is in flower, but it is expensive and would have to be repeated every year. Even then, there could be problems. Injections might encourage two other enemies of chestnut trees, both of which are bacterial. Whereas leaf miners are rarer at altitudes of 500 feet or more, these bacteria are active in the north of Britain too, including Scotland.

Bacteria have had less publicity but they are the supreme menace to the chestnut's future. For years we have known one of them, a basic 'bleeding canker', which attacks the crowns and lower branches of horse chestnuts and causes them to ooze a black drip. This sort of attack is due to two forms of that fungal hold-all, *Phytophthora*, a word which is based on Greek and simply means 'plant destruction'. The symptoms look nasty but these bacteria do not kill bigger trees and the only option is to try to ignore them. The other type of bacteria is far worse. It is a newly active one which is at present traced to the *Pseudomonas syringae* group. Unfortunately, it causes more of a tree's bark to drop off and quickly cuts a circle around the stem of bigger branches. It is a killer and will wipe out a tree in one year. Other members of the pseudomonas family can be controlled but not destroyed, but unfortunately, the one which attacks chestnuts cannot as yet be killed. Here, too, we need a chemical and when we find it we need to be less fussy about rules for its use by farmers and gardeners in a crisis. The one bit of good news is that this particular bacterium seems less active on big old trees. Usually it destroys trees between ten and thirty years of age.

The dangers, then, are multiple. If you have a horse chestnut whose bark is loose and sticky, you should wait and see whether it is the deadly pseudomonas or not. If in doubt, do nothing meanwhile, because it may only be phytophthora. It seems, however, that the red-flowered horse chestnut is much less susceptible to the killer variety. Unfortunately, the lovely white-flowered chestnut is most at risk. As ever, neighbours like to depress us. One of my neighbours has a bleeding avenue and has raised the possibility that there will soon be blood on my avenue too. I have a line of tall limes which are close to intervening houses. They are not horse chestnuts, but my neighbour tells me that the more dangerous of the two bacteria may well travel by wind and attack limes, too. At present he is downwind from me but if he exports his bacteria, I think I will move to a high-rise flat.

Lotuses and Lilies

Unsettled by brown chestnut trees, I try to look outwards in July, at gardens further afield where the disease is less in evidence. From time to time I visit a garden and have a transcendental moment. Sometimes I have two, a twinned excitement which lives in the annals of a gardening lifetime.

One such excitement arose from a horse-ride through south-west France, where the chestnuts are sweet chestnuts and the horses were hired for the occasion. Turning for home, I rescued a brochure before my mount could eat it and found that the two of us were within cantering distance of the garden of Monsieur Latour-Marliac. So what, you might wonder? So almost everything, I would reply, because this particular monsieur was the man behind the water lilies which we all enjoy. Until he began his life's work, we were limited to a vigorous white-flowered variety, the only hardy water lily in Europe. From 1879 onwards, Latour-Marliac crossed this variety with wonderfully coloured forms from tropical climates. Meticulously he selected the results and in 1889 dared to display them for six months in the water gardens at Bagatelle on the edge of the Bois de Boulogne in Paris. They were a sensation, so he repeated the display. Two years later they caught the most distinguished eye in the history of the water lily: Claude Monet. Monet had just become the tenant of the ground at Giverny which he was to make into his famous garden. In 1893 he acquired the right to extend it round its big lake, and the rest is art history. When his paintings of water lilies are shown in museum exhibitions, they are still the biggest magnet for crowds of visitors.

Where did Monet find the water lilies which he painted? He ordered them directly from Latour-Marliac, and amazingly the breeder's ponds, flowerpots and nurseries are still in commercial existence at Temple-sur-Lot in the Lot-et-Garonne, east of Bordeaux and not far from the town of Agen. Here, Marliac lived, studied and

Water lilies in the Latour-Marliac garden

experimented after giving up his work as a lawyer. He built water-basin after water-basin and it is possible to visit the remains of his nursery and see the best of his hybrid lilies in place. Better still, if you penetrate to the nursery's tool shed, you will find copies of Latour-Marliac's replies to the orders of Monet himself. These exchanges of letters are great documentary survivors. Through them the most famous lily pond in the history of art was furnished with flowers. Monet had a fine eye and it was he who introduced a Japanese bridge at Giverny and added an upper storey to it to support wisteria. Nobody knows if Monet came down to see Marliac among his lily-ponds. Marliac certainly went to see Monet because he imitated the Japanese bridge. His compressed version of it still stands in his garden.

In ponds all over the world, the water lily follows the schedule of elderly academic life. The flowers wake up after 10 a.m. to face the daylight and then fall pleasantly asleep around teatime. You would never find one in a place like Goldman Sachs. The Latour-Marliac garden contains more than 200 such varieties, many of which were bred by Marliac himself. They float in long narrow canals or in circular ponds where they have been tended for years by the devoted Sylvie Benedetti. A Corsican by birth, she explained the lilies' needs to me while holding a sharply toothed knife of the sort which I last saw being used to castrate a pig. She was preparing to take cuttings and divisions to sell to the garden's daily visitors.

In Marliac's day, young lily plants were allowed to float in hundreds of shallow circular pots which he placed on the edges of his network of concreted canals. The pots are still there but there is nothing in them. '*Voleurs*,' Sylvie explained to me: the French would steal them if they were set out in Marliac's trusting style. Before you feel smug, the English are even worse. When I last opened my garden, I lost several of my rare alpines in one afternoon, probably to the middle-aged ladies who arrived with handbags.

So many of the great water lilies are still in Marliac's canals: the rose-pink 'Nigel' which he bred in 1892, the famous yellow 'Marliacea Chromatella', a stronger yellow called 'Texas Dawn' and some tender blue varieties around the big Victoria lily, *Victoria amazonica*, which lives in a necessary greenhouse. If you time your visit correctly you will be enchanted.

In the 1990s the collection in France had a link with Britain's own Stapeley Water Gardens, near Nantwich in Cheshire, who hold and sell many of the same varieties. Whatever happens to this link, I hope that their historic French nursery will continue to thrive. In 2004 the garden was declared a '*jardin remarquable*' in French national listings, but over time, its long raised ponds have inevitably started to leak. The honour should encourage French funding to restore it because the nursery is a doubly remarkable site.

Water lilies are not its only heavenly item. Latour-Marliac also grew semi-hardy forms of lotus which will survive outdoors at temperatures down to minus 7 °C. We can see from the surviving bills that Monet ordered lotuses too but soon lost them, refuting Marliac's belief that they would be hardy in the Giverny area. Down at Temple-sur-Lot, however, Marliac went on crossing lotuses and selecting superior forms. They still flower briefly there above their glistening grey-green leaves and when I called, the pink forms were at their exquisite best. Behind the pink lotus stretches the shadow of another genius, Alexander the Great. It was he who found the pink lotus

The pink-flowered lotus

flowering in India and who reached a conclusion which I now understand. When he saw it, he was on the river Indus, but he believed that he was at the head of Egypt's Nile. 'Egyptian beans,' he thought, were growing along the banks of the Indian river, proving that it was linked to Egypt. After his conquests a pink-flowered lotus ended up in northern Greece near his native Macedon, where it was a great wonder. I quite see why, but I now understand the muddle of the 'Egyptian beans' too. The Nelumbo lotus has the most exquisite flower, the sacred symbol of Indian religions. Its seed-heads look like green watering cans and if you look closely inside, as you can in Marliac's garden, you will see that the seeds are hard, black and shiny, exactly like a type of bean. Alexander was not such an idiot as some historians like to claim. As I looked at the pink lotus I might well have made his mistake too.

Is there anything lovelier in the natural world than the leaf and flower of a lotus at a moment of perfection? Its loveliness inspired a Chinese essay on 'Love for the Lotus' in the eleventh century AD which praises its subtle scent and the purity of its flowers above the muddy floor of a lake. It is particularly lovely when it is safe from mud in the concrete breeding-pens of the French genius who transformed our awareness of the family. He sold specimens to Monet and added to the parcels some plants of the water lilies which became subjects of the most famous stretches of canvas in the world. Despite Marliac's optimism I cannot believe that a pink-flowered lotus will survive outdoors in Oxford, even in a modern winter. It will have to go indoors in a confined tank. I am starting to think about sinking one in my college's ante-chapel, where it will float as an object of veneration.

Sociable Deutzias

A few years ago I went into deutzias, a family of plants which continues to intrigue visitors to western China but never makes it into the British limelight. June and July are the deutzias' cue. There are dozens of them, all extremely easy to grow. They put up with lime soil, unlike many of the best white-flowering shrubs from south-east Asia, and they do not droop in the drought. The best forms have to be tracked down and are much better than the limited range which is on display in an average garden centre. Deutzias are very sociable and can be pruned and contained in a convenient shape. They are classic companions for shrub roses, with whose flowering most of them coincide. They look pretty in such company but they are even better in quiet isolation or at the backs of a mixed border. My favourites include the brightest and boldest, the excellent white hybrid *Deutzia × magnifica*. It is a big plant but its flowers make a strong impact, confounding critics who think that deutzias' flowers are small and for fanciers only. It has a squashed pink relation which is separately listed as *Deutzia × hybrida* 'Strawberry Fields'. Nearly twenty nurseries in Britain now offer this excellent hybrid which has an unusual colour. It flowers with exceptional freedom, but I do not rate it so highly as 'Magicien', its brother hybrid, which has a touch of lilac in its mixture of pink.

The deepest pink deutzia is upright and very useful in the middle-to-back row of a big border. *Deutzia × elegantissima* 'Rosealind' is a product of the old Slieve Donard nursery in Ireland and has small flowers of a deep pink. It grows up to five feet high and puzzles visitors who have forgotten how useful this old variety still is. These hybrids are all very pretty but I prefer forms which are closer to their wild Chinese origins. They must be a beautiful sight among low bushes in Yunnan, but the first collectors in China chose to idolize rhododendrons instead. I first discovered *Deutzia monbeigii* in the wilder parts of the garden of my first landlady, Nancy Lancaster, who grew it in rough grass, lightly shaded by tall trees. This Yunnan native is in full flower by late June, is hardy and reaches a height of seven feet or so. I am glad I encountered it early in life. It is one of a group of taller deutzias, all of which can be trimmed, or even thinned, after flowering. Thinning is the classic advice in the old handbooks which tell us to cut out shoots of our deutzias once they have flowered and prune them to the ground like raspberry canes. From time to time, I thin but I am never so drastic. The alternative is to reduce the bulk of these taller shrubs enough to slim them down, a reason why they are so convenient in a mixed border. After their flowering, if a late summer clematis is planted beside them, it will scramble prettily up through the deutzia's branches.

Two of my best deutzias resulted from a raid on the excellent nursery at Longstock Park, near Stockbridge in Hampshire. On one golden afternoon, I came back with a large white-flowered *Deutzia longifolia* 'Veitchii', which commemorates a great nurseryman. It is spectacularly pretty, and I also bought the unusual *Deutzia × wilsonii* which commemorates the great plant-hunter Ernest Wilson. It seems to be smaller than 'Veitchii' but is equally good. The stars in the family, however, are two other Chinese forms which are distinctive. Ever since I began to read books on plant-hunting, I have had a dreamy mental image of the Ningpo mountains. On them grows *Deutzia ningpoensis* which is now offered by a dozen or so suppliers in Britain and is unusual in having long and narrow leaves and flowering late in July. It seems to be extremely easy and I expect it to reach about seven feet, surprising me with its late cool show of flowers. Fine though it is, the winner is the good deutzia from Sichuan, *Deutzia setchuenensis*, especially the *corymbiflora* variety. It is not the easiest deutzia to propagate, a reason why it is scarce in standard garden centres, and in a very cold winter it may die out. It is not the right deutzia for a cold, exposed place, but it lasts in flower longer than the others and has a slight bloom on its small leaves which sets off the white flowers delightfully. I expect my plants to stop at about four feet, the height at which I first saw spectacular specimens in the paved pool garden at Kiftsgate Court in Gloucestershire. They start to flower in July and persist on through the month long after the other deutzias are over. Casting around for complaints, critics observe that it has no

Deutzia setchuensis corymbiflora at Kiftsgate

scent. Instead, it has elegance and its little clusters of unopened white buds are enchanting. We are unfair to deutzias which add such class to thoughtful gardens during July.

We have also forgotten an old trick, practised by thoughtful gardeners until the 1930s. Youngish deutzias can be grown in a reserve bed and potted up in early November for sheltering in a moderately heated greenhouse (up to 14 °C). Plants can be brought under glass in sequence, some in mid-November, some in early January and February, and if they are sprayed quite often with warm water, they will break into leaf and bud, giving a fine, unseasonal show which can be shown off indoors. After flowering, the flowered stems should be cut to their base to promote new growth for next season's display and to keep the plants within bounds. Obviously, the smaller deutzias are best suited to the purpose and in due course, after a couple of indoor winters, they can be planted outdoors and younger plants brought in to replace them.

Blue Flax

What would the world look like if the sky were green and the ground were blue? In early July, a few fortunate parts of England have a chance to see a hint of the result. Whole hillsides in the south of the country are a shimmering sea of sky-blue as their crops of flowering flax glisten in the wind. In full flower, flax looks heavenly. When Moses and the elders saw the God of Israel, we are told that 'there was under his feet as it were a pavement of sapphire, like the very heaven for clearness'. A field of flax is a reflection of it.

Early July is an excellent time to start flaxing. Seeds of the best perennial varieties can be bought easily from the leading seedsmen and sown in trays of light compost where their firm, glossy seeds are easily spaced and persuaded to germinate. They are extremely satisfying as they grow quickly and prepare to flower in the following summer. The seed needs no special heat or protection and before the seedlings become too straggly, they can be moved on into separate trays, about twenty to the normal size of seed-tray. They can then be potted up and transplanted in late April.

The flax family has some singular beauties and a few peculiarities. One of the best is a small variety with brilliant yellow flowers, known as *Linum flavum* 'Gemmell's Hybrid', which cannot be raised true from seed. It has to be increased by cuttings, but they are not easy to root. Nonetheless, I have grown it on and off for years, but even on the poor soil which it prefers, 'Gemmell's Hybrid' is quicker to go off than on. It is not a long-lived plant and cannot take credit for stamina. It remains a lovely thing, but thoughtful gardeners are not much worse off with *Linum arboreum* or the small *Linum flavum* 'Compactum'. These yellow-flowered varieties show up clearly at the edge of the flowerbed and are well worth the effort. The blue ones, however, are what we want under a summer sky. The best known is *Linum perenne*, which is a shimmering sky-blue and comes in several varieties, includ-

View to flax fields, near Stow-on-the-Wold, Gloucestershire

ing 'Blue Sapphire' and *alpinum* 'Alice Blue'. All of them are good, but none is as lovely as the darker blue of *Linum narbonense*, which grows wild in parts of southern France. From a seed packet, this dark blue form is the one to prefer. Potted plants cost about £3 each but are no better than the scores of seedlings which you can raise by sowing seed for the following year. Unlike the flax in the fields of our farmers, these blue forms will go on flowering for many weeks, but they must stand in sunshine so that their flowers open fully and show off the heavenly sheen on their petals. The plants are slender so as to thrive in poor conditions without too much water and the leaves are minimal so that the plants can survive wherever the soil is poor and stony. Flaxes thrive in Mediterranean surroundings, but few British gardeners remember to try them round their summer bolt-holes. I clip them lightly in late summer and instead of hacking them down to ground

Linum narbonnense 'Heavenly Blue'

level in autumn, I allow them to regrow freely in spring. They seem to live longer if they are starved and left alone.

In my mind's eye, I picture a sapphire pavement of flax emerging from plants which spread rapidly across the ground from late July onwards. The airy pink flowers of the low-growing *Gypsophila* 'Rosy Veil' would be one possibility, perhaps with the freer-flowering forms of herbaceous potentilla, especially the unstoppable 'Gibson's Scarlet'. The last of the flax would coincide with the first exhalation of flower on the pink 'Rosy Veil' and then the brilliant red of the potentilla would take over. These plants are all happiest in a dry soil in sunshine.

The Tivoli Garden

Flax flowers most freely in a sunny summer, but in the heat of such summers I soon dream of water extravagantly used. I do not mean gallons of water leaking from the pipes of the local water authority. I mean tumbling waterfalls, foaming fountains and rushing streams with no ambition except to look good. Recently I took the plunge and in a hot spell went to revisit the most famous water garden in Europe, the Villa d'Este at Tivoli near Rome.

When I told a distinguished garden designer that I was going to the villa, he looked pained and told me that I should not bother. It was the sort of place, he thought, which is only popular with tours and coaches. Many of the best things are, and I think he was muddling the villa with those later copies called Tivoli Gardens which make a feeble use of water. The real villa's gardens are magnificent. They are even more magnificent nowadays because they have been given a new life as part of Italy's clean-up for the millennium. In Britain, we suffered the Millennium Dome. In Italy, they cleaned historic buildings and restored garden fountains which work. At the Villa d'Este, more fountains now run at one time than I have seen previously. They power up to a great height and make the fountains at Marble Arch in London look pathetic.

Visitors to the Villa d'Este enter a garden which is more than 400 years old. In the 1550s it was laid out by a patron who defied rules which would now restrict it. He was a frustrated candidate for the papacy whose unfettered attitude to the surrounding landscape demolished anything in his way and took anything worth burgling in the neighbourhood. Nowadays he would be sued on at least five counts and would be regarded as a crowning scandal of the Catholic Church. Instead, his garden is a national heritage monument.

Ippolito d'Este was a grand cardinal who found himself appointed to govern the town of Tivoli. He was the son of the scandalous Lucrezia Borgia, and was so handsome that he had been fancied in his youth by the King of France. His family was immensely grand. The d'Estes had long patronized the arts and all the refinements of court living at Ferrara, their charming seat in northern Italy. Few families could meet them as equals, but the Farnese family was one, already enmeshed in the history of the Roman papacy. The d'Estes wanted a pope too, but the honour continued to elude them. Ippolito made two attempts to be elected and one way of understanding his garden is to see it as his compensation for a failed electoral bid at the Vatican.

It was not an unpleasant compensation. Ippolito's name recalled the ancient Greek hero Hippolytus who was famous for his love of hunting: 'hunting he loved,' as Shakespeare put it, 'but love he laughed to scorn.' Ippolito d'Este followed his namesake's example. The 1550s were a time when every self-respecting cardinal would withdraw from Rome during the season for blood sports, maintaining the Gospel while chasing anything on four legs. Round the Villa d'Este, Ippolito annexed large areas of land in his property's main view and preserved it for duck-shooting and deer-hunting, his cardinal pleasures in life. He also had an informed mind. He kept several historical advisers, of whom the most learned was Pirro Ligorio, the Papal adviser on classical archaeology. His Tivoli villa lay near the vast garden-park of the Roman Emperor Hadrian and like several popes before him, Ippolito would visit the site with his archaeological adviser and remove any pillars and bits of stonework which caught his fancy.

Up on his hill, he then set about improving the dull façade of an old Benedictine monastery. The monks had had no idea of the potential genius of their place. During the next twenty years the cardinal had the hillside excavated by hand and arranged for steep staircases to descend from one level to the next. Each level made a terrace with a cross-view on which he could install extraordinary displays of water. While serving in France, Ippolito had seen great waterworks in European gardens, powered by devices of a new mechanical era. He set out to surpass them. The result was a garden which visitors to the house cannot fully appreciate nowadays. In the cardinal's day, the entry was from the bottom of the hillside so that visitors would be humbled by the ascent to his main terrace. We first see the garden nowadays only from the first-floor windows where the slope is so steep that the intricacy of the descending terraces is

Fountains at Villa d'Este.

hardly visible. The bold entrance-prospect is lost to us.

On his terraced slope the cardinal installed running stairways of water and a long line of 100 fountains beside which floated model boats and items with mythical allusions. Four enormous set-pieces spouted water to tremendous heights and even played musical tunes. Ippolito was helped by the natural landscape of surrounding Tivoli, which had once been the site of ancient Roman aqueducts and stylish villas. Its local rivers had already powered the water supplies for ostentatious ancient Roman owners of nearby country seats. The cardinal diverted part of Tivoli's main water supply in the hills and dug out his own aqueduct-tunnel with an unchristian indifference to the community, an attitude which garden owners, restricted by modern laws, both fear and secretly admire.

The result is one of the most spectacular designs in the world. If you arrive in the garden early or during the last hour of its opening, the crowds are hardly visible and the water seems to be running everywhere. The intricacies of the fountains have never been better displayed in modern times. One of the few losses is the cardinal's sculpted display of Rome's seven hills, but the fountain connected with them is now being restored. The Fountain of the Birds is running merrily again and the rocky seat of Tivoli's mythical sibyl is in gushing form. The gigantic water organ has never been heard to better advantage and nearby, the water rushes again down the main staircases and fills three serene fishponds. There is even a Diana grotto, which eclipses the one on the lower floor of Fayed's Harrods store in London. In the evenings, Cardinal Ippolito and his educated friends would read ancient lives by Plutarch and the matchless Latin poetry of the local villa owner, Horace. I think that there are many undercurrents to his villa which nobody has recently understood. Through a haze of spray I thought of two.

On one of the terraces the famous fountains of Rome stand at one end while the other end is closed off by a vast representation of Tivoli. Surely the cardinal and his visitors thought here of the poet Horace, the first man to immortalize the modern commuter's sentiment: 'When in Rome, I love Tivoli, fickle as I am; when at Tivoli, I love Rome.' This famous line of poetry was surely in the minds of visitors who could walk here between a model Rome and a model Tivoli on one and the same terrace. Further down, the great fountain which powers the water organ was controlled to pour forward in a deluge and obscure the cave of the ancient Sibyl which opens on to the terrace behind. Spectators would have known that the Sibyl was thought to have prophesied great apocalyptic floods, including the one which washed away the world in the Biblical story. In his garden, I think, the cardinal recreated the event. It explains why visitors were then treated to a second, calmer array of fountains along the fishponds. As they sat there, these lesser fountains caught the light and shimmered, we are told, like rainbows. I think this effect was deliberate. First, the ancient sibyl foretold the flood. Then, the water fountains simulated it. Then, these smaller fountains recreated the rainbow by which God was believed to have promised that the world would never be washed away again.

I would not wish the garden to seem too cryptic. It has these thoughtful dimensions but it also has such a sense of fun. Since 2000, brilliant engineers have restored the water and the wind-powered music which issues from the fountains. Once again we can hear the twittering birds and the hooting owl in the cardinal's fountain of birdsong. We can even hear tunes on a version of his original water organ. Great gardens often have a complex underlying meaning, but like the Villa d'Este, they are great if they are also capable of setting solemnity aside.

Coneflowers

As an alternative to waterfalls in hot summers, 'New Wave' planters and writers keep telling me to turn the garden into a prairie. I find this advice ironic, because I have spent years trying to turn an impoverished flat patch like a prairie into a garden. Nor do I want great swathes of their favourite 'prairie' plants: those bilious pink knotweeds with flowers like pipe cleaners or their ornamental grasses which flutter delightfully in the wind and seed themselves where they are least wanted for the next five years. I am happy to plunder the prairie-school, pinch its best idea and leave its enthusiasts to cope with their own sea of dead-heads, scruffy leaves and hours with the strimmer among dripping winter stems.

Their best idea is a family which nurserymen have recently improved. Gardeners want something tall and classy which will last well from August onwards, and here the family of echinaceas has come into its own. For years, I used to believe that echinaceas would only look good on damp soil. White-flowered varieties with names like 'White Lustre' and 'White Swan' were recommended for cool, damp surroundings where they could keep company with the damp-loving blue of *Salvia guaranitica* 'Argentina Skies'. The prairie-planters established the opposite: many echinaceas do not need to be damp at all.

Perhaps you need to be reminded what their daisy flowers look like. They are close relatives of that other self-descriptive coneflower, the rudbeckia. They have a prominent yellow or dark central cone made up of tiny florets, attached to spiny bracts. These tough little spines in the central boss explain their curious name, which derives from the ancient Greek word for a hedgehog. The central cone is surrounded by daisy-like ray petals which come in shades of purple, rose or white. Some of the best forms come from the American Midwest, where they once earned a reputation as a herbal remedy. Chief Sitting Bull was probably given a dose of echinacea whenever he caught a chill. Extracts of the plant were also used against snake bite, giving it the name 'snake root'. The most fascinating use of the plant was as an insulation for feet and mouths. An extract of echinacea was turned into a juice which protected Native American fire-walkers and fire-eaters during their antics. Herbalists are fascinated by the properties of this prairie flower, which are still not fully understood.

Echinaceas are best compared in the National Collections which have sprung up in Britain. The most varied is at the Herb Garden, Chesterfield Road, Hardstoft, Pilsley, Chesterfield, Derbyshire, but even the National Collections are struggling to keep up with the latest varieties, the best of which are coming from Germany. Echinaceas hate a wet winter soil, not a dry summer one. As a result they are not good on clay, but they are excellent in gardens which are dry from mid-July onwards. The older varieties and the natural forms have the habit of holding their petals at a reflex angle, so that they look as if they have started to put their ears back in anxiety. I like this habit, but breeders have struggled to correct it by aiming for varieties which hold their petals horizontally. In most gardens, the usual choices are variations on the purple coneflower, *Echinacea purpurea*, from eastern North America. There are some rich colours available, especially the new 'Augustkönigin' which is more pink than purple and holds its petals horizontally. The older 'Robert Bloom' is about four feet high and flowers in a splendid combination of purple petals and orange cones which I still recommend. Any number of white forms are now on the market, but the simple *purpurea* 'Alba' remains one of the easiest and most charming. The tallest variety is 'The King', with bright crimson flowers on stems as much as five feet high. I value this height, although breeders have done their best to reduce it in other varieties.

Exciting new echinaceas are now waiting to spread over our gardens. One is 'Purple Knight' with dark purple stems and flat purple-pink flowers at a modest height of about two feet. On my soil, a winner is the pale pink coneflower, *Echinacea pallida*, which comes from Midwestern America and is well up to life in the Cotswolds. Its petals are finely divided, about three inches long, and wave elegantly in a slight breeze, best seen in the variety 'Hula Dancer'. Usefully, it puts up with bone-hard soil and refutes the old view that this family only grows well in a swamp. Other recent excitements are *purpurea*

'Rubinglow' and 'Rubinstern', two excellent short-stemmed varieties, one with big, heavily petalled red-purple flowers around dark brown centres, the other with huge ruby-red flowers from August till early October. 'Rubinglow' is about two feet high, 'Rubinstern' a little taller. They are outstandingly good new plants, first choices for thoughtful gardeners.

I cannot yet endorse the latest range of colours, the oranges, yellows and reds with names like 'Art's Pride' and 'Harvest Moon'. For the moment I am content with whites and rubies, less usual in August's range. There is no need to have a vast prairie carpet of these easy, bright flowers. Instead, fit them into your existing borders where they will prolong the season when the campanulas are gone and the phloxes are looking tired. It took a new style of gardening to bring them to prominence, but the style is not essential for their enjoyment. Ten years ago echinaceas seemed likely to be much more fussy, but we now know that they will survive a tough summer. The rose-purples and ruby reds are fresh colours for thoughtful gardeners to add among stylish white dahlias and the first blue flowers on a haze of small-flowered Michaelmas daisies.

Asphodels of the Negroes

Exile induces nostalgia for one's home flora. In the 1940s, during self-imposed exile in South Africa, the great Greek poet George Seferis surveyed the landscape and felt profoundly homesick. There were no olives, no cypress trees, so he transposed his memory of Greece's flowers to those along the African roadsides. In a fine poem, he described the stands of blue and white agapanthus as the 'asphodels of the negroes'. From the Mediterranean to the Cotswolds, early August is the peak of the agapanthus season. I much prefer their flowers to the 'romantic' flowers of asphodel, a wishy-washy thing. However, the agapanthus has enjoyed an uneven fate in our gardens. At first, it was regarded by Edwardian gardeners as a tender and exotic beauty which had to live in glasshouses during the winter and was only a flower for the rich. The first agapanthuses to reach Britain from the Cape were the least hardy, so it took a second wave of introductions to bring in hardier varieties. The breeding of the hardy sorts is famously associated with the Hampshire experiments of Lewis Palmer whose results are still commemorated in the Headbourne hybrids. In the 1950s Palmer did much to publicize the strength of these stunning flowers when he crossed them for hardiness and found them to be admirably suited to life on the warm chalk of his Hampshire garden.

While he worked, many gardeners still associated agapanthuses with the French Riviera gardens of the pre-war rich. In them, varieties with thick leaves flourished on hillsides running down to the sea. The agapanthus is still a star performer for anyone caught in a hot zone of France during summer, but Palmer opened the way to a wider use of agapanthus in Britain. He bred hybrids that could survive the winter. Headbourne hybrids are widely advertised nowadays, although their connection with Palmer's original crosses is tenuous. As the agapanthus is easy to raise from seed, it has developed dozens of natural hybrids in the past fifty years. Named hybrid varieties can only be

My *Agapanthus* × 'Ardernei'

truly transmitted by controlled propagation of stock plants. We can all buy an agapanthus from a big garden store, but there are few suppliers who understand what they are offering and why. Hence the importance of the endeavours of Dick Fulcher in mid-Devon. He holds the National Collection of agapanthus and lists about forty of them for sale through his nursery, Pine Cottage Plants, Fourways, Eggesford, Chulmleigh, Devon. From September to June he sends out young plants by mail, but stocks of the best older named varieties are still scarce and his customers need to list substitutes with their order. On principle, Fulcher has tracked down parents of known provenance, but his list goes far beyond the hybrids which Palmer introduced. He even has young plants of my particular favourite, the hardy 'Ardernei' which was bred before Headbourne was a name to drop. *Agapanthus* 'Ardernei' has white flowers with a grey line down their middle and holds them for a longer season than many of those which purport to be Palmer's blues. Mr Ardern has been unjustly forgotten in the annals of the agapanthus and we ought to reinstate him. Newer named forms range in colour from the excellent 'Bressingham White', raised in the heyday of Alan Bloom and his nursery, to the unusual 'Lady Grey', whose flowers are violet and white, and the splendid late-flowering 'Lilac Time'.

Meanwhile, extremely important work is continuing to be done to the family in New Zealand. The lovely results could be rebranded as the 'asphodels of the Kiwis'. The colours of these Antipodean agapan-thuses are distinctive and many of the best varieties are hardy. They also flower for so long, surpassing the brief fortnight in August when the hardy Headbourne varieties are at their best. Two New Zealanders to look for are 'Jack's Blue' and the vivid 'Timaru'. They will still be sending up flowers in early October and are extremely free-flowering, though at different heights. 'Jack's Blue' is tall, with stems up to four feet, and the flowers appear in quantity in a shade of rich purple-blue. Marginally, I prefer 'Timaru', which is about two feet high and generous with a long succession of strong blue flowers on many separate stems. The most conspicuous variety is the excellent 'Purple Cloud', which takes the family into a new colour-range as its strong heads of flower are a shade of deep purple. These new varieties suffer from no diseases and are well up to everything which the English winter throws at them. In open ground they all survived the snow and frost of early and late 2009. There is even a prolific pure white variety which is about a foot high, an excellent arrival known as 'Snowdrops'. I recommend it for the front of any border which looks tired in mid-August. Two years ago, I also bought a single plant of *Agapanthus* 'Streamline' and I rate this one, too, as a winner. The flowers are a grey-blue with dark lines, a combination which never occurred in Palmer's old Hampshire range. The remarkable virtue of 'Streamline' is that it goes on flowering for about two months. It is now quite widespread in the trade and is better than the low-growing 'Tinker-bell', which tends to be promoted with it.

There is nothing difficult about growing these lovely flowers. I have never known any of them to be attacked by slugs. They like sunshine, a south or west aspect which is not a frost-pocket, and a light soil which is full of lime. Their central clump of roots soon becomes a thick tangle but unlike snowdrops, the plants do not flower more freely if they are regularly divided. They can, however, be split very easily into another dozen plants when new green shoots begin to appear like tabs in April. If they are given a liquid feed with Tomorite when the leaves first show they build up strength more quickly.

Fine though these new arrivals are, the finest agapanthuses in the world are not in gardens. They are in Monet's late paintings where they stand out brilliantly, outclassing his lilac-pink water lilies or his muddy views of the Giverny garden's main walks. The best of them live on canvas in the basement of the Marmottan Museum in Paris. If anyone would like to send me an offshoot, I would treat it with grateful respect.

Dead-Heading

If I go to a godless heaven, I hope to spend an hour every evening on the business of dead-heading. An hour of help each day from fellow faithless gardeners should ensure a perpetual season. Dead-heading is the most enchanting of garden tasks and is timely in early August.

Gardeners who complain that their gardens look wretched after mid-July have usually failed to dead-head them sensibly. This careful cutting helps in several ways. It removes the mess on popular early-flowering plants like the hardy geraniums. Geraniums which flower in late May and June are sometimes attributed a longer season by their hopeful nursery's catalogues, but they have this longer season only if they are dead-headed. A good recent arrival is *Geranium* 'Patricia', a lower-growing variation on the tall magenta *psilostemon* which is the mainstay of many borders in early July. 'Patricia' responds nobly to dead-heading from August onwards and will then flower again in early September. Another good arrival, the starry-flowered deep purple 'Nimbus', is also responsive. It will flower from June to November at a height of about eighteen inches if its span of two feet or so is regularly trimmed. Other varieties like violet-blue 'Spinners' or 'Johnson's Blue' have to be tidied at once. They finish flowering in early July and until you have cut them back to a central clump of leaves about a foot high, you cannot imagine what an improvement the tidying makes.

The most rewarding dead-heading is aimed at encouraging a second flush of flowers. I set about the willing varieties with nothing more than the kitchen scissors, reckoning that I will cut back as often as cutting off. Dead-heading, pinching out and shortening of stems are affiliated skills. Excellent candidates for shortening in early August are the lemon-flowered forms of anthemis, the daisy-flowered family which is potentially such a long flowerer. As you cut off the discs of the first dying flowers, you will often find that a second crop of buds is

Dead-headed *Cosmos bipinnatus* 'Purity' in September

already breaking from the leaves beneath. My favourite is still the tall lemon-yellow *Anthemis tinctoria* 'Wargrave Variety', a great repeater when carefully dead-headed. The job is seldom the simple one of heading and usually requires a cut further down the anthemis's stem to a point where side-shoots will develop. The natural pair for this treatment is the admirable helenium. This daisy-flowered plant will often break into side-shoots and flower again. One of the winners in its family is the wonderful 'Moerheim Beauty', which quickly sends up a second mass of flower-buds below the first dead-headed crop. It has now been overtaken by an even better performer, 'Sahin's Early Flowerer'. Its main British supplier, Bob Brown of Cotswold Garden Flowers, used to remark in his nursery catalogue that 'like *Come Dancing*, it goes on for ever and ever'. *Come Dancing* has added *Strictly* . . . on television, but 'Sahin's Early Flowerer' is flowering on and on. The flowers are a mixture of orange and red-brown markings and some gentle dead-heading will keep it going happily until autumn.

Phloxes are also responsive to an informed snip. Immediately after flowering they need to be cut back to their upper pair of leaves, and then if the weather is not too dry, a worthwhile second round of flowers emerges. To help this second coming, you are advised to feed the plants with a weekly spray of Phostrogen which helps them to

Dead-Heading

My dead-headed *Penstemon* 'Pensham Freshwater Pearl' in September

regain their stamina. It also helps delphiniums, which are so conspicu-
ously ugly after flowering that it is essential to cut off the dead spikes
at once. If the plants are then fed with a regular spray of Phostrogen
on their leaves, they develop shorter side-stems of flower which open
in early autumn.

Younger plants are more capable of repeating their season. This sad
fact of life is particularly obvious in the penstemons, among which old
plants in their third year or more flower earlier but tend not to repeat
themselves. Younger ones will have a second or third flowering if you
continue to dead-head them and feed them gently. I need hardly say,

too, how important dead-heading is for annuals from August onwards. The botany is simple. The annuals are hurrying to set and ripen seed in one season, and if we can stop them, they will continue to flower, hoping to outwit us. It is a pleasant race to prolong the best of the bedding plants' display, from heavenly blue cornflowers to brown-orange rudbeckias, feathery cosmos daisies and all types of scabious. If you maintain a constant war on their seed-heads, you can keep them going until early October.

Dead-heading is the one profoundly rewarding war. It tidies away the signs of death and encourages yet another show of flowers. It was wonderfully understood by Vita Sackville-West, in her garden at Sissinghurst Castle. 'Dead-heading roses on a summer evening,' she wrote, 'is an occupation that carries us back into a calmer age and a different century. Queen Victoria might still be on the throne. There is no sound except the hoot of an owl and the rhythmic snip-snip of our secateurs.'

Gendered Landscape

In mid-July, when dead-heading becomes urgent, the first flowers begin to open on border phloxes. As a gardener in a university, I associate them with the last of the questions which have to be marked in the papers for university exams. The questions are hard enough for the hordes who have to answer them, but a thought should be spared for those who set and mark them. Summer is punctuated by unimaginable attempts at answers and by unthinkable questions which some of my brilliant colleagues set.

One such question haunts me, long after the results of its exam were published. In a General Paper you might think that historians are asked to write generally about class war, economic growth or social identity. You would be wrong, even in Oxford. 'What,' one of my fellow examiners recently wished to ask the under-23s, 'is the relation between gender and landscape?' Until now, gender studies may not have shaped your interpretation of green, rolling countryside. Nonetheless, they are everywhere. Sexual distinctions are biological, but gender ones are cultural. Your body parts, to be blunt, are sexual. The fact that females think of buying high heels, whereas I buy semi-brogue shoes, is gendered. So where does gender show up in the landscape?

After an hour's thought, I could think of little as an answer, except that separate lavatories for men and women have been placed by the National Trust along the acres of English coastline which have been preserved by its Operation Neptune. So I wrote to the examiner who set the question and asked what she had in mind. 'There is a list here,' she said, 'which lays out areas in which questions can be asked: one is landscape, one is gender, and as I could not think of a question on either, I ran them together and asked a question on both.' None of the candidates answered it.

Nonetheless, it has not gone away. Once you start looking for answers, they turn up in casual reading, even in reports of the most recent researches on two great British gardens, one at Stowe, the other at West Wycombe. At Stowe, the theory now is that the inscriptions on some of the garden temples referred to the ageing libido and decreasing prowess of the garden's male owner in the early eighteenth century. They might have been subtitled 'Waiting for Viagra'. In reply, witty and outrageous guests at the nearby West Wycombe Park encouraged its owner to lay out one part of his garden in the shape of a naked woman lying flat on her back. There were mounds in appropriate places and a sort of entrance tunnel, surrounded by a thicket of brambles. Their gendered garden was a vigorous answer to Stowe's gendered Georgian inscriptions. Would these researches count as a first-class answer?

My fellow examiner was not giving up. No, she said, the answers need to be much more general and not just show knowledge of a few odd things about odd places in the middle of England. Snubbed, I started to think again and have been thinking ever since. My conclusion is that the landscape is highly gendered but nobody talks about it. In Britain, the whole of it is overwhelmingly male. Men have owned most of it. Men have farmed it, fertilized it and cultivated it. Men, for the most part, have designed it. Why have we all been so slow to point this out?

Half of you, perhaps, are already protesting and saying that this conclusion is untrue. There have been women gardeners and land-scapers, even if we exclude the present era in which the professions are finally open and both sexes can gender gardens as they wish. Women's earlier activity is most easily traced through the upper social classes, where a well-studied line runs through women of the nobility from 1600 onwards and includes several members of the royal family. It begins with Lucy, Countess of Bedford, who married at the age of thirteen in 1594 and then had the fortune to have a husband who was permanently mute after a fall from a horse. She liaised with King James I's wife, Anne of Denmark, who had a parallel problem: her husband's homosexuality. The two of them took to gardening and befriended artists and poets, including John Donne and Ben Jonson. The most impressive result was Lucy's second garden at Moor Park in Hertfordshire, whose symbolic and architectural design cost a fortune. Lucy never put a spade in the ground herself, but she is one of the first

English patronesses who contributed to grand gardening, a socially acceptable outlet for frustrated females.

Several members of Britain's royal families shared this outlet, especially Queen Mary of William and Mary, and Queen Caroline, wife of George II. Queen Mary had a real interest in plants, although I doubt that she ever put them in the ground. Caroline enjoyed the help of the enchanting William Kent and built a famous garden at Richmond Lodge which contained an array of allusions to Great Britons of the past. In a Gothic cottage, she even maintained a poetic hermit, who represented the supposed prophecy of Merlin that the kings of ancient Britain would one day return to rule as the Georgian House of Hanover. The garden was a fascinating comment on the idea of Britishness, another hardy perennial in general exam-papers for historians.

These women and others plainly enjoyed gardens, but were prevented by convention from enjoying gardening. It is not entirely clear when that convention began to change. The mid nineteenth century is the likely turning point, represented in books with titles like *Every Lady Her Own Flower Gardener* (1837) and in the famous output of Jane Loudon who started *The Lady's Magazine of Gardening* in 1840. Even then, it was assumed that 'ladies' would not occupy themselves in vegetable gardens or in growing their own fruit. They might manage a flower garden, no doubt with a male labourer under their direction, but it was not considered wise for them to bend over for any length of time. Up to this point, their main contributions had been patronage and spending their husband's money.

So far as I know, the change to practice comes in the 1890s and in 1902 the first School for Lady Gardeners was founded by Frances Wolseley at Glynde in Sussex. Women had become fit students of the practical art of gardening. From the 1890s onwards, therefore, trained female gardeners began to invade Adam's sphere. By 1896, females were working at Kew Gardens. 'Who wants to see blooms now you've bloomers at Kew?' asked a witty magazine in 1900. Since then, the gender balance has continued to even up. Female landscapers include Sylvia Crowe and Brenda Colvin, both of whom laid out acres of ground. At Sissinghurst, there was Vita Sackville-West. In America, there was Beatrix Farrand. In Surrey, there was Gertrude Jekyll. In

Sixty years of gendered gardening at Kiftsgate Court: Anne Chambers and her mother Mrs Binny

Germany, there was Elisabeth von Arnim, famous for her book *In a German Garden*.

Indeed there were, and there still are, others, but were they not gardening in a gendered male slipstream? Vita wrote frankly: 'I could not have done it by myself.' She depended for her great garden's structure and design on her talented husband, Harold Nicolson. Beatrix and Gertrude were extremely good at planting, but were they ever effective in a wider landscape, and did they ever come up with a distinctively feminine style of design? Out in Germany, Elisabeth certainly did not. She was always tip-toeing around her awesome male partner, whom she called the Man of Wrath. If Mr Wrath wanted a big alley on the estate, I am sure he drove one into the landscape in an imperious, masculine way without ever asking her advice.

There is a famous letter, written in 1749, which nearly refutes men's dominance, but turns out to confirm it. The valiant Lady Luxborough wrote to the poet and landscape gardener William Shenstone detailing all the alterations which she had just carried out in her garden. 'The upper garden is now ungravelled and is making into a bowling-green; the pavilion will be set up next . . .' However, she begins and ends by thanking Shenstone for his book and sketch-plans, and hopes that he will go on helping her. She has only one idea of her own, and she puts it to him as a 'proposal'. She is evidently wanting assurance from a differently gendered hand.

I have excluded the recent, dysfunctional fountain in memory of the Princess of Wales. Instead, I should mention the May Day style of celebrations at America's all-female university, Bryn Mawr College. Recently, the ladies banned the traditional maypole because it was wrongly gendered and too erect. Instead, they dug a cleft in the ground and welcomed the dawn of May by sitting round their May-hole. They gendered the festival, but the idea has not caught on. To understand why, I suggest you look out of a train window and ponder while it speeds into the concrete jungles of a town. Those haystacks and hedges, those pleasant little coverts, those magical clumps of beech trees: all of them go back to men in the landscape, imposing their masculine gender for the sake of artistry, profit and their beloved country sports. The landscape has a masculine orientation. It is so masculine that I even risked putting the fact to a free-thinking feminist over lunch and asking her what she thought. How would she feel driving home now that she realized that the landscape is imprinted with the tyranny of the phallus and the patriarch? 'Sexy,' she answered, 'incredibly sexy: it really grabs me.' An alternatively gendered landscape is not what the other gender wants.

Lacecaps Under Trees

In a corner of my male-gendered landscape, near the drainpipe for my washing machine, I have an old pink lacecap hydrangea, which my father and I bought in 1963 after a visit to Hidcote Manor gardens in August, where the lacecap hydrangeas are so good. It is a historic hydrangea because it was acquired on a visit which opened my gardening eyes. For five years I had already been keenly growing alpines and annuals but at Hidcote I first realized that there was so much more to shrubs and climbers than our family gardens contained at home. Ever encouraging, my father agreed. We planted this lacecap hydrangea in the angle of two evergreen thuja hedges, a site of dry shade. Remarkably, it survived. It then moved house once, to my home as an adult, and it has never been better than in the years of its late middle age.

Intrigued by it, I set off on a hunt for a place where hydrangeas look really good. In England their qualities remain the subject of controversy. Some of you may be thinking that I should have gone to a major racecourse where mophead hydrangeas are such a frequent decoration of the stands. Others may be thinking of a bad hotel by the seaside where the hydrangeas in the front garden are neither pink nor blue. In fact, I went to Normandy, where hydrangeas are in their element. On the Normandy coast, almost every garden uses them because they love the dampness in the air and the days of sea mist. In an open field near Varengeville-sur-mer, hydrangeas are tended in the National Conservation Collection of the Shamrock gardens. The gardens can be visited on any day of the week as French growers take hydrangeas seriously. Their nurseries list many more varieties than ours do. In Angers there is even an association which takes a scientific approach to one major branch of the family.

The Shamrock gardens are remarkable. They have been built up by Robert Mallet, whose family's great garden at Parc des Moutiers was partly designed by England's Edwin Lutyens. In 2001 Robert and his wife Corinne had to think carefully about how to transfer their prized collection to a new site, and came up with an unexpected answer. They planted a thick canopy of paulownia trees, which have big leaves like green handkerchiefs and flowers like purple-blue foxgloves if they are not caught in England by spring frosts. Paulownias grow extremely fast, and I would have imagined that hydrangeas would hate to try to grow around their trunks. In fact, they love it, even more than they loved my father's thuja hedge.

The Mallets had studied paulownias and realized that their roots drive deeply down through the soil and draw up water like pumps. In the classic days of old Japanese gardens, the paulownia was highly prized for other reasons: its flowers and its distinctive wood. Parents would make boxes from paulownia wood and give them to their daughters when they married so that they could keep the last dress of their virgin years in a safe, dry place. Nowadays, such a dress would probably be an ageing party dress from childhood, but even so, the paulownia is a tree with a future. Its big leaves open late in the year and fall early, but its roots can draw up water even in the sandiest soil and spread it around, making a garden possible. This brilliant combination is in action in the Shamrock gardens. Their paulownia trees are only six years old but great mounds of hydrangeas are already hugging their trunks. This pairing will work even on very dry soil and this excellent collection has changed my ideas of the hydrangea family's prospects.

It is odd to think that hydrangeas did not even arrive in Europe before the late nineteenth century: Wordsworth and Milton never saw one. They are at home, above all, in Asia, especially in Japan where there are hundreds in the wild which we have yet to collect and understand. I remember Germaine Greer remarking that the sound of the word 'hydrangea' in Australian-English nearly scared her off gardening for life. Actually, the family is popular down under and there are several named Australian forms. A visit to Shamrock trans-forms our ideas about what is globally available. All over the world growers are busy breeding new forms and we are seriously behind the game in Britain. The soil at Shamrock is acid, and therefore the blue varieties flower in a proper shade of blue. Forget those old varieties like *macrophylla* 'Blue Wave'. The Swiss have bred a blue mophead called 'Blaumeise' which is in a different class. Over in Germany

My lacecap hydrangea, now 47 years old

breeders are developing low-growing forms with big flowers and
naming them after leading European cities. 'Eibtal' is a cracking blue
and they may be telling us something when the one called 'London'
is big-headed in a boozy shade of wine-purple.

It will be hard for the Shamrock collection to keep up with the rate
of progress. New varieties are pouring in, more than 100 every year.
There is also a historic obligation to track down prize varieties raised
by great breeders in past decades. One of them was England's
H. I. Jones, whose Hertfordshire hydrangeas have almost disappeared
from English lists. There is the further problem of uncollected var-

Hydrangea macrophylla 'London'

ieties. Corinne Mallet made a recent trip to the Japanese mountains
and found several low-growing unnamed lacecaps which have yet to
appear in gardens anywhere.

In cultivation, no branch of the hydrangea family has been spared
improvement. Some gardeners grow the paniculata forms, which have
long, pointed heads of flower, but most of them are unaware that they
vary in season and hardiness between their homes in north and south
Japan. Paniculatas from the north flower early and should be pruned
immediately after flowering because they set buds on the previous
year's wood. Paniculatas from the south of Japan flower late and can be
pruned later. There are even some low-growing ones with names like
'Dart's Little Dot'. Many of the best are grown in Alabama and are
unknown to English gardeners. So, too, are good forms of the much-
loved quercifolia, which is popular for its oak-shaped leaves and white
heads of flower in August. There have been many recent improvements, some of which flower earlier and make a better show. As for
the rest of the family, if anyone offers you a *serrata* 'Miranda' or a
'Mousseline', accept them with delight.

Hydrangea macrophylla 'Blaumeise'

Two problems face everyone who tries to grow hydrangeas: how do you make the flowers go a true shade of pink or blue? How do you prune them? Most of the pink-flowered forms need an alkaline soil, but should be given extra lime between April and July if they stray towards purple-blue. True blue forms need an acid soil but can be maintained elsewhere with a good colour if you dose them on Sequestrene or any chemical compound which allows azaleas to survive on limey ground. The pruning is easy when you know the trick. It is wrong to leave the dead-heads on hydrangeas for months after flowering as if they will protect the plant against damage from frost. At Shamrock they cut them off as soon as they can. Each stem should be traced back to a pair of leaves by a visible pair of lower buds and cut back to that point. The buds are quite easily found on the stem when you look for them.

I set out on my travels thinking that hydrangeas live for ever and that my father's lacecap will outlive me. I returned realizing mopheads have a bright future too, and much more variety than I imagined. If you think they are fit only for the seaside, you are missing the point of a worldwide story.

Le Jardin Plume

Not so far from this garden of hydrangeas lies the best garden with a modern twist which has come my way in years. It represents a thoughtful vision which combines the traditions of several nationalities into an independent and intelligent style. There is a superb sting in the tail. I hate to say it but it makes an excellent use of ornamental grasses. Almost nothing in the vegetable kingdom has had a worse press from me during the past ten years, but I am forced to moderate my convictions. At last, I have seen them ingeniously employed.

During the past decade, Patrick and Sylvie Quibel have quietly been making a remarkable garden on a patch of Normandy so difficult it would have deterred me from even starting. For more than twenty years they have been nursery people with a critical eye for the changing styles of modern gardening. In 1996 they started to imprint their personal vision on a difficult landscape scarcely ten miles from Rouen. On their chosen site, the wind is severe and the soil is unfavourable clay. They had to garden on eight acres of it, but without much external help. Their site would have struck me as a flat, forsaken pancake, but they saw possibilities in it which would allow a plan to come true. The result is Le Jardin Plume, Le Thil, 76116 Auzouville-sur-Ry in Normandy. The garden is open every afternoon from Wednesday until Saturday with a few morning openings listed on the website at www.lejardinplume.com. In 2003 they won a prize for the best modern garden in France. They must have won by a distance. I have not seen a better modern garden anywhere. In 2009 they won a similar award from London's Garden Museum.

At Le Jardin Plume they have combined geometrical formality with natural freedom, arranged so that symmetry and solidity lead out into unregulated wildness. What does this planning mean in practice? They began with a flat expanse of ground which stretched away from undistinguished buildings, now modernized to serve as their house, and

A corner of Le Jardin Plume in July

nursery's barns. They raised the ground immediately around the house by the height of a single step and began to adorn it with a strict formal pattern of clipped green box and a tightly controlled planting whose flowers are mainly strong, pure yellow. From this one step up, you look down into a brilliant innovation, a rectangular pond which sits without edging or paving in the surrounding ground. It acts like a mirror and sounds even better in French: *un bassin miroir*. Beyond it, between fruit trees, stretches a carefully planned sequence of rectangular patches of the ornamental grasses which I most deplore. Here, they look brilliant because they are contained in rectangular borders and interplanted with flowering perennials which cheer up their brown waving plumes and give an impression of a man-made wilderness. These rectangles extend for more than an acre down the view across a flat prairie. They are many times prettier than the wildflower meadows which obsess gardeners in Britain and then look a mess for five months of the year. Here, the 'meadows' are rigidly controlled by a formal French eye and

Meadow perennials in Le Jardin Plume

the mown paths between them are given the width of a boulevard. It is
a fine experience to look down the central length of this extraordinary
garden which is not in the least hostile to flowers. There is no brutal
modernism, no silly sculpture and no unsympathetic concrete. There
is an orderly sense of tightly controlled nature. I love it.

Round the house the colour is intense in several different sections.
When I first visited in July the main terrace was a blaze of strong
yellow from excellent types of coreopsis, emerging rudbeckias,
carefully chosen dahlias and so forth. The strong colour goes well
with the fresh green of the clipped box and makes an excellent contrast with the directed wilderness of grasses and perennials beyond.
The wilderness is not like the shaggy banks of a British motorway,
even when they are dotted with meadow geraniums.

The Quibels are excellent nursery people. They have worked out
exactly which types of veronicastrum, tall thalictrum and desirable
sanguisorba will compete and survive in a general setting of waving

Part of the potager in Le Jardin Plume

grasses. Like all patrons of '*les graminées*', known to me as eurograss, they emphasize the way in which this type of planting waves in the wind and fluctuates like waves when breezes penetrate the surrounding hedges. What differentiates the style at Le Jardin Plume is the intelligent interplanting with flowering perennials and the strict controlling vision which has not lost a reassuring formality underneath the seed-heads.

Patrick is most likely to take you round the garden and talk about its plan. It sounds so chic in French and makes me think of the formal mind of Descartes applied to a flat patch of the natural world. As it is a deeply thought garden, it does not stop with beds of grass or a single season. On one side of the house the spring garden faces east towards the rising sun and is cheered in the autumn by plantings of lowly *Aster divaricatus*. On the west side of the house, a segregated autumn garden includes very tall plants with flowers like spires. Clear yellow daisies rise here among clumps of bright pink and purple Michaelmas daisies and a central backbone of silvery grass. I can well imagine that it is spectacular when in season.

As you stand on the terrace's single step and look out, to your half-right is an enchanting potager which has rambling gourds, clumps of flowery coriander, the right kind of woven hurdles and a good display of upturned flowerpots. They are just like the pots from which Laurence Olivier used to extract earwigs while playing John Mortimer's blind father in his *Voyage Round My Father*, reliving those memorable scenes among dahlias which Mortimer's father would never see. The style in the potager is highly cultivated, intimate and immediately lovable. Beyond it you enter a forest of grassy miscanthus, the rampant grass which, for once, is rather exciting. Beyond it again, the white-flowered willowherb, or epilobium, has run wild in magnificent profusion. In spring, the flat rectangles of grasses on the main axis are full of brilliantly coloured bulbs. As an informal Englishman I might have been tempted to vary the rectangles and include one rectangle of flowering perennials to every two of grass. No doubt it would have looked awful but I would like to try. Meanwhile, I urge you to go and see the existing plan.

When you talk to Patrick and Sylvie you realize how considered and how serious is their engagement with nature and gardens. This quality does not always belong to the people who become most famous or who write the most books. The Quibels knew what they wanted to do. They looked carefully at the new styles of wild gardening in the Netherlands and adapted ideas which they found there, giving them a personal turn which transforms them. So often I found that they put into French what I quietly think in English. I am sure they will never exhibit at fancy Chelsea but I give them a gold medal. They also run an excellent nursery whose prices depend on the British pound's rate to the euro. Before the pound fell, they were lower than specialists' prices in England. There are no fewer than fourteen kinds of excellent helenium, eight of which are new to me, and eleven varieties of the sanguisorbas which they use so well but which are not easy to propagate. If you have a car boot, I suggest you fill it, because there is plenty there which you will not easily find back in England. All the plants are properly grown, not in peat-based compost, but proper soil, what is called in French '*terre universelle*'.

Dealing With Dry Shade

In August, those of us at home can put the garden under critical review. In sunny weather, the first problems which hit the eye are areas of dry shade. We all have dry shade and not many of us make much of it. When the sun is hot, we retire towards it and then realize the space we are wasting. After many experiments I have a core of reliable colonizers which survive on these awkward sites. I am not thinking of dry shade under a wall so much as the shade cast by tall trees, a difficult constraint, especially on a light soil. The answer is not to aim for anything exotic and not to plant phloxes, which may like light shade but are miserable without water. Go for something quieter which will not look as if it is struggling.

One of the best choices is a first cousin to our Michaelmas daisies, an aster called *schreberi*. Its flowers are star-shaped and white above leaves which are an excellent shade of dark green. *Aster schreberi* is quite without diseases and never catches grey mildew. It flowers for about three months, starting in July, and is even more robust than its striking blue relation, the daisy-flowered *Aster macrophyllus* 'Twilight' which will also put up with difficult conditions. 'Twilight' does not cover the ground but it shows up well from August onwards in a pretty shade of blue. It is excellent to see its fresh flowers among other survivors which have had their season. In front of it I plant groups of the pleasantly sprawling *Aster divaricatus*, another neglected winner with small starry white flowers, dark black stems and exceptional stamina in drought.

The greatest such survivors are the hardy geraniums, many of which throw out long stems of flower and fall forwards untidily after midsummer. They must be cut back promptly with a pair of lawn shears and reduced to a central clump. Some of these sprawlers will grow well in difficult settings, but my standby is a tidier one, *Geranium macrorrhizum* 'Album'. It is a quiet plant but never seems to fail, although the flowers are not actually white, as the third of its Latin names implies, but a pale shade of pink-white from May onwards. The leaves are tidy and it is fun to discover that they are pleasantly scented of the geranium oil which is used for bath essence. One or two plants can soon be divided and multiplied to make a long line. The plant is a godsend in dry conditions.

If you also choose shade-lovers with height, they will break up the lower layers of this cover and stop them looking like an effort to block the ground. An excellent option is to plant the deeper blue form of what is sometimes wrongly known as 'chicory'. *Cicerbita plumieri* is an indestructible plant which gives great pleasure in high summer at a height of about four feet. It is not the sky-blue 'chicory' which is often seen flowering by roadsides in Mediterranean countries. Its flowers have a deeper colouring, almost violet-blue, and its thick, water-retentive roots will grow where the going is tough.

Shrubs also give a layer of height and the best of them flowers in late spring, although it is happy with minimal water. The familiar choisya, or Mexican orange blossom, is a surprisingly good performer under tall deciduous trees, a discovery which has come late in my experience. A choisya's leaves have a shiny green coating and although they are not at their seasonal best when the flowers appear in May, they soon recover and remain a glossy green presence which is cheering from June onwards. The entire plant is tougher than was thought forty years ago, when there were fears that it might not be hardy. Few modern winters are going to trouble it in the shelter of tall trees and it is good to discover that a dried-out summer does not bother it, either. I am also puzzled why an equally tough form of honeysuckle is not more widely available. *Lonicera tatarica*, preferably the form called 'Hacks Red', is a reliable shrub with an exceptional ability to put up with next to no water wherever the developing roots of trees cause problems. Its leaves look dusty in dry weather but it is almost in-destructible and the red flowers in the joints of the leaves are pretty. They puzzle people who know honeysuckles only as climbers.

If you prefer to allow a small, narrow strip of a dry bed to be invaded so that it never needs attention, I recommend a wild runner, a relation of comfrey but one which never seeds itself widely. *Sym-phytum cooperi* is not yet in the *RHS Plant Finder* but is excellent value if given its head in a dark, dry corner. The flowers are tubular, com-

Aster schreberi

bining a hint of dark purple with blue and white without being over-powering. Alternatively, I would choose evergreen *Phlomis russeliana*, which has quite big leaves and sends up green-yellow flowers to a height of about three feet. The leaves will flag if the weather is persist-ently dry, but the plant never dies.

In August, it is easy to think only of yet more flowers for August but the best plants in dry shade flower much earlier. Even when they are in competition with sycamore roots, hellebores will make an excellent show in dry ground from February until April. The ones to choose are the many varieties of the Lenten rose, *Helleborus orientalis* and the × *hybridus* garden forms. From August onwards, in dry places, it is worth feeding their clumps once a fortnight with diluted fertilizer to be sure of spectacular shows of flower in the following spring. Some of their experts write as if they must have a deep soil, lightly shaded, but in fact, they will grow in less than a foot of soil over a stony subsoil, only six feet away from the trunks of tall sycamores and chestnuts. I know, because I tried them there, at first with a sinking heart, as I had ordered them before I discovered with a crowbar how bad their chosen position was to be. An autumn feeding has helped them but in these tough conditions they are as beautiful as those in more favoured parts of the garden.

In the past ten years, crossing and selecting have extended the charm of these excellent plants. The good work has accelerated through the positive attitude of Ashwood Nurseries at Kingswinford, near Kidderminster, whose owners took a splendidly contrary view. For years, there had been fears that hellebores would deteriorate when their famous keepers gave up or died. Two of the great experts were Helen Ballard in Worcestershire and Elizabeth Strangman in Kent, and fortunately they had the generosity of true experts and were prepared to make their best plants available to the Ashwood team. While other experts were inclined to moan that all the good forms were dying out, Ashwood rose to the challenge and set out to breed even better ones. You can now go to their splendid nursery and buy the results in selected colours. The Ashwood crosses will ensure that you have high-class winners of your own, although other forms have been bred elsewhere and are often very good. I have had excellent value from an ugly-sounding hybrid, *Helleborus × nigercors*, which is a cross between the Christmas rose and the vigorous green-flowered Corsican helle-bore. The big white flowers come in bunches and last very well and the Corsican bloodline gives the leaves a point and the plant some extra strength.

Dry shade is not a disaster for gardeners. It is a challenge which limits options and needs thought if it is to be turned to good effect.

Rosemary Revisited

Dry shade was the sort of challenge which Rosemary Verey liked to overcome with a forgotten cure. Ever resourceful, she became the Queen of English gardening until her death in June 2001, and I still reflect on her fame and style. As a writer, lecturer, planter and gardener, she became celebrated throughout the English-speaking world for her densely planted garden at Barnsley House in Gloucestershire. It was promptly sold by her heirs, but was bought and turned into a hotel by neighbours who had admired Rosemary in action. The garden remains open in her memory.

Rosemary was first propelled to fame by the book *The English-woman's Garden*, which she wrote with the talented gardener Alvilde Lees-Milne, famous for her fine garden, also in Gloucestershire, at Alderley Grange near Wootton-under-Edge. The title caught a mood of gentle feminism and showy gardening in the early 1980s, although with hindsight, many of the gardens in the book were made by men or jointly with men as partners. On the strength of it, Alvilde became a garden designer for Mick Jagger and Rosemary, too, would soon be advising a male celebrity world. Increasingly known from her writing, she emerged as a garden designer with influence. In imitation of her Gloucestershire garden, ever more people wanted to own a tunnel of trained laburnum, dripping with yellow flowers. She emerged in middle age, an achievement which seems unusual now because subsequent garden-princesses have been launched through television, for which youth and beauty are a help. Whereas Alvilde had gardened for decades, having known (and loved) Vita Sackville-West in the 1950s, Rosemary only began gardening in her early fifties when her children had grown up and her husband was encouraging her to fill the empty spaces in the garden with flowers. One of her shining qualities was that she was always clear and generous about the people who inspired her to try to garden seriously. She recalled how Russell Page, the landscape gardener, had just brought out his classic book *The Education of a Gardener* and it caught her fancy. She often told me of the encouragement she received from Arthur Hellyer, the impulse behind so many well-known gardeners.

Her gardening career took off at an age when many people think of downsizing their garden or giving up. Undaunted, she showed what a female gardener could do through her own talent at an older age. Rosemary was extremely well organized and had a clear, efficient mind. In her youth she had read for a degree in Economics in London and throughout her years of motherhood she was a skilled horse-woman, applying her talents for organization to the horse-shows and local Pony Club meetings around her Gloucestershire home. The death of her beloved husband David, himself an architect and man of style, impelled Rosemary to apply her skills to a new, absorbing occupation. She chose gardening in which she had already progressed but in a different era and place she might well have chosen a public career.

Rosemary Verey began late, but she hit on the right style at the right moment. She coincided with a new wave of English-style gardening, propelled by economics and a subtle change in technology. The technical change was not horticultural. It was a change in book-production which encouraged the rise of the book-packager and book-designer: English publishers realized that good, cheap colour printing could be bought in from Italy or Hong Kong. As a result hers was the first grand garden to be stunningly photographed and mar-keted through full-page colour spreads in such affordable books as her *Making of a Garden* (1995) and *Garden Plans* (1993), among the most rewarding of her titles. She soon began to think clearly in photo-graphic terms. In the 1960s, most colour picture books had been feebler: Rosemary's set a new standard by the way in which her gardens were presented.

The revolution in presentation went together with various social novelties and a particular character of her own. Until the late 1970s, the main theme in most gardens had been the continuing urge to 'save labour'. Gardeners were still struggling to use 'ground cover' and surmount the shock to their parents or themselves caused by the disappearance of cheap labour since 1945. Rosemary went in the opposite direction, helped by an increasing team of gardeners. She

Rosemary under the laburnum arch

liked themed features, colour, thick layers of planting, and anything which was not drab. As her fame and fortunes grew, the variety of features at Barnsley grew too and the lavishness of the planting and upkeep were able to be sustained by the profits of her advice. In the early 1980s, a new free-market mood in Britain made riches and their display more accessible and more acceptable and gardening regained a scale and extravagance lost since the 1930s. The Prince of Wales, recently married, set high society an example of grandiose gardening round his newly bought home at Highgrove, on whose themed gardens Rosemary gave early advice. In the new social climate well-off garden-owners began to want to compete with the illusory perfection which was caught in the photographs of her plantings. She stood for a new affirmation of a generous 'English style', one which had been in retreat for fifty years.

English gardening had always been popular in America, especially on the East Coast, and the newly lavish style of her flower gardening appealed to American owners too, who were also prospering in a free-market age. Rosemary was quick to develop transatlantic contacts which multiplied through mutual friends, impressed by her garden, her royal contacts and her clear views. She had the special cachet of being a woman, one who was at ease in high society and very well presented as a lecturer. She became a major bridge between keen American gardeners and English gardeners who had previously written off much of America's gardening out of ignorance. Back in Gloucestershire, she found in her friend and neighbour, the dress-designer Hardy Amies, exactly the person to dress her in style for lectures and meetings on her transatlantic circuit. They had a splendid rapport, as Sir Hardy was also a sharp-eyed gardener of taste and independence, with a fine eye for old-fashioned roses, his 'last collec-tion', he would tell me, while showing off his roses with French names as if they were ladies in a couturier's salon. Characteristically, Rose-mary loved learning from the many fine American gardens which she was now able to visit: she especially admired the artistic style of Bob Dash on Long Island and the exceptional planting by Ryan Gainey in Atlanta, Georgia. 'The dry brown hills,' she once wrote, 'of the Yakima Reservation in Oregon, with their tawny look, remind me of the brown stems and trunks of my winter shrubs and trees at Barnsley.

It has taught me to think about the expansiveness of nature . . .'

As the books and their authoress travelled, Rosemary became in demand as a designer and garden-planter to a degree which no Englishwoman in recent decades had equalled. Throughout, she retained a concern for natural solutions to the artificial art of garden-ing. She liked to look for such practices in older garden books which dated back to the 1600s and before. Her strength was to suggest ideas, not to design on paper, an art which she never mastered. She could not draw. Instead, she liked novel experiments, so much so that she was one of those who urged me to mulch my garden with cocoa-shells, a fashionable war cry in the battle against peat, and one which I am glad I never followed. Her 'countrywoman's notes' from Gloucestershire are some of her most enjoyable writings, but here too her fancies can seem idiosyncratic in the modern world. 'If your son or daughter is facing an important examination,' she once suggested, 'encourage them with angelica ("inspiration"), red clover ("industry") and pink cherry blossom ("education") . . .' From my practical observations, the young recipients' first thought would be to try to smoke them.

At Barnsley, her knot garden was a brilliant revival of an old fash-ion, using forgotten green germander as well as box. Her laburnum tunnel was not an original idea, but it was a master-stroke to under-plant it with the tall purple onion-heads of *Allium aflatunense*, a choice which she told me she owed to the Dutch nurseryman van Tubergen. It was, however, her own happy idea to plant the long paved path from the main rooms of her house with bright helianthemums, or sun roses, a scheme which ought to be imitated. By the mid 1980s, she had also planted a formal vegetable garden, or potager, which became famous through photographs of its standard gooseberry trees and richly coloured Swiss chard. It was a difficult space to visit, not least with the owner, who would bend among the elegant cloches and accentuate a visitor's sense of fighting for space, like a car-parker in Knightsbridge. Here, especially, she had thought to a photographic scale, rather than to a workable width for a long-term garden.

Monarchs are also adept at looking past people, or putting them down, arts which Rosemary sometimes failed to realize she possessed. To those whom she acknowledged, she was extremely loyal and generous, but at her packed memorial service in Cirencester, one of her many beneficiaries, the fine plant photographer Andrew Lawson, recalled how he once came to photograph the Barnsley garden. He started work very early in the morning, a garden photographer's necessary licence. He went to the yellow laburnum tunnel and found a few flowers fallen on the ground beneath, so he brushed them away to suit his picture. Breakfast followed, and Rosemary surprised him by remarking on his tidying of her tunnel's appearance. There was a pause and while Andrew reached for a reply, Rosemary cut him short. 'I preferred it,' she told him, 'the way it was.'

I am not sure that she always preferred the garden the way that it became. Winters in Gloucestershire can be bleak, and as the years passed, a bottle or two of spirits used to help her through dark, solitary evenings. In due course her own garden became a victim of the very photography which made it wondrous. Photographs fix a perfect instant, but as time passed and plants grew too freely, she was prone to pass off the jungle of her later decades as a 'meadow style'. She was a great magpie and noticer, but how deep and broad was her knowledge? Once, when we returned from a walk to admire her orange-flowered asclepias, I responded to her offer of a shrub from her plant stall. I asked for a plain old ceratostigma, the prince of blue-flowering autumn shrubs, which grows well enough at Barnsley. Rosemary surprised me by saying she did not know it and certainly did not have it.

Television viewers may share a different memory. In front of the camera, Rosemary Verey was magnificently poised and true to her class, but she was seen on one widely watched programme walking down the broad borders of a lovely Cumberland garden with its panama-hatted owner. After passing some fine urns, he turned to her to ask for advice, as he felt the garden needed a bit of a lift at the point where they were standing. There was a brief silence and she replied: 'Urns, more urns . . .'

Rosemary remains justly honoured as a great ambassador for English gardening, here and abroad. One of her clients was the singer Elton John and she once wrote that she loved to hear him singing, and even hoped that 'one day, it will be a song about the orange marigold that has found its way into his white garden'. Was she chiding him for the oversight, or was she celebrating nature's wayward manner? Either intention would be true to her way with gardeners and gardens.

Swinging Baskets

Up and down historic Britain, sweaty August brings the public crop of hanging baskets into overheated bloom. They dangle on the lamp-posts in heritage Oxford (twinned with Leon, Nicaragua), conservation Bath is crawling with them, and they are swinging far and wide in Leamington Spa.

Why ever have councils assumed that their taxpayers want to pay for this public fiesta? The cost is not only the cost of the baskets. Cast-iron poles have to be drilled into the pavements to hold them above head height. While publicizing their low-emission buses and writing on their nuclear-free notepaper, councils send out teams of water-carriers to soak their hanging baskets with precious water which could otherwise help them in their mission to 'save our planet'. The watering is done in the twilight before dawn, away from spectators who might question it. In a vivid image, Germaine Greer has given the display a new meaning. Hanging baskets in our city centres remind her, she has written, of 'severed heads on the way to the Roman Forum'. Were there really heads on show in the central space of ancient Rome? Romans were capable head-hunters, and they first cut the head off a presiding consul and displayed it in the Forum in 87 BC. Forty years later, Julius Caesar had a neat little bout of head-hunting at the expense of his enemy Pompey's remaining men in Spain. In celebration, his troops stuck the heads on the fortifications of Spanish towns. In 43 BC, there was the beheading of poor old Cicero, the acknowledged master of oratory. Head-hunters sent his head to his enemy Mark Antony, whose wife is then said to have pierced the tongue with hairpins. Head-hunting has ancient roots in the history of Western civilization.

Severed heads in Rome's forum were always male, but is the most thought-provoking analogy for baskets in a crowded town centre a Cicero with petunia-dreadlocks or a Gaul with a grimace of busy Lizzie? Not according to one of my former gardening suppliers in the Vale of Evesham. He declared himself king of the hanging basket and delighted both sexes by offering them a choice of hanging baskets in cup-sizes ranging upwards from double-D. He changed my perception of a council's underwired basket of blue lobelia, delicately lined with green moss. In return I told him about Queen Pheretima, attested in Herodotus' ancient histories. She took revenge on the women of a Libyan city by cutting off their breasts and fixing them on the outside of the city wall. In her honour he introduced a special basket called Pheretima's Revenge. When you next see the municipal baskets on city walls, think of Pheretima and look again.

Why are these great balls of colour so often an affront? One reason is their context, another, their contents. They have become part of the mission to jolly up town centres and give them a festive mood. Poles topped with streaky petunias are a strange idea of a festival. They derive from the municipal obsession to turn town centres into a vision of Toy Town, spattered with pointless signposts and multi-coloured distractions. Towns with serious architecture are lucky enough not to need them, as they have their own dignity without being told to join in a frolic. Has anyone seen a row of hanging baskets in the centre of Venice or Paris?

Perhaps you wonder why petunias, trailing 'surfinias', lobelias, 'geraniums' and busy Lizzie are the overwhelming types of planting in each severed basket. The reason is commercial. These particular types of plant are raised in vast quantities by wholesalers who then pass them on as young 'plugs' or ready-grown plants, to the 'gardening' departments of local authorities. If you wrote and suggested that the baskets might be filled next year with trailing morning glory, the problem would be that somebody locally would have to germinate it and grow it. This pre-selection is an anathema to thoughtful gardeners. They look on the contents of a typical hanging basket much as keen cooks look on supermarkets' rock-hard apologies for 'fresh nectarines' or Class One pears.

Is there a suitable place for rounded holders of colour, clamped above head-height on posts or on buildings' façades? If you live in a festive building like a pub, you might as well go festive and cover it with anything which flowers. The problem is not the basket itself but the transfer of decoration fit for a pub to settings which have no need of it. Why, too, does the container always have to be a basket? In the

Hanging baskets in Oxford (twinned with Leon, Nicaragua, and Perm, Russia)

south of France or in Italy a cluster of single flowerpots often stands beside steps or windows and shows plantings of a carefully chosen scarlet geranium or a flower of the homeowner's choice. On the walls of a big square in Cordoba the trailing geraniums are spectacular. In bright sunlight, these single flowerpots are so charming because they lack the over-stuffing which comes with a double-D basket in full flow. They also avoid the carmine colours which are chosen by city parks departments without thought for their setting in a sober street. Breeders have proudly developed trailing petunias which will flower for weeks and 'add value'. The trouble is that most of these varieties are available only in veined or streaky colours.

It is time for council taxpayers to answer back. Each year, busy judges go out and assess the annual planting which local authorities, 'working with the environment', have plastered over their town centres. They then give them prizes in the name of Britain in Bloom. Then the taxpayers pay all over again so that a winning of this prize can be inscribed on the road signs which identify the city and its foreign twins. Instead, the judges should request that slips be sent out with each demand for council tax, asking the payers whether they continue to want baskets and artificial watering all over their environment at their own cost. There could be a space for comments and another for suggestions of colour-coding. The extravaganza would then disappear, along with the pretensions which introduced it.

Forcing Nature

'The French build gardens and the English like to think that only they can plant them.' Is this bit of popular garden history true? I have been checking it out at one of those dreamy French country houses which activate the planting instincts of English gardeners as soon as they see avenues of trimmed limes and beech trees.

Near Bayeux and within sight of the 'Gold Beach' of the Normandy landings in 1944, the Château de Brécy is a rare delight. Formal French designs for gardens are usually on such a grand scale that modern gardeners struggle to apply them to their own setting. They 'force nature', we are taught, but at Brécy nature looks as if she has been happily seduced into submission. Neither the château nor the formal garden is impossibly large. Nonetheless the virtues of fine stonework and mathematical planning are in evidence on the three terraces, which ascend in due proportions from the main vista. Their former owner and partial restorer, the man of letters Jacques de Lacretelle, described the garden as the 'finery of an Italian princess thrown over the shoulders of a little Normandy peasant girl'. It was thrown there in the 1660s and has lived on wondrously as the backbone for a medium-sized formal garden, which is once again at its peak. I wish I could inherit it.

Plagued by small black thunder-flies, I stood on the roof of the château with the present genius of the place, Didier Wirth, and asked him to take me through the evolution of the garden beneath us. Its mastermind is still unknown, although some have suggested a genius of formal landscaping, François Mansart, who worked earlier in the vicinity and helped to teach the great Le Nôtre. Its patron is better known, a local man of law, Jacques Le Bas. His supplementary fees while in office would fascinate the modern British press but they were also the income on which his plans for Brécy's house and its ascending garden of steps, parterres and balustrades were based. Their main vista

The clipped hornbeam cloister at Brécy

is a triumph of rational French calculation and demonstrates that mathematical proportion applies to all houses and homes, whatever their extent.

Brécy's garden lies on the site of a former monastic seat for Benedictine monks. Even now Didier Wirth and his gardeners hit on the bones of holy brothers when they dig the foundations for new hedges and plantings near the surviving priory church. In the French Revolution this church and its lands were taken over by the villagers. The sculpted entrance gates and formal backbone of the Brécy garden survived in gentle decay, until they were encountered by the renowned French actress Rachel Boyer on holiday in the summer of 1912. Enchanted by them, she bought the place on sight and even acquired the superfluous priory. Everybody's property had sunk to the value of nobody's property. She paid 101 francs for the church, one of history's great post-Revolutionary buys.

In her care Brécy first benefited from the attentions of French professionals, experts who cared for the preservation of '*monuments historiques*'. A lull followed, including a merciful escape from shelling in 1944, when Brécy was taken without a fight in the first flush of the Allied landings. In 1955 the writer de Lacretelle bought the place and set to work on the formal garden near the house. He reintroduced a smart box parterre and a formal pattern of diagonal lines for the main terraces. He based his patterns on drawings by the master designer André Mollet, preserved in the classic handbooks of the period when Brécy was built. Brécy began to smile again, but its smile has been lengthened and greatly improved by Barbara and Didier Wirth, owners since 1992.

As I looked at their excellently chosen old roses round the church, I remembered the cliché about English planting and French building. Modern Brécy challenges it. At home, on the hedges of my English old vicarage, I have sheets of white flower from the apt climbing rose 'Rambling Rector'. Beside the Church of 101 Francs, the Wirths have 'Rambling Rectors' too. I had left for France while two valiant tree-cutters struggled to restore shape to my English avenues of hornbeam and evergreen *Pyrus calleryana* 'Chanticleer', a self-inflicted penance which drains money every two years. At Brécy, Wirth's gardeners keep a long run of hornbeams to the shape of a green cloister, complete with arched windows. They emerge on ladders through this cloister's green ceiling and clip every twig in sight. Neat cones of hornbeam flank a path by the church, clipped so tightly that you could bounce a ball off them. In England my avenues of hornbeam become so fluffy before their clipping that I have sometimes thought of felling them. The difference is that Brécy's hornbeams are cut three times a year from a French platform which makes my platform at home look like a clumsy parody of a guillotine. Brécy is proof that hornbeam hedging, tightly clipped, is the right choice for sites in full sun, whereas beech hedging is best in partial shade.

Brécy is fortunate in its present owners. They have emphasized the garden's strong architectural lines by intelligently extending its green hedging. On the far end of its main axis they have added formal barriers of limes and hornbeams in a style which struck a distant English chord in my mind. A widely spaced line of pleached trees stands as a back row with its trunks neatly clipped. In front of it runs a line of tightly clipped hedging, matching the variety of tree behind it. I remembered the excellent green lines of similarly clipped hedging in the Buckinghamshire garden of the famous decorator and designer David Hicks. It was not a random memory. Barbara Wirth, I then learned, had run the David Hicks shop in Paris and had been a good friend of the designer, whose garden had indeed influenced her style.

Clichés begin to become fuzzy. Here is a formal French garden with lessons in planting and maintenance for English gardeners. Its formal style is a supreme witness to the classic age of French planning, but one of its initiatives owes a debt to an English designer's example. Happily confounded, I turned back to consider the garden's most unusual keynote, globe artichokes modelled in stone on the garden's impressively restored fountains. Wirth explained the underlying idea. They imitate the globe artichokes which survive scarved in stone near the top of the property's Benedictine priory church. They puzzled later historians, but the answer lies in medieval Benedictine bibles. The globe artichoke is not a symbol of the hors d'oeuvres which await us in a starred French restaurant in paradise. It represents our human relation to God. God is in the artichoke's heart, below the layers of choking fluff and prickles. We are the artichoke's leaves which surround His presence at the centre. Is that why I often find the artichoke's heart so indigestible? At Brécy, I am happy to accept that the designs on the Wirths' new fountains are telling us that the garden is close to heaven.

Later Clematis

Clematis which flower in late summer are the most reliable members of their family. The best of them never catch the disease of clematis wilt and are able, too, to survive a long dry spell. The best of all is *Clematis* 'Bill MacKenzie'. It is a tangutica hybrid with yellow flowers, but the flowers are larger and more open than in close relations, and it is a name on which you should insist. Tangutica comes from Mongolia and north-west China and should not be confused with the smaller-flowered *Clematis orientalis*. The 'Bill MacKenzie' name commemorates a great gardener who did much for London's admired Chelsea Physic Garden during the 1960s. It was he who selected this exceptionally good variety while visiting Valerie Finnis at the Horticultural College which flourished at Waterperry, Oxford. It was the happiest selection, and you should insist on it when you are shopping.

The reason is that it flowers spectacularly, grows strongly and makes an exceptional show. The flowers have four broad yellow 'petals' which open out and show a contrasting cluster in the centre. It grows more than fifteen feet high with great speed and is not fussy about a dry place below a tall wall. For years, I never realized that it would thrive when facing south on the front of a house. I now wonder why I bother with anything else. 'Bill MacKenzie' goes on and on flowering and is still at its best in early October on my walls. Not only does it have the best flowers in the yellow group, it also has the enchanting grey-silver fluffy seed heads of the main species. An *FT* reader once wrote to describe them to me as resembling 'imitators of the early Beatles' haircuts, now in their late middle age'. Indeed, they look like grey-haired survivors from those carefully styled fans whom I saw screaming in the Hammersmith Palais in late 1963. Fortunately, Bill MacKenzie's clematis is silent.

One of my other late favourites is a useful sprawler. *Clematis* × *jouiniana* was raised as a cross between two wild parents, one of which is the vigorous Traveller's Joy of hedgerows. It falls around happily at ground

Beatle heads on *Clematis* 'Bill Mackenzie'

level and makes a mound, off which long side-growths spread. The small
flowers are shaped like an X and are a pleasing shade of milky blue-white.
The advantage of this plant is that it will spread and hide gaps or ugliness
at ground level. It is not evergreen, but it makes a good job of hiding an
old tree stump or a big drain cover if you plant it some distance away and
fix wide-meshed netting over the offending object. If you ever need to
open the drain cover, the stems of ×*jouiniana* can easily be brushed aside.
Alternatively, you can build it a frame of pea-sticks and leave it to
scramble into a longish thicket about three feet high. It will also grow up
a wall, but it is as a late sprawler that I value it most. On poor soil, I have
found that its flowers are much smaller, but they are always better in a
wet year. There is an earlier form, conventionally called ×*jouiniana*
praecox, but I think that this name is freely applied in the trade, irrespec-
tive of the start of the plant's flowering season. A true *praecox* should
already be in flower in July.

One of the main ambitions of breeders nowadays is to create a
late-summer clematis which will stay small and flower well as a pot plant.
None of the candidates has yet persuaded me, but there is one established
item, a neat little number from Guernsey called 'Petit Faucon'. The merit
of this plant is its exceptional length of flowering, which sometimes
stretches across three months. The height is not more than a metre, but
the flowers are prolific from the tips of new growth and open to a good
shade of deep blue. They twist round as they open, showing pretty
orange-yellow stamens, and then the colour becomes more pure. 'Petit
Faucon' is a good choice for the middle row of a flower border, where it

can be centrally supported on a cane. Alternatively, it can be placed to fill in the bare space which develops at the base of many climbing roses, especially if they have not been pruned sufficiently hard in their early years. 'Petit Faucon' is an excellent plant which fills a gap in gardens and in its family.

Over early-flowering shrubs I grow late-flowering clematis, a cloak which gives these shrubs a second season. The best ones for the purpose are members of the Viticella Group, coloured from white to deep velvety maroon-red. They grow to a convenient routine. In February, they should be cut down to within a foot of ground level, a cutting which keeps their stems off the flowering growth of forsythias, viburnums and early shrub roses. When the shrubs have flowered, the viticellas begin to spread through them, but not so quickly that the shrubs, too, cannot be pruned lightly after flowering. In August my white-flowered *Viburnum* × *carlcephalum* would look dull and dusty without their covering of white-flowered *Clematis* 'Alba Luxurians'. This white variety with green markings shows up best on a shrub, whereas the darker purple and red viticella forms are blurred by the branches over which they run. For this purpose, a clematis should be planted on a cane about three feet away from the shrub's main stems. The cane should be tilted towards the shrub's lower branches, so as to guide the clematis to clamber in the right direction.

On quite a different scale, another winner was bred in the Crimea about forty years ago, also by capitalizing on vigorous Traveller's Joy as a parent. It is called now correctly 'Paul Farges' (formerly, *fargesioides* 'Summer Snow') and is one to watch. The flowers are small, but they are cream-white with a slight scent and a long season. It is a favourite with beekeepers because bees love it and turn it into palatable honey. 'Paul Farges' is a favourite with me because it is so vigorous that it will bolt up a tall tree or hedge. I have even let it loose up a shaggy barrier of Leyland cypress. I am now thinking of aiming it up a big pine tree which a passer-by has kindly killed by lobbing a cigarette over the garden wall from the nearby footpath.

One place not to put this rampageous Russian is in a pot on a terrace, where I saw it, lovingly labelled, in Fulham. Thoughtful gardeners have much scope for placing clematis, old and new, but a pot is no place for varieties with so much energy.

Autumn

I remember a clear morning in the ninth month when it had been raining all night. Despite the bright sun, dew was still dripping from the chrysanthemums in the garden. On the bamboo fences and criss-cross hedges I saw tatters of spider webs; and where the threads were broken the raindrops hung on them like strings of white pearls. I was greatly moved and delighted.

As it became sunnier, the dew gradually vanished from the clover and the other plants where it had lain so heavily: the branches began to stir, then suddenly sprang up of their own accord. Later I described to people how beautiful it all was. What most impressed me was that they were not at all impressed.

Sei Shōnagon, *The Pillow Book* (*c.* AD 1000), translated by Ivan Morris

Vita Sackville-West, the most beguiling of garden writers, once compared the seasons of the year to the stages of human life. March and April, she thought, were youth, and May to June ran up to one's thirtieth birthday, 'that disagreeable milestone'. June to July 'is the stage between thirty and forty, or should we say fifty?' In August 'we enter the painful stage when we know we are going on for sixty, and then comes September when we approach seventy'. Her garden at Sissinghurst had some fine features in September and October, including a border of bulbous pink-flowered nerines and blue *Aster* × *frikartii*, two essential autumn plants for us all. Her pessimism has not survived our new attitudes to our advancing years and our wider range of garden plants.

Autumn's first six weeks are often the loveliest in the garden's entire year and they have regained the limelight as barriers of prejudice have fallen away. I emphasize in this section the exceptional beauty of dahlias, Michaelmas daisies and chrysanthemums, but each of them has been frowned on in my lifetime by gardeners who preferred pale colours and plants without links to the florist's trade. At least we can all agree that the blue flowers on *Ceratostigma willmottianum* are one of the entire year's high points. This shrub is entirely hardy in modern winters and is one of the indispensable plants for a garden. I still leave its top growth uncut in winter in honour of the old advice that it will protect the plant in case of an extreme frost. I am less confident that many hebes will survive hard weather, but as they grow so quickly and flower so young, they are worth the risk and regular replacement. My two favourites are among the hardiest: *Hebe* 'Watson's Pink', which is a magnificent survivor up at Kiftsgate Court, even higher than my garden in the Cotswolds, and 'Nicola's Blush', which goes on producing pale pink flowers until early December on bushes about three feet high. There is usually a 'Watson's Pink' for sale on Kiftsgate's excellent

top: Autumn in the Picton Garden, Colwall, near Malvern   above: Autumn in Le Jardin Plume's meadow

Hebe 'Watson's Pink' at Kiftsgate

plant stall in summer, from which I acquired my original plant and learned how good this variety is. 'Nicola's Blush' originated at Rushfields Nursery, near Ledbury in Herefordshire, whose owners once told me that they had named it after a young garden assistant who was prone to blush during conversation. Nicola's name and habit are now commemorated nationwide and I rate her namesake as one of the best buys for a later season.

Lemon-yellow tall *Helianthus* 'Lemon Queen' ran back into favour about twenty years ago, an excellent choice for a border's back row and only slightly invasive, though best in soil which is not too dry. It gives valuable height at six feet behind clumps of middle-ranking asters and it goes very well with the blues of the tough aconitums, *carmichaelii* being my mainstay here, though newer ones, named after

English rivers, have just appeared on sale and need careful study. September and October are months in which it is very easy nowadays to plant a classic border with graded height through a back row, middle row and front row. As in spring, that old 'colour wheel' is irrelevant, because the autumn light is mostly softer and the effect of a multi-coloured finale does not need to obey artificial rules of visual 'harmony'.

Older gardeners used to look on 15 October as the cut-off point for the half-hardy bedding, the date at which salvias, heliotropes and marguerites must all be brought under cover. Nowadays, they can flower on outdoors until the end of the month, often later, especially in London gardens warmed by their neighbours' hot air. I pick only five of the better salvias here, but they could as easily have been twenty choices, some of which will survive modest winters outdoors. Remember that plants in pots are more sheltered if the pots are pulled back in late autumn against a sunny wall. Terracotta pots are best kept safe in winter propped above hard paving on pairs of bricks, allowing the winter rains to drain through safely. If left on the paving itself, the bottom of the pot may freeze on to the hard surface with water which has drained from it, and when the pot is moved in a thaw, the bottom will break off it. I admire solid terracotta work and have two big urns, made in Impruneta near Florence, which once belonged to Nancy Lancaster. Nonetheless their decoration has been frozen off in various winters and I would not now buy specialized terracotta purely for garden purposes. At prices up to £10, supermarkets offer thin but acceptable clay alternatives which will last for quite a while. If their colour annoys you, the answer is to paint them in your favourite shade of Majorelle blue or dove-grey. Paint will even hide the horror of chunky plastic substitutes, making them welcome too in a garden's green surrounds.

Until mid-October I am still picking flowers off perennial pen-stemons, the essential family for the front rows of autumn flowerbeds. Young plants flower best, so it pays to take cuttings off a parent and root them in September, ready to be potted on and grown for the following season. I remember the fuss which used to surround the scarlet-red *Penstemon* 'Schoenholtzeri' even before it changed its trade name to 'Firebird'. Was it hardy? How could ghostly gardening cope with its strong red? Some gardeners were even persuaded to plant *Penstemon* 'Garnet' instead, on the grounds that its flowers were a muted shade of purple-red. It is not just that 'Garnet' then changed its name correctly to 'Andenken an Friedrich Hahn', making it unsaleable in Britain. Its colour had a stale drabness which is outside my personal limits. Scarlet-red 'Firebird', meanwhile, turned out to be entirely hardy, willing to flower well for several years, and a welcome shade of red at a time when colour needs to be cheerful. Dozens of less hardy penstemons have now appeared on sale in its wake, of which dark black-purple 'Blackbird' and white 'Snow Storm' are good, but among the least hardy. The way forward is to track down the new 'Pensham' varieties, which have a long season, near-hardiness, varying height and a marked willingness to flower until October. Bred in the Vale of Evesham they are fine additions to the autumn armoury and are very easy to root from early September cuttings.

Not that the first frosts finish a thoughtful garden's interest. Berries are not just a subject for columnists out of season. As I reiterate in this section and exemplify under 'Crabs in Flower', they are a high point of the year. Mine begin on the admirable *Sorbus americana* in August, the most unjustly neglected tree in this book. They end with late cotoneasters, especially the good *lacteus*, big red *frigidus* 'Cornubia' and yellow-berried 'Exburiensis', two strong growers for any soil. In between come the maluses, of which I write with a new, clearer knowledge. I now regret my choice of *Malus* 'Golden Hornet' among the yellow-fruited varieties, for reasons which I explain. Books on thoughtful gardening are not written by faultlessly thoughtful gardeners.

Fluttering Buddleias

When it is too cold and wet in English gardens and too hot for Mediterranean ones, is there anything seasonal in August which will grow well in them both? My answer is one of my favourite floral families: the buddleias. Many gardeners think of buddleias only as tall, easy shrubs with coarse leaves and plumes of flower in shades of purple or white which are beloved by butterflies. Their seedlings blow all over the place and have a troublesome way of lodging themselves in walls or stonework. They have been great uninvited colonizers on bomb sites, but there is so much more charm in the family's members. They have been on a five-year trial in the Royal Horticultural Society gardens at Wisley but until the trial's results settle down I prefer to consult a grower whose livelihood is linked to the family. The biggest buddleia collection in England is in the fine nursery at Longstock Park, near Stockbridge in Hampshire. Longstock Park is owned by the John Lewis Partnership and the nursery lies in the grounds of its enlightened founder, the late John Spedan Lewis. Buddleias have yet to appear at the tills of the Waitrose stores in the John Lewis group but the nursery sells more than a thousand pot-grown specimens yearly. Mature specimens can be viewed in beds outside the nursery's walled garden on any day of the week because Longstock's owners have had the good fortune to employ a buddleia fanatic and breeder, Peter Moore. Peter worked for years for the nearby nursery of Hillier's, but has found his true home in Longstock's smaller enterprise. There, he can attempt to improve on nature by breeding exciting new hybrids in popular families of shrubs.

In the Longstock collection I thought I had made an instructive study of the parent buddleias until I dared to interrupt Moore while he was active nearby in his Waitrose working overalls. We spent another hour-and-a-half studying the buddleias which I had overlooked. The lessons included many of the most important specimens on the site. There are spring-flowering buddleias, pale pink-flowered buddleias and even a Mexican one, *Buddleja cordata*, which attracts flies rather than butterflies. I am about to become a buddleia bore, not least because I have bought too many varieties and have no idea where I can fit them into my gardens. Mainstream buddleias are very easy to look after. They like a sunny site and are unfussy about soil. Most of them are best cut down to about a foot above ground level every spring. At Longstock they are cut down in late March, a job which needs a leap of faith, because the yearly top-growth of a buddleia looks so luxuriant. It is so dense that veterans even do the cutting with their powered hedge-clippers. The plants survive it well and then regrow to a manageable height, liberally covered in flower by August. The other essential is to continue dead-heading the bushes so as to treble their flowering season. As we walked round the collection I noticed how Peter Moore would cut the dead and half-dead flowers off his buddleia-children, reproaching himself for not having done so for at least two days. Gardeners are obsessed about dead-heading their roses but never think of dead-heading their buddleias so carefully. Many varieties show dead brown plumes of flower among their fresh flowers but if the dead ones are cut off, their stems will usually send up new, short plumes from their lower leaf-joints. When dead-headed, most of the popular varieties will flower on into mid-September.

If your mental image of the best buddleia is still an old *davidii* hybrid like 'Royal Red' or 'Black Knight', you are contending with coarse untidy leaves and a tall habit which is hard to fit into a border. At the entrance to the Longstock collection, I realized how far I had fallen behind the new age. A five-foot-high beauty called *davidii* 'Adonis Blue' was showing dark, slaty blue spikes of neat flower above tidy, slender leaves. It had been bred at Notcutts nursery in Suffolk. In front of it were the striking short white-grey leaves of 'Silver Anniversary', a new silver-leaved buddleia which stands out in a crowd. Its terminal flowers of white even have a honey scent. It has been bred at Longstock by Moore himself, so I bought one of each variety, thinking how well they will look in the driest part of my garden. 'Adonis Blue' and 'Silver Anniversary' are both hardy and would flourish in a hot garden nearer the Mediterranean. Many buddleias are native to dry parts of China, and in Europe they colonize dry, untended ground along railway lines.

Buddleja 'Autumn Surprise', a late flowering new hybrid bred by Peter Moore at Longstock Gardens

If their flower spikes droop in hot weather, water the plants in the evening, whereupon they will recover and continue to attract butter-flies. To us, these flowers smell like the hair-oil of an old-style city slicker but to male butterflies they smell like female butterfly-flappers.

Over-stocked with buddleias in my garden, I asked Moore to name his top picks for keen gardeners. I coaxed him into naming two of his own, the shining white 'Silver Anniversary' and the palish blue *davidii* 'Summer House Blue'. He even recommends the former for big pots which can be brought indoors in November so that their 'Silver Anniversaries' can be persuaded to go on producing scented white flowers in winter. 'Summer House Blue' is a taller variety but it is not coarse and is easily contained by annual pruning. It arose at Longstock as a random seedling by the property's golf course and was never part of a breeding programme. Such are the wonders of plants in national collections, where marriages are free and easy. We then argued about the third choice, concentrating on *davidii* varieties. I much like the recent 'Nanho Blue', which has chic leaves and good blue flowers. Moore picked 'Nanho Purple' instead, insisting that its rose-purple flowers were far better when lit up by late sunlight. I think he was being very precise. We agreed that 'Camberwell Beauty' is another pink-purple possibility, with the agreeable habit of holding little sprays of flowers above a main plume. Many know the similar habit of 'Dartmoor', but 'Camberwell Beauty' is less rampant. Among the whites, you should choose 'White Profusion', which is still the best of this class. Among the yellows with balls of flower, the best is *Buddleja* × *weyeriana* 'Sungold'.

I listened, noted and tested the flowers like a happy butterfly while many more varieties pressed forwards to be bought. The buddleia is now so varied and improved that it deserves to be sent fluttering out across Europe.

Sorrel Soup

When did you last see sorrel in a supermarket? I have kept the same three plants going for fifteen years and if archaeologists were ever to analyse my diet they would be hard put to identify the source of its natural acidity. The answer is sorrel, picked in green leaf and consumed in heavy quantities. I even have a recipe sorrel for soup which was written out for me in ballpoint pen on an old payslip by the great French chef Raymond Blanc. It involves sweating a chopped carrot and an onion in butter and adding torn sorrel leaves late in the process. Reading hungrily, I then hit on a neglected wonder in that unsurpassed classic, *French Provincial Cooking* by Elizabeth David: the recipe for a sorrel omelette. It involves making an omelette in the usual pan and putting some chopped sorrel leaves in the centre just before you roll it up. Sorrel omelette is delicious and puzzles even the most serious food bores. Miss David's firm advice is often neglected: never put too much of a filling in an omelette, especially a sorrel one. A few finely chopped leaves give the distinctive tang of lemon which transforms a simple dish. *Omelette à l'oseille* is not to be found on menus nowadays in France. The only person to recognize it at my table was a Russian visitor. In Russia, sorrel is a staple survival from peasant life.

My third sorrel trick is Greek. It consists of top-dressing a stew of diced lamb with sorrel leaves added to finely beaten egg yolks. The top dressing goes on at the last minute and must not be allowed to set. I ate this excellent dish in an ordinary establishment in Athens in the early 1990s and took the recipe away with me, written in Greek on the back of the bill. I then found it given as Arni Fricassée in Claudia Roden's *Mediterranean Cookery*, although the sorrel leaves ought to go in nearer to the last minute than she implies, as their strips become too soggy otherwise. Lamb and sorrel have gone down well, except when I forewarned a guest, a brilliant cook, that the recipe was Greek. She promptly assumed that the lamb cubes were goat and left them untouched on the plate.

Between them, these options consume masses of my sorrel between April and September. It is as well that the plants earn their keep because I bought my three original sorrels as pot-grown plants for a silly price. Actually you can raise them easily from seed sown outdoors, one source of which is the interesting 'heirloom' list of vegetable seeds from Pennard Plants at East Pennard, Shepton Mallet, Somerset BA4 6TU. 'Growing the dream' is its slogan and it offers two types of sorrel at £1 each per packet. I do not like the sound of the red-veined one, which is described as a 'staple in French cooking' and is compared with a sprightly spinach or chard. The green one is better, although the list calls it 'Cuckoo's Sorrow', claiming that birds are believed to use its sharp lemony leaf to clear their throats. I had just slashed my old sorrels to the ground and dumped the top growth when I heard the call of the cuckoo for the first time in years. I do not believe it had been at the compost heap but I do believe in cutting the tall stems off sorrel plants in mid-May. Otherwise they bolt, set seed and deteriorate. Pennard Plants has several other rare types of forgotten vegetable, including strawberry spinach with salad leaves and shiny fruits like mulberries.

Elizabeth David is my source for another classic summer dish: chicken with tarragon. Her real thing, *poulet à l'estragon*, is unafraid of the necessary cream and is unsurpassed. The trick here is the variety of tarragon. Supermarkets sometimes offer pots of a useless herb, the Russian tarragon, which is hardy in British winters and quite tasteless. The only cookable variety is the frost-prone French tarragon, which smells exactly right when you pinch its leaves. I buy it as a named plant from reliable garden centres which offer both types separately and know their business. The plants grow freely in light soil until mid-November but are then at high risk to most winters' frosts. Dig up some pieces, plant them in pots and protect them until spring.

The other con on the market is chainstore 'spinach', which is labelled 'French spinach' and packaged as pale heart-shaped leaves. This bland browse is fit only for a pet hamster. It is a tame sort of beet, justly called *Beta*, as the labelling admits in small print on the pre-packed plastic bag. The true alpha spinach is dark green and totally different. To find it you must grow your own from seed: true dark green English spinach, the only type which will make the classic salad with chopped, darkly fried bacon and a dressing which is strong on vinegar, added to the leaves after the bacon fat has been poured on from the pan. True spinach prefers a wet summer in rich soil.

Even if you are a minimal gardener, flatter your skills by sowing radish seed, too. The seeds come up so easily and are ideal as a crop for children who need some summer amusement at home. Like everything from basil to tomatoes, radishes now come in shapes and colours which have left the prototype far behind. I link my first years of radish-growing with a short story by H. E. Bates, the supreme describer of hot English summer days. It involved an elderly man with a round bald head, reddened in the sun like a radish, who intruded on a neighbouring lady's garden and was set to work by her, tossing lettuce and helping in the kitchen. Slightly drunk on her cocktails, he fell slightly in love and stayed, I remember, for days. Modern radishes could no longer be compared with his bald head because they are white, long or twisty, or something called 'mooli'. In honour of H. E. Bates's story, I sow 'Rougette', an all-red rounded variety with a root like a sunburnt head. It is not very hot on the palate but I use it in this classic pasta dish which I met near Naples, a radish-growing area. Lightly fry an onion, put in about two dozen sliced radishes and the chopped leaves from their tops. Add garlic and cook until the leaves flop. Add the mixture to a big spoon of the water in which you have just cooked some tagliatelle. Mix in the pasta, add grated cheese (strong Cheddar does the trick) and top it all with fresh parsley. The result is remarkably satisfying, a *pasta del giardino* which is within the competence of us all.

Founded on Love

For readers, the one great garden on Long Island is the garden of a literary mind. 'There was music from my neighbour's house through the summer nights', music which still echoes to readers of F. Scott Fitzgerald and his tale of the rise and fall of Jay Gatsby who 'told me once he was an Oxford man'. On Mondays, there were eight servants in his pay, including an extra gardener, and at weekends there were the parties. 'In his blue gardens men and girls came and went like moths among the whisperings and the champagne and the stars.' Young Englishmen were dotted about, 'all looking a little hungry, and all talking in low, earnest voices to solid and prosperous Americans . . . agonizingly aware of the easy money in the vicinity and convinced it was theirs for a few words in the right key'.

For gardeners, there is a finer garden on Long Island, also founded on love, but not on a desire to impress or on deals done on the wrong side of the law. In 1903, the son of Andrew Carnegie's first partner in business went down on one knee in the heather in Scotland and proposed to his young English bride. If you will marry me, he told her, and come and live in America, I will make you a garden as fine as any abroad. She accepted, so her husband, J. S. Phipps, took her to Long Island, to Old Westbury Gardens where the gates are carved with emblems of the sport of hunting and you can scent the sea between the driveway's avenues of limes. True to his word, Phipps began to make the garden which now draws 80,000 visitors a year. I owe the story of Phipps's promise to the authority of his surviving daughter, then in her nineties, who remained a presiding genius of the place.

Like other great gardens, Westbury has been made from a marriage of English and American talents. Phipps's English bride introduced an English style of planting, and entrusted the design of the house and garden to George Crawley from England, a name no longer honoured as it deserves in the annals of English gardening. Crawley's plan is still

Early summer in a corner of Westbury Gardens.

impressive in its American setting and is marked out by broad hedges of hemlock, fine trees, bold steps and a stylish use of water. The Phipps family were Crawley's patrons and have continued to influence the garden, the scene of their halcyon days since 1903. Old Westbury Gardens is now run by a board which draws on the family's endowment but it retains its original character as it has never called in an outside group and been forced to diverge from the family's sense of style.

Westbury Gardens runs on a budget of $2.6 million a year, about a fifth of which comes from gate money and as much again from annual fund-raising. Four horticulturists and five working gardeners are assisted by part-timers who are each paid by the hour. There are also interns, up to six in any one year. Money alone never makes a great garden, and when I entered the walled enclosure, some way from the house, I was enchanted by the mixing of plants and colours which went beyond the usual English range. Huge standard bushes of purple-flowered tibouchina stood as backing to the drooping flowers of tall white tobacco plants. Familiar cosmos daisies fluttered beside unusual types of salvia and groups of *Pentas lanceolata*, a plant which never seems to be grown from seed in England. In borders by the wall, a tall *Abelmoschus* had flowers which looked like a clear yellow hibiscus, and its forthright woman supervisor said that it grows with such ease that even an Englishman should try it. Sky-blue plumbago covers another brick wall beside cotoneaster clipped in an espalier shape. Perhaps we English should try that combination too. A cross-vista divides the walled garden and at one end a curving pergola concludes the view across a semicircle of water. It is made as exotic as New York's Lotus Club by the leaves and seed-heads of the vivid lotuses which are growing in its depths.

Long Island's sea-driven climate is not so relentless that the garden is browned by winds in autumn. Great maples, limes and beeches luxuriate, including a gigantic beech tree which was moved to be nearer the side terrace in days when the moving of such a big tree cost only $100. Very large gardens risk losing their atmosphere, but Westbury's is secure in the careful attention given to its bedding and to the green views through parkland and clipped hedges which run away from the house. Order and scale have not been lost in flowery detail, even where unusual ipomoeas romp in the walled garden beside *Clematis terniflora* and big groups of pale *Salvia coccinea* 'Snow Nymph'. The trees, the ground plan and the yearly succession of such well-chosen flowers are a reminder that gardens may indeed grow best on a founding promise of love. It could never be a place like Gatsby's where 'a sudden emptiness seemed to flow from the windows and the great doors, endowing with complete isolation the figure of the host who stood on the porch, his hand up in a formal gesture of farewell'. Westbury was made for happy family life and was duly blessed by it.

Back To The Fuchsia

If you think European winters are permanently warming, the fuchsia should be your first stop. So many varieties have hovered on the borders of hardiness, showing a willingness to survive in all but the hardest frosts. Now that frost is proving less of a problem, the boundaries of the fuchsia family have been noticeably advanced. Following the climate, I am going back to the fuchsia and profiting from the cool summers which they love.

The facts have been clear for years in California. British gardeners are mostly unaware that fuchsia growing has a long history in parts of California where the winter temperatures are far removed from frost, and the summer humidity reaches the high level which fuchsias enjoy. Not for nothing are so many of the best varieties named after sites around the Los Angeles area. In the 1930s, breeders developed vigorous varieties with names like 'Beverly Hills' and 'Hollywood Park' which flower all year round and have to be stopped by a firm pruning in the new year. In Britain one of the best suppliers of fuchsias is Roualeyn Nursery at Trefriw, Conwy, North Wales, who prefer to supply rooted plants by mail in spring, when their prices are extremely reasonable. Their catalogue now lists more than forty varieties which their years of Welsh experience show to be hardy. I have had confidence in their choices and have not lost a single one of their recommended range in the past eight years.

If you buy a young fuchsia, you can train it up quickly into a special shape. In spring, standard fuchsias with tall stems come on sale at prices up to £100 but there is no magic about training a fuchsia into this form, except patience and basic knowledge. Take a normal bush variety and cut off all side shoots except for the main stem and its growing tip. The stem should be supported on a cane and when it has grown up to two or three feet, about a foot less than the height you want, the side shoots should be left to develop freely without being pinched out. Traditionally, four or five pairs of side shoots are left to grow free at this height and then the growing tip is snipped out to limit the plant's height. The entire operation is simple but the result looks exotic and somebody, somewhere will pay extraordinary prices for it. Standards are less hardy than ordinary branched varieties and as they become bulky to protect under glass in winter, it is convenient if only the hardy forms are chosen for the purpose. They have the strength to survive in unheated settings.

One of the best is the excellent red-flowered 'Rufus', which was bred nearly fifty years ago. It flowers madly and has an upright habit which trains well into a standard. If you start a 'Rufus' off now and trim it, you will have an excellent standard specimen within eighteen months. It pairs well with the larger-flowered 'Blue Gown', which is double-flowered and a classic combination of scarlet and blue, changing to purple. 'Blue Gown' flowers heavily, and as it always needs staking, it might as well be staked as a standard. Roualeyn Nursery classes it as hardy nowadays.

Down at ground level, there is a neat combination for gardeners who are more lazy than they care to admit. If they lay out box-edged beds in a formal pattern of evergreen compartments, they can plant the gaps with hardy fuchsias for the summer and underplant the fuchsias with small narcissi for a spring display. The results look dreadful in late May when the narcissi's leaves are dying down and the dead stems on the fuchsia are breaking into growth. If you can live with them for this one drab fortnight, they then give you two seasons of colour for minimal effort without the bother of yearly bedding-out. In autumn, the fuchsias take over and look charming in full flower against the clipped evergreen box. A good group of fuchsias to choose here is the low-growing range with names of the seven dwarfs from Snow White: 'Sleepy', 'Dopy' and so forth. In early spring, low-growing small-flowered narcissi make a patchwork of flower in the bare earth between the dwarfs' bare stems.

I have two other tips about fuchsia growing, one nutritious, the other historical. It pays to feed all fuchsias with regular doses of balanced Phostrogen, directed at them through a watering can from July onwards, because they revel in humidity and an inorganic supplement to their health. Historically, the family is the subject of a famous story for entrepreneurs. It does not involve liquid fertilizer, but it does involve some fertile business practice.

Traditionally, the flowering fuchsia is said to have originated at Wapping in east London in the 1780s, before anyone thought of printing newspapers on the site. A great nurseryman, James Lee of Hammersmith, is said to have heard news of an exotic new plant with hanging flowers which was growing in the window box of a Wapping housewife. She said that it had been brought to her by her husband from the West Indies. Though tempted to retain the fuchsia, she was more tempted by the colour of Mr Lee's money and handed over her stock plant for about £10. The nurseryman then stripped it for cuttings, multiplied the stock and began the next season with 300 plants which were already showing buds. Smart society rushed to buy them, propelled by competitive females. Their 'horses smoked off to the suburb', breaking the speed limit in order to buy the remaining stock, but, justly, Lee gave the housewife one of the first of the new batch so that she could keep it safe for her husband. Lee himself sold so many fuchsias in one year that he turned £10 into more than £300, all from a woman's memento.

Quite probably, this story is exaggerated. It emerged only fifty years later on the authority of a curator at the Botanical Gardens in Liverpool, and in its first published form, the newspaper which told it seems to have misprinted the plant's point of origin as a 'widow' in Wapping, not a 'window'. Authorities therefore argue whether the housewife lost her husband as well as her fuchsia. However, nobody can dispute that James Lee the entrepreneur brought gardeners a flower from which they have derived ceaseless pleasure.

Botanical Palermo

Throughout Europe there is a truth much neglected by travelling gardeners: always head for the botanic garden. Across the ages most of their founders were inspired by the arts of herbal medicine and the results linger on, gardens which are not fully about gardening and centres of botany which are not fully at the centre of genetic science. For decades, I have visited such gardens from Leiden to Vienna, Urbino to Berlin. There are many more in waiting, but there is one where the plants, history and design are an ageing paradise on an unlikely plot of earth.

In Palermo, in north-west Sicily, the Botanic Garden is a witness to the enlightened ideas of the 1790s. The place still gives off a neo-classical atmosphere. By its entrance, three regular, classical buildings express the values of order and reason which their mustard-yellow paint cannot conceal. They still have friezes, pilasters and pediments, with sphinxes in front and statues inside. By the garden's original entrance, two pillars support statues of the great ancient botanists Theophrastus and Dioscorides on honey-coloured stone at a height of thirty feet. The two classical masters survey a formal setting whose flowerbeds have been laid out on the sexual system of the Swedish botanist Linnaeus.

There is a pleasant irony of time and culture in this garden's archi-tectural form. Work on it began in early 1789, just before the events in France which ended in revolution. A French architect laid the plans for the garden buildings and was ably supported by Italian sculptors and collaborators, encouraged by the Bourbon King Frederick II and his courtiers. Local Palermitan notables and prominent clergymen also contributed funds, but when the garden opened in 1795, its classical style had acquired new overtones after six French revolutionary years. The garden's backbone is a bold series of straight avenues which are endowed with names of significant figures in its history. These

Glasshouse in Palermo Botanic Gardens

avenues, or *viali*, radiate at a series of angles and each one is flanked by different types of tree. Evergreen oaks edge one, palms and pelargoniums another. The roots of huge old specimens of *Ficus magnoloides* and its relation, the sideways-rooting banyan tree, unsettle the central pathway beside tall oriental planes and rare eastern neighbours. Some of these fine trees are nearly two centuries old, great survivors from thoughtful curators of the past. To walk down these uneven avenues is to recapture a sense of the main avenue in the fine garden at Tresco in the Scilly Isles before a storm in the late 1980s destroyed its canopy of tender trees.

The avenues are a challenge for tree-lovers, but they are not the garden's only distinction. The central *viale* ends at a circular garden of water, donated by Palermo's archbishop in 1796. Ice-blue water lilies, lotus, papyrus and much else float in the neatly divided sections of its pool, and around it a forest of bamboos makes a tall green fluttering curtain. Big banyan trees are in the background and even the skeletal shape of the modern gasworks beyond the boundary makes little impact on the immediate view. Down each of the avenues run hundreds of flowerpots, carefully labelled, and in autumn showing few signs of growth. The empty, labelled flowerpot is a speciality of Italian botanic gardens, but at Palermo the pots are planted with bulbs for all seasons and are very much alive. A few autumn-flowering varieties suggest what the spring will also bring. On the flowerpots, the bust of a sphinx is stamped as a hallmark, matching the sphinx which stands in sculpture outside the garden's main buildings. In the 1790s, sphinxes acquired new meaning through Napoleon's Egyptian conquests, but I doubt if the Palermo garden was moving to this rhythm.

In Palermo, there is hardly any rain between April and mid-September, but some spectacular residents are not deterred. Huge spiky specimens of *Dracaena draco* stand near an artificial mound of rocks. Old plants of *Yucca elephantipes* rise to a height of thirty feet, while hundreds of cacti, cycads and agaves are tended in yet more flowerpots. I treasure the sight of a scarlet bougainvillea, which scrambles over an outbuilding in the company of sky-high yuccas. The nearby garden has orderly greenhouses, one of which was given by Queen Maria Carolina in the 1840s and based on French design. Like the flowerpots, the greenhouses are lovingly maintained in a city whose public services are not exactly overfunded. The houses are an excuse for yet more collections of flowerpots, holding anything from aloes to mimosa.

Among the dry fallen leaves and the highs and lows of the surviving trees, one spectacular avenue flowers prolifically in September. In a far side of the garden, Palermo's curators have planted a long run of the flowering false kapok tree, or chorisia, from South America. They have become huge trees, thirty to forty feet high. In nature their trunks swell with age like bulging bottles and are fitted with botanical prickles to deter animals. Their flowers are a five-petalled mixture of pink and yellow, and drop by the hundred on to the garden's paths. Fully mature and swollen, the trees are an astonishing sight.

This botanic garden has also become a home for the mother of all Palermitan plants, one which the garden's earliest foreign admirer, Goethe, never saw when he visited in the 1790s. About fifty years after Goethe's visit, gardeners in Palermo discovered the charms and strengths of the frangipani. In Palermo, this superb flower is everywhere. It has been the subject of a special exhibition at the Botanic

Garden, and there are tremendous trees of it in front of Palermo's older houses and dozens of specimens on private balconies. It even has its own folklore. Experts from the Botanic Garden described the frangipani to me as the object of an all-female cult. Women, they tell me, are the 'priestesses responsible for tending it'. When a girl marries, her mother traditionally gives her a piece of the family's frangipani for her new balcony. If it fails, it is a bad omen. Frangipani plants on balconies 'remain a female province from which males of the family are excluded'. Men are allowed to look after them only outdoors, and preferably they are 'retired males and experienced gardeners'.

The plant has the most extraordinary history. Technically, it is plumeria, the name under which it appears in nursery catalogues. Our name, frangipani, commemorates a titled count of that name who invented a similarly scented compound in seventeenth-century France. The people of Palermo call it 'pomelia', a name which reflects the plant's wide diffusion. This marvellously scented flower goes back to the brutal empire of the Aztecs in America, who venerated it, mainly because its bark and juice were so good for healing wounds. The earliest picture of the plant is in the famous *Codex Badianus* which dates from 1552 and shows plants known to the Aztecs. There are four main species, all of which centre on tropical America or the Caribbean, but nowadays the tree is all over India and the Far East and is famous as the source of flowery necklaces in Polynesia, where Paul Gauguin's girls loved to wear them. Spanish travellers carried bits of the plant with them to the Far East, and established them away from its native habitat. On Hawaii, frangipani is believed to originate from plants brought by an American diplomat in 1860.

The mild climate in Palermo was well suited to frangipani, so it multiplied rapidly, spreading outwards from the gardens of the rich nobility in the early nineteenth century. The frangipani is such a brilliant traveller because cuttings from it root easily and are even able to come into flower on a branch which has been cut from a parent-tree. In the Far East, the public were delighted by this rare ability which seemed to symbolize eternal life, so they planted frangipani by burial grounds and temples. In the Palermo Botanic Garden there are no fewer than eighteen types of frangipani, arranged against a wall beside the greenhouses. The flowers range from pink through yellow

Frangipani in Palermo

to white and the garden has been important in spreading this plant to the balconies of well-trained Sicilian women. It is one of the many American imports which make the plants of the Botanic Garden much richer than its architect's original classicizing conception.

In Britain, frangipani is not too difficult if grown in a heated greenhouse until frosts are over. The plants should be kept in pots, with or without sphinxes, and will survive the tender care of an English male. They lose their leaves in late autumn and should be brought back into a heated house before the danger of frost in October. Out in Palermo, the ladies of the balcony sometimes protect the tips of their plant's branches by capping them with empty eggshells, making them into a sort of egg tree. With female cunning, they have found that this ovarian trick protects the growing points against frost. In Britain, the climate is too cold and the eggshell trick is superfluous.

Great modern botanic gardens hum with technology, order and research. Palermo's is now under reconstruction with help from the European Union and is at grave risk of unwary modernizing. Even so, it has a great basic design, teeming contents and an enchanting contrast of age and youth. Delighted by it, I went up to one of the garden's blue-overalled interns and told him that his botanic garden was the best in Italy. No, he corrected me, with winning local patriotism, not just in Italy, but in Europe, perhaps the world. There are so many pots to water and a reconstruction to survive, but work with a hose-pipe has not dimmed the staff's affection for their home.

The Haunt of Ancient Peace

In hot weather, flower gardens have the worst of it, but architectural gardens retain their style. They depend on big evergreen building-blocks, strong design and an elegant use of stone and hard surfacing. The best are often the gardens of architects, whose sense of space and proportion stops a flowerless garden from being dull.

Just to the south of Bath, but still in Wiltshire, the garden at Iford Manor is a calm architectural masterpiece. Its design goes back across a hundred years to 1899 when it was bought by a genius of landscape design, the architect Harold Peto. He had matured in the late Victorian era when many still wrongly think that the style of gardens was bizarre. Peto had a superb eye, an architectural training and no family ties to hold him down. By his mid thirties, he had travelled widely and discovered the charm and artistry of Italy. He had also opened his eyes to gardens in North Africa and Japan. Twenty years before the great planter Miss Jekyll began to extol her herbaceous borders, Harold Peto had laid out gardens with an architectural mastery which was quite beyond the famous old lady's skills. One of his early assistants was Edwin Lutyens, the man who would later put the backbone into many of Miss Jekyll's plantings.

At Iford Manor, this master-architect's design survives around the house which he chose for himself. It stands on a steep hillside which he shaped and landscaped with great skill. The result is not just a flower garden. In its central core, Peto found room for superb flights of ascending steps, a noble Italian-style terrace complete with ancient pillars, a small Mediterranean-style house (his 'casita') and a most remarkable private cloister.

In the 1880s, geometric patterns of bedding plants were popular, even when set among patterns of pebbles and reflecting glass. Peto the architect wanted none of them. He reintroduced English gardening to architectural Italian style while the same style was independently

A Mediterranean corner at Iford Manor

reaching the new mansions of East Coast America through the work of Charles Platt. In garden history, he is a forerunner of the formal style which shaped the theories of Sir George Sitwell in Derbyshire and is so dramatic at Hidcote Manor, where it blossomed in his younger American contemporary, Lawrence Johnston. Iford remained in the Peto family until 1964, and thanks to restoration and the dedication of the present owners, Elisabeth Cartwright and John Hignett, it now attracts 10,000 visitors a year. Until the mid 1980s John had been a farmer on nearby land, but he then turned his energy to restoring Peto's buildings and stonework, which had started to crack after years of neglect, not least because they stood on a hillside whose geology is unstable. Elisabeth Cartwright had arrived in her mid twenties from the classic Georgian mansion at Aynho in Northamptonshire. She, too, had a family background which could warm to the challenge of Iford, and with her came Leon Butler, her mother's garden boy. Appointed as head gardener, he has just retired after nearly forty years of work on Iford's behalf.

Those forty years have been well spent. The place has a natural holiness which Peto's style has helped to enhance. He believed that a garden of nothing but flowers would be boring, so he introduced stonework because stone is as expressive as plants. At Iford, he introduced some very remarkable stones, the spoils of his collecting and travelling in Spain and Italy. Every piece was honestly bought, and nobody has yet made a fuss about repatriating the Peto Marbles, but it is astonishing what this artful magpie was able to bring back to Wiltshire. His terrace has some fine ancient Roman sarcophagi and his stairway has a spare column from one of the greatest churches at Ravenna, constructed in the sixth century. His cloister contains fragments of fine Italian doorways, coats of arms, rare marble pillars and a relief of the Virgin Mary protecting survivors from a great plague. All of them would be treasured antiquities nowadays, but in the early twentieth century, Peto bought them because nobody else wanted them. He even acquired twelfth-century stone lions and some pieces from the Ca' d'Oro in Venice.

Iford Manor is a charming house of many different periods, but it is Peto who intuited a particular quality in its setting and overgrown hillside. On a hot afternoon, there is no more tranquil landscape in

England than the view from his antique colonnade to the grass-green meadows beside the River Frome. Peto had a well-formed culture and taste which guided his canny expenditure. He was not extravagant and he had a public dimension to his art: he expressed increasing distress at the breakdown of the uneasy balance of power in Europe. In 1907 he put up an unusual memorial to King Edward VII as a peacemaker and then built his rectangular cloisters, basing them on the cloisters which he had seen and loved at Granada in the Alhambra. He was enchanted by Granada's great gardens because Granada, he rightly saw, was a place which could match up to the artistic standards set by Venice, Rome and Florence. When he returned to London after a Spanish tour, he wrote how he had 'sat next to a Spaniard at dinner who had been in London and said he should really die if he lived there a year: everything is black, the sheep, grass, houses, even birds'. Spaniards can be rather macabre. Peto's landscape gardening is an expression of a brighter vision which was rooted in an undergrowth of contemporary taste in English society. In his early lifetime, polite society had redis-covered Florence; millionaires were bidding competitively for Italian master-paintings and Florence was seen as the wellhead of the arts and crafts. As so often before, Italy had jolted England out of barbarity.

Iford is only one of Peto's gardens but it is the most personal. His public masterpiece is Ilnacullin on the island of Garinish in Ireland's Bantry Bay. He was also taken up by rich Edwardian migrants who used his talents freely, not least on Cap Ferrat in the South of France. Would a new Peto be possible nowadays? Iford is not a big garden, but our age of global tourism has a weakened awareness of the classical underpinning of Western art, and so Peto's Italian taste has a different emphasis to modern eyes. We no longer take his assumptions for granted. Sharing them, I cherish his inscription in the year in which he finished Iford's cloisters. He carved into the stone: 'The Haunt of Ancient Peace'. The year was 1914. In our own late summers, the words have a contemporary resonance.

Space Invaders

Gardeners draw some fine lines, and none is finer than the line between nature and culture. Standing back, I have been thinking that parts of my garden are at last full of plants which look after themselves. They knit together and spread into self-sustaining communities. They are not scrupulously tidy but they survive the winter, and one day they may even survive me.

In Europe this style of planting is fashionable and much photographed. In America, I now find, many of its components are listed as 'menaces'. I have been checking them in a fascinating guide, *Invasive Plants, Weeds of the Global Garden* which was published in 1996 by the Brooklyn Botanic Garden in New York. In 1993 the Congressional Office of Technology Assessment compiled a report entitled 'Harmful Non-Indigenous Species in the United States', which tried to quantify the main dangers and their damage. It concluded that seventy-nine of them have caused losses worth $97 billion and that fifteen 'high impact species' will cause another $134 billion of damage in future. What neither they nor I realized is that I have been lovingly planting some of their most dangerous 'weeds of the global garden' for my own pleasure. A hit squad needs to come over and poison my anti-global garden, using compounds like picloram or imazapyr, which is sold in America under the blunt name of Arsenal. It is not that I am growing the dreadful Japanese knotweed. I have a relation of the lovely giant hogweed, but its habits are restrained. I am looking after some ground elder, but it is the elegantly variegated form and I wage vigilant war on the green-leaved variety. I have banished almost all milky euphorbias, whose juice is so painful if it ever sprays into an eye. My invaders are plants which other British gardeners also choose and admire.

Like many of them, I look forward in May to the flowers on the silver-leaved Russian olive, the suckering *Elaeagnus angustifolia*, which has intensely scented, small yellow flowers. There is even a selected form called 'Quicksilver', which is especially silver in May. It becomes rather dingy by July, a fault which disqualifies it as a shrub for a main vista, and it spreads slightly, but the American assessors are having none of it. Since it arrived in the States, it is 'choking out native vegetation', particularly in the western plains, and should be attacked by 'girdling, stump-burning and depositing rock salt into holes drilled into the stump'. For years, I have been even more fond of the green-leaved *Elaeagnus umbellata*, which is equally well scented when in flower. It is now a declared enemy in the Midwest, where it arrived in 1917, and unfortunately, the register tells me, 'periodic fires' do not control it. What about the good old guelder rose, the *Viburnum opulus* which was so beloved by Britain's revered Miss Jekyll? Advisers to the Pennsylvania Department of Conservation would have gone straight into her Munstead Wood and attacked in hard hats: 'Natural area managers recommend a 20 per cent solution of glyphosate herbicide to the cut stump and chipping the brush to prevent seed dispersal'. Apparently, it has started to interbreed with native highbush cranberry and may soon produce 'a truly innovative child'.

In southern Britain we treasure big paulownia trees and their occasional displays of lavender flowers like foxgloves whenever they survive the late spring frosts. In colder counties, many of us enjoy this big-leaved tree as a showy shrub for a border, where we cut it down every year and cause it to sprout again with emphatic foliage. In my view, we should plant more shrubs around it as its roots are such helpful pumps of water from the subsoil. Over in the Great Smokey Mountains National Park, however, they want us to declare war on this 'princess tree', which is capable of producing twenty million seeds and colonizing banks, roadsides and 'utility rights of way'. 'Treat cut stumps immediately with triclopyr herbicide to prevent sprouting.' Last year, unwarned, I planted three more paulownias to give a bold emphasis to three of my garden's strategic points.

Instead, you might be tempted by thoughts of the shimmering leaves of a white poplar tree in the middle distance, or foolish enough to risk the Far Eastern *Acer ginnala* as an ornamental tree. Forget them both. The poplar suckers horribly and has escaped into American landscapes since the Colonial era. The acer produces thousands of seeds which 'have the potential' to become a major weed, even in

Canada. Burn them both, Americans are warned, and spray herbicide over the stumps. As for the old English holly, abandon it. It is now a 'recent invader of the American north-west' and is changing the structure of forests not by adding a foreign hint of Christmas but by bringing in a layer of tall vegetation, which casts shade and competes with native plants. When birds eat the fruits, they drop the seeds far and wide, but at least this invader is vulnerable. 'Fortunately, English holly is easy to remove mechanically.' It is fortunate that these machines have not been prowling round English churchyards.

Much of my planting at home turns out to be on America's most unwanted list of immigrants: Chinese privet (costing £7.50 a plant in garden centres); *Nandina domestica*, an evergreen bamboo which is infiltrating 'pine flatwood communities in the south-east'; and even Scotch broom, which 'currently occupies more than 2 million acres in Washington, Oregon and bits of California' and needs to be removed with a 'brush hog machine'. It has been a hard horticultural slog to grow anything in my garden of Cotswold glacial shingle, and I plead for mercy if most of the shrubs which I have established are classed as anti-American terrorists.

At least, you may think, English herbaceous borders are safe havens. On poor soil, I am glad to grow *Hesperis matronalis*, or sweet rocket, in late May, perennial potentilla in June and baby's breath in July, with a few clumps of ornamental silver-leaved cardoons and some Michaelmas daisy species for autumn. Please do not tell the American Office of Assessment. After next year's poppy-spraying mission in Afghanistan, agents may descend on me and spray them all to death. The cardoons had occurred in 'thirty-one counties' by the 1950s and are classed as an American agricultural pest. Sweet rocket is spreading rapidly from seed and 'should never be included in roadside plantings of wild flowers'. I treasure my pale yellow *Potentilla recta sulphurea* and the vivid yellow *recta* 'Warrenii', two plants which a highly decorated member of the Royal Horticultural Society once described to me as her favourite herbaceous plants. In the northern Rockies, forget her: this potentilla is becoming a 'serious wild land invader' and people are being told to remove it by 'slipping a sturdy digging tool under the crown'. Michaelmas daisies are a pest on the edges of woodland and as for baby's breath, it is a feared problem in Michigan and is likely to try to terrorize the 'open dune habitat' on the surrounds of the Great Lakes.

I have just been cutting back my beloved form of baby's breath, *Gypsophila* 'Rosy Veil', and blessing the day when I discovered this plant whose stems spread so usefully in late summer. The Michigan Department of Natural Resources has a different view. 'Early in the growing season, spot-burn all plants with a hand-held propane torch.' The line between 'gardening' and 'wilderness' is drawn differently in our two allied lands. In the garden, as in other areas, England and voices in America are fighting different wars.

Odessan Odyssey

Gardens do not have to be perfect to be rewarding. They are often evocative in ways which depend on their viewer, not their level of care. No two people see quite the same when they look beyond the surface, and often it is easiest to see more in gardens abroad, partly because they use a different flora, partly because these sites can evoke a world remembered by an outsider's restless eye.

When I looked recently at Ukrainian gardening, I found an interest which went deeper than appearances. In the Black Sea city of Odessa, first impressions are curiously familiar. Horse chestnut trees line many of the central streets, and like their British brothers, they turn brown in August in a premature announcement of autumn. They too are beset with the chestnut-infesting insect which has spread as fast as the internet in the past ten years. Its presence in southern Ukraine supports the theory that its ultimate home lies further east, probably in China, from where its natural predators have yet to pack their bags and fly in pursuit.

Under these browning chestnuts, Odessa's city gardeners surprised me by the plantings of lines of narrow-leaved hostas. English gardeners reserve these plants for richer soil and never plant them round tree trunks, but Odessans ignore our rules. I watched as hundreds of hostas were planted out and saw how their gardeners begin by removing a spade's depth of the surface soil and replacing it with rich compost. In prominent places they add leaking hosepipe below the surface to irrigate the new arrivals. In Odessa, too, preparation is more than half the battle.

In the elegant main city square, gardeners must also be irrigating their splendid cannas. Newspaper readers used to send me postcards from former Soviet countries of hideous beds of cannas, sometimes with an exclamation mark on the back of the card. The sight of them made me glad to be living in the free West. Christopher Lloyd then began to champion the charms of cannas in his garden at Great Dixter, but I pictured a bust of Lenin glowering over them when he took up their cause as if it was new. In Odessa, gardeners have not been reading Lloyd's books. They exclude the forms with purple leaves and rose-purple flowers. In the city's main square only clear scarlet or yellow cannas are used in masses, and then only in forms with clear green leaves.

What happens, I wondered, in the Odessan botanical garden marked 'Botanichesky Sad' on my city map? Up in Kiev the botanical garden is remembered for its fine display of the little-known flora of the Ukraine. In the Crimea, just outside Yalta, the huge Nikitsky Sad includes a yew tree which is more than 500 years old. This vast horticultural enclave became the experimental centre of agriculture in the Soviet era, extending over 600 acres with another 1,500 acres of out-stations. It has remained almost wholly unknown to Western lovers of plants. Odessa's botanical garden has a very different air. In Odessa, a port-city, the pride of the botanical garden is the oak tree which once made the English navy great. Superb specimens of our beloved English oak tower over a garden of evocative neglect. Under the oaks are yet more hostas, freshly watered, as if somebody, somewhere is still trying to do their best. I recalled how the garden historian Edward Hyams wrote of this very garden in 1969: 'It consoled us for its neglect by producing hoopoes for our delight.'

Instead of hoopoe birds among the acacias, it consoled me with its personnel. In the heart of the garden, I watched the only gardener, an elderly lady who was hosing the last of the hibiscus and rose-pink gladioli. She was wearing a smock whose style had surely not changed in the last hundred years. An aged magnolia sagged in the background and panes were missing in the nearby greenhouse, whose heating chimney had corroded. Inside the house, cacti and tender plants were jumbled in big clay pots. Outside, pear and plum trees overlooked the Black Sea and, with a sudden shock of recognition, I realized I had been in such a garden before. It evoked for me the garden of the Bolkonsky family outside Moscow, to which Prince Andrei returns before battle in the matchless pages of Tolstoy's *War and Peace*. Andrei, too, found panes gone from the greenhouse and plants lying on their sides in tubs. In his garden, too, there was a magnolia with broken branches and only one worker was visible: not a woman watering the hibiscus, but an old man weaving a shoe from raffia-twine. He, too, was undistracted among adversity, as if life must simply go on. There were fruit trees, too, in the Bolkonsky garden. A group of young girls, Andrei found, had been pillaging them in their noble owners' absence. These girls ran unawares into their former master while carrying stolen fruit in the folds of their dresses.

Andrei had come to say farewell to his home 'from a characteristic desire', so Tolstoy tells us, 'to aggravate his own suffering'. I had come to say hello, out of a gardener's curiosity. Amazingly there were sounds of a scuffle in the bushes and fiction became fact before me. Three young girls appeared by a hovel, two of whom were carrying plums, like the girls in Tolstoy's novel. The old lady went on with her work, watering, not weaving, but as unconcerned as Tolstoy's old man by a spectator's existence. The plane trees which towered above the five of us were old enough to have existed in Odessa's garden in the year when Tolstoy was writing his chapter.

Andrei had turned away, 'unwilling to let his girls see that they had been observed'. He sympathized with them and 'a new sensation of comfort and relief came over him when he realized the existence of other human interests entirely aloof from his own and just as legit-imate as those that occupied him'. The girls in his garden ran away through the meadow-grass, carrying their stolen fruit and showing their bare, sunburned legs. Instead, my girls pushed the eldest to the front so that she could ask if I needed a guide to the garden. She was riding a Western-made bicycle. Like Andrei, I 'shared their wish for the success of their enterprise', but I needed no guide because I could retrace my path by following the English oak trees.

Desirable Dahlias

By September, dahlias are at their brilliant best. They have had a chequered history because they were not at first a success with gardeners, and even now many people fail to exploit their beauty. Dahlias were discovered by Spanish settlers in Mexico but at first were thought to have a bright future as vegetables. The local Indians used to eat their fat tubers, and when a few plants were sent to Madrid the hope was that they would vary the fashionable diet of potatoes. It took a while for the British to catch on to them and only in the 1810s do we hear of dahlia seeds and species being sent for experiment to a titled lady in London. Her gardener failed to make anything of them, and it was left to Napoleon's wife Josephine to see their potential. French contemporaries slyly called her 'the lubricious Creole', but she showed excellent taste in plants. At her Malmaison garden she paid for superb roses and lilacs, immortalized by her painter Pierre-Joseph Redouté. She also patronized new forms of the dahlia, flowers which shared her connection with the New World. Back in Mexico the Indians had been calling the dahlia *cocoxochitl*. I would like to hear the Empress Josephine pronounce that teaser in a Creole accent. Fortunately, the botanists came up with a pronounceable name. It was given in honour of Andreas Dahl, one of the favoured 'apostles' who travelled the world to bring back new plants for classification by Linnaeus in Sweden.

Even then, many gardeners looked down on the new wonder in their midst. It became entangled with boundaries of social snobbery, as if it was fit only for the bungalow-gardens of the working class. Polite English society banished many of the available colours to kitchen gardens, where they could be grown in hiding and used as cut flowers. Breeders continued their work, but in the south-east of England there was a prejudice against many of the new shapes, as if they were all balls of lilac-mauve. It took years for dahlias to be integrated in full glory into mixed borders, where they prolong the season in a flush of fine colour.

Like many gardeners, I was alerted to the best dahlias' potential by the autumn exhibits which Aylett's of Hertfordshire used to put on at the Royal Horticultural Society halls in London. During September it is still a treat to see these dahlias on their home ground at Aylett's garden centre near London Colney in Hertfordshire. Off the M25 at Junction 22, on the A414, Aylett Nurseries have kept up high standards in the cultivation of the dahlia for more than fifty years. In 2005, I attended the celebration of their fiftieth anniversary. It was held in a temporary tent installed by the main garden centre. The displays of dahlias were backed by a brass jazz band.

Aylett's began trading in 1955 when Roger Aylett and his family took on seven-and-a-half bare acres and set up premises in a former chicken shed. They were quick to pick on dahlias as their speciality and found that exhibiting was in their blood. Their first show was coordinated by Muriel, mother of the family, in the Harpenden Public Hall. They then staged their own dahlia festival, charging an entrance fee of 15p, to include a cup of tea. By 1977 the company had won one of the highest medals in the RHS. It continued to exhibit until the late 1990s when it stopped, having won most of the other major medals too. Exhibiting in London had made little difference to the company's business at home.

Back in Hertfordshire the garden centre grew far beyond the old chicken shed. It now employs 120 people and turns over £5 million a year. It has remained a family business with a firm grip on what it stocks, but it is the dahlias which bring in migrating customers. In spring there are even enthusiasts who come all the way from Norfolk to buy them, because Aylett's sell young pot-grown plants. They are so convenient for those of us who have no frost-proof greenhouse or shed.

I first realized dahlias' tremendous presence in a mixed border when I saw them beautifully grown by the brilliant head gardener, Jimmy Hancock, at the National Trust's property at Powis Castle in Shropshire. Dahlias in beautiful colours filled the middle and back rows of his great borders on the main terraces and made my August gardens look extraordinarily boring by comparison. Since then, dahlias have gained from the warmer climate. Converts to the family

Roger Aylett directing his dahlia fields in June

find that nowadays they are usually able to leave the tubers lazily in the ground even when a frost has killed the top growth. Until early 2009 the winters were so mild that the plants came through in strong form for a second year. I still shy away from this idle habit, and the early months of 2009 and 2010 were so cold that they exposed it as bad practice. If you still want to take the risk, put straw or chopped compost on top of the dahlias after cutting their shoots down. Do not try to plant them deeply in the belief that they will come through the winter more easily. They do not.

After fifty years, I asked Mr Aylett which dahlias are his favourites. While a tuba and trombone played in the background, he evaded the question by telling me the variety which his wife likes best. Mrs Aylett votes for the shell-pink decorative variety 'Dawn Sky', perhaps because it has a long stem and is excellent for picking. Her husband then came up with three selections. The first is the salmon-pink blend of 'Scaur Swinton', a colour which I would never have chosen but which he knows as a grower and guarantees as a fine performer with level, steady growth. The second is my personal number one, although stocks of it have now dwindled and my plants are rarities: the superb 'Maltby Whisper', which is a small-flowered cactus variety in clear yellow, a star which flowers freely in large pots or in the middle-to-front of a border. At shows in the 1990s I made a note of the alluring 'Vicky Crutchfield', a pink variety which has served me well ever since. However, Mr Aylett thinks that 'Vicky' has had her day and that the silver-pink waterlily dahlia, 'Pearl of Heemstede', is much better. Over the canapés I felt I had extracted fifty years of wisdom. Like me, the Ayletts are not sentimental about many of the old varieties, not least because they have grown them and understand that many of them are mediocre, long before conservationists feared they were being 'lost' and tried to bring them back.

Old or new, dahlias grow well only if given plenty of water. I plant mine with a dusting of Vitax Q4 fertilizer beneath them and I feed them until late July with a growth-promoting fertilizer, Miracle-Gro being my choice. Advised by the experts, I then turn to Tomorite to prepare for good buds and flowers. Before that, I harden my heart and stop the young plants at least once, preferably twice. Stopping means removing the tips of the main growing shoot when about four pairs of leaves are showing. It is something beginners hate to do, but it is crucial. It encourages strong side shoots which will in turn bear flowers. If your dahlias have only two or three buds of flower you are shirking the stopping. Mr Aylett also recommends careful disbudding, the removal of buds which appear on side shoots between mid-July and early August. So long as you then stake the bigger dahlias properly, you will have nothing but pleasure.

How popular are dahlias nowadays? Aylett's raise 120,000 cuttings a year, but dahlias account for only 1 per cent of their garden centre's turnover. They suffer from being gardeners' plants in an era when gardening has become so much less popular than the idea of gardens. They give me exceptional pleasure and each year, the mild sense of satisfaction of having done my best by them. In return, I can take credit for one innovation in the Aylett repertoire. In the late 1980s I reproduced beside my column a picture of Aylett's prize-winning London exhibit of dahlias with young Julie Aylett, the boss's daughter, captioned beside it. The photograph was seen by Adam Wigglesworth, then a commodity trader in vegetable oil, while delayed at an airport in Holland. He had already been wooing Miss Aylett, but when he saw her displayed in the *Financial Times*, his daily bible, he realized that her speciality was even more esteemed than his. Shortly afterwards they married, and he is now a director of the family's garden business. They have been married for twenty years and the dahlias have continued to shine. When my son married too, it was for me to supply the flowers for his church wedding. Naturally, I turned in September to dahlias, and except for the bride, Aylett's pale cream *Dahlia* 'Cameo' and the wondrous yellow 'Glorie van Heemstede' were the beauties of the day. Say it with dahlias, and you too will join the revived fashion of our age.

Appreciating Asters

Whenever I can, I pay a late September visit to the National Collection of Michaelmas daisies, which is beautifully kept by the Picton family at Old Court Nurseries near Malvern in Worcestershire. Paul Picton is the latest member of a distinguished family of gardeners to be involved with the aster family. He has grown them and much else since he was a boy and his family's nursery at Colwall shows England's finest collection of asters, on which Paul is an acknowledged expert and grower. His book *The Gardener's Guide to Growing Asters* was published in Britain and America in 1999 and remains one of my most consulted and most admired recent gardening books.

If you mistrust Michaelmas daisies, you need to look at them more closely. Traditionally, their enemy was mildew. If it spared the old varieties they made a heavy mass of dark leaves and blocked up a border for months before flowering. Most of the mildewed plants were hybrid *novi-belgii* varieties which flowered in brilliant colours and had names which ranged from 'Percy Thrower' to 'Winston S. Churchill'. From August onwards they looked as if they had been showered with grey powder, and steadily went into decline. Thirty years ago, sensitive gardeners never even mentioned them in memories of their gardening progress. They were felt to be plants which the Edwardians had wisely reserved for special Michaelmas borders and which were best reserved nowadays for the sort of bungalow which surrounds itself with purple dahlias.

There is much more to the family than mildew, mites and wilt. For years, I blamed *novi-belgii* asters on Belgium because of their name. They are not Belgian at all. Their name was an early attempt to render New York in botanical Latin, so they are the New York asters, which were rampant on Park Avenue and in Times Square before the human Astors took over. They still grow wild up America's east coast as far as Maine.

Aster 'Kylie'

Paul Picton's book gives informed advice about coping with the problems in this lovely section of the family, from the early lilac-blue 'Ada Ballard' to the purple-red 'Winston S. Churchill', which spoils in wet weather. I urge you to read his instructions and to pay attention to his personal list at the end of the book. It gives the varieties which his long experience has found to be less prone to mildew. His personal favourite is the double blue 'Marie Ballard', the best blue of all autumn daisies and an exquisite variety wherever it remains healthy. New York asters were not much developed by New Yorkers or Americans, although their varieties are widespread in the American trade.

It is odd, too, that the other great branch of the family, the *novae-angliae* varieties, are under-represented in American gardens. These asters are also American, deriving their name from New England, and in the wild they grow as far south as Carolina. In Europe, gardeners have been defecting to the New England aster because it is so much stronger and not prone to mildew. The best varieties have lilac to purple-blue flowers, although there are whites and a well-known 'Harrington's Pink'. 'Rosa Sieger' is a valuable tall pink, and the purple-red 'Lou Williams' is six feet high at the back of a border. It was only bred in 1995. I like many of them, but they are not as sensational as the New York forms. The most sensational turned out to be a disappointment. 'Andenken an Alma Pötschke' began by promising to be a brilliant splash of autumn colour in Britain but the flowers did not open well, especially in wet years, and recent autumns have left it looking its worst. Hopes of its cherry-red flowers, fully open in October, have faded in the past decade.

The exciting revivals belong to related species, on which Picton's book is excellent. America's favourite aster is *Aster × frikartii*, and many British gardeners too would rate this lavender-flowered single variety in their top half-dozen of all border plants. Confusions about the true variety are neatly cleared up in Picton's text and I would only add that this aster is a brilliant plant for twining and propping among other plants from July onwards while the first summer flush of flowers in the front of a border is fading. Staking is essential for a proper display of almost all asters, and the best method is to use bamboo canes of moderate height, artfully placed and secured.

In America, there is a great following for the long-flowering

Aster novi-belgii 'Ada Ballard'

violet-blue 'Fanny's Aster', which we hardly grow in Britain. It owes
its name to a grower's housemaid, whereas names from domestic
servants are more usually found among English varieties of the past.
In Florida and the south-east, gardeners also grow the remarkable
climbing *Aster carolinianus*. It is rather untidy but shows thousands of
flowers in a shade of pale purple to a height of more than ten feet. In
Britain, not even the Pictons have been able to grow it. British gardeners, however, have at last woken up to the beauty of early-flowering
Aster sedifolius and the small-flowered variations of *Aster cordifolius*. If I
could have only one of them, I would choose the metallic single blue

top: *Aster* × *frikartii* 'Wunder von Staffa'   above: *Aster* 'Little Carlow'

'Little Carlow', which is wonderfully vigorous. I owe my first know-ledge of its excellence to a passing remark by John Sales, former adviser to the National Trust's gardens in England. When he was confronted with miles of flowerbed needing colour until the end of the public season, 'Little Carlow' was his suggestion, a great aster with thousands of smallish flowers in a shade of steely clear blue so intense that I find it almost best against the dark background of a green yew hedge. The time to plant and divide 'Little Carlow' is early spring, because it dislikes a wet winter and, when young, is susceptible to slugs. As my own asters multiply and add an entire month to the high point of my garden, I have to say that this easy variety remains top of my list.

My other star turn is tall, pale blue *cordifolius* 'Chieftain', which holds a handsome place towards the back of the border, growing up to five feet high. It is even taller than the light sprays of flower on *Aster turbinellus* or the little white stars which then begin to open on admir-able *Aster tradescantii*. Again, these varieties prefer the opposite condi-tions to modern mildewed hybrids. They like a light, well-drained soil and will tolerate dry weather, although it turns their leaves brown.

The broader range of asters shows us that the season is far longer than we usually realize. With me, it begins with the pale blue *Aster thomsonii* 'Nanus' in early August, joined a little later by the admirably easy *Aster sedifolius*. Without mildew, the focus then moves to the *novae-angliae* varieties, and it is usually mid-October before we see the best from *Aster amellus* 'King George' and its wonderful flush of violet-blue. October is the season for the low-growing *Aster lateriflorus* 'Prince', which has very small flowers of pink-white and stems and leaves of a remarkably dark purple. These dark-stemmed asters are always worth watching and I am particularly keen on the tall *Aster laevis* 'Calliope'.

From August till late October thoughtful gardeners can have asters without diseases and a prairie of first-class colours. Michaelmas daisies are no longer limited to Michaelmas and the strongest of them give the garden a good two months of colour.

Coloured Crabs

In Britain, our trees' autumn colour may be disappointing, but their berries and fruits are another matter. They are an excellent way of prolonging a garden's impact and are invaluable for those of us who like arranging seasonal displays indoors. In August there are already undamaged bunches of big scarlet fruit on one of my top tips, *Sorbus americana*, an upright tree which is untroubled by dry summers. This tree is always good, but it excels itself now that so many garden birds are in hiding. Maybe the birds are on the run from the aggressive wildlife which we are being encouraged to cherish in our gardens.

It is worth planning carefully for a good blaze of fruits. For a small garden in Britain, Europe or America, I would turn first to the family of *Malus* or flowering crabs. The best of them are extraordinarily tough. They are beautiful in flower, fruit and autumn leaf, with two high seasons of special interest. Most of them will grow in dry or cold climates and are more or less foolproof. My deepening knowledge is based on visits to an outstanding nursery collection of the best maluses, where I realize that my view of them needs revision. I have learnt my lessons from Landford Trees at Landford Lodge, Salisbury, Wiltshire whose catalogue has grown gratifyingly during the twenty years in which I have been using and recommending it.

The stock is grown on thirty acres of exposed Wiltshire farmland and is the backbone of a nursery which hardly ever buys in its trees from other sources. An alphabetical collection of the maluses on offer has been steadily developed in and around an area of its walled garden, and I met the proprietor, Christopher Pilkington, beside his visible catalogue of maluses in green growth. We walked up and down his densely planted lines and tried to rank them in an order which would help gardeners to find their way to the best. To my initial relief, we agreed on the one which holds its fine red fruits for the longest time and continues to catch the eye throughout the winter. *Malus* 'Red

Malus × *robusta* 'Red Sentinel'

Sentinel' is an old favourite and ranks near the top after Landford's careful assessment of many of its rivals. It holds its red fruit from November until February in my college garden in Oxford, at least until one of the fellows discovers that the fruits can be turned into jam. 'Red Sentinel' is healthy, arching in outline, and pretty in pink-white flower. So long as you do not expect a tree of a simple, upright form, it is a superb choice.

We also agreed on a lesser-known species which has the prettiest combination of flower, fresh young leaf and sideways-spreading growth. *Malus transitoria* has my favourite leaf in the entire family. It is extremely tough, drought-resistant and delicate in its young greenery. The yellow fruits are a further pleasure and should earn the tree a wider public.

Some of my other initial choices turn out to be not so well advised. 'Golden Hornet' is as common in the trade as *transitoria* is not. It is a tough variety, but its shape is upright, the leaves look dusty and drab, and the brilliant yellow fruits have a way of vanishing by early November. For years, I have blamed birds for their disappearance, but Pilkington remarks that the culprit is always the first hard frost. He rates *Malus* × *robusta* 'Yellow Siberian' much more highly and considers it the best of the yellow fruiters. I am stuck with two 'Hornets', my penance for life.

Several of the most popular types of malus have dark-purple flushed leaves. I would probably have named 'Profusion' as a top variety in this group, but the expert assures me that it looks increasingly wretched as the summer proceeds and is not especially healthy. We hear much less about the related *Malus × moerlandsii*, which is unusual in the trade but happy in the Landford nursery. I saw it growing strongly to a height of about fifteen feet and its red-purple leaves and healthy nature deserve more attention. A combination of dark red flowers and shiny purple leaves is also an attractive possibility, best found in 'Liset', an upright variety which is selected from × *moerlandsii* but more widely available. The red colouring of many maluses' leaves has a way of fading and looking tired as the years go by, but the most persistent red is the one called 'Royalty', which begins by growing straight before spreading pleasantly outwards in later years. The darkest shades of red come from fruits, not leaves, and are best seen on a dark-fruited new arrival, *Malus* 'Indian Magic'. The big fruits are distinctive and when stocks of this fine variety build up, they ought to be widely planted.

My favour for 'Golden Hornet' and 'Profusion' has been misplaced. It is pleasant, then, to agree on the virtues of varieties which others wrongly consider to be ordinary. *Malus × robusta* is the Siberian crab from which 'Red Sentinel' and others are derived. It is a very good tree itself in flower and fruit, retaining red crab-apples well into the winter. It is as robust as its name and an excellent choice for a double season of beauty in flower and fruit. Its close relation is the Japanese crab, *Malus floribunda*, which is spectacular in flower, making a conveniently small tree whose crimson-red buds open to white flowers. It becomes more wide than high and allows itself to be clipped into a pretty, semi-floral shape. It is very strong, and although I thought it was too hackneyed when I was first offered it, I have learned to love it as one of the best of the family when in flower.

Finally, two modern varieties which are on the up and are difficult to kill. Pilkington's first choice is 'Evereste', a transatlantic variety with white flowers and green leaves which age unusually well. Its masses of orange-red fruits are pretty in October. I appreciate the expert's tact in choosing this one as 'idiot-proof'. 'Evereste' is the variety to which I gave a central position in my garden some years ago and which I have prided myself on growing with unusual success. That pride can now be transferred. In Landford's maloretum there is a new variety which suits me particularly well. Known as *Malus × zumi* 'Professor Springer' it bears masses of orange-red fruits on a super-healthy tree. At Landford they know it as the 'zoomy professor'. I have zoomed in, and given it a prime place at home.

Cutting Corners With Chrysanthemums

Thoughtful gardeners can prolong their gardens' late flowering by the clever use of chrysanthemums. These flowers have had all sorts of symbolic associations across the world, from China to France. They represent love or death or scholarly perfection, and in parts of China their leaves would be infused in water to make a liquid which was supposed to give eternal youth. Elsewhere in China admirers used to examine them and mark them on a scale used in the exam for entrance into the Chinese civil service. I like the idea of coaching chrysanthemums for an Oxford degree and deciding which of them deserves a low second ranking. In Britain, there is an obstacle: like dahlias, chrysanthemums are bound up with the British sense of class.

Up the social scale, garden-owners look down on chrysanthemums as if they are common. They scorn mounds of them in simple front gardens and dislike those yellow-flowered varieties in plastic pots from florists. Anything which calls itself a 'Mum' and flowers like a fancy cushion is beyond the bounds of acceptability. As a result, chrysanthemums have receded into vegetable gardens, where they can be visited but never confronted in the main view.

The family should not be damned because a few members of it are used in odd ways. The choice is not between a Mums' outing or a complicated system of training spray-chrysanthemums under glass. Nowadays I enjoy ten weeks of chrysanthemums by the dozen because I cheat. I grow chrysanthemums only from the end of April and have none of the bother of rooting, rotting or prolonged heating which deters beginners. In busy times, thoughtful gardeners can let others do the initial work. I turn to Halls of Heddon-on-the-Wall, Northumberland NE15 0JS, who specialize in dahlias and chrysanthemums and are committed to helping customers cut corners. If customers send in orders for chrysanthemums before early March, Halls will deliver rooted cuttings of named varieties in late April or early May. Each

Chrysanthemum
'Bronze Max Riley'

rooted piece should then be set in a four-inch pot filled with a good
garden compost and kept in a sheltered place. Watch for warnings of
a late frost, and if forewarned, bring the plants indoors for the night
only. I use no heat, no glass and receive my plants at the end of April,
potting them and growing them on for planting outdoors on 15 May.
It is so easy, and in ten years I have not lost a single one.

The results are extremely pleasing, especially from early-flowering
varieties which give such a lift to the garden from the third week in
August onwards. My winners are the old and well-loved 'Bronze Max
Riley', flame-red 'Membury' and pale yellow 'Dana', which is good
for cutting. The range of colours is widened by the stalwart 'Allouise'
and the sports from it in many colours. They come in shades of white,
peach, red and gold and flower early enough to be at their best long
before the weather turns in mid-November. Experts emphasize the
importance of stopping the early varieties in order to encourage side
shoots and many more flowers by removing the growing tip, or upper
few inches, of a young plant. I stop mine at the end of May, whereupon the side shoots multiply and keep the season going. Feeding and
spraying are important too. I fork the fertilizer fish, blood and bone
into the soil a day before planting out the young cuttings. From
mid-July until mid-August, I spray the developing plants with diluted
Phostrogen, but I stop the fertilizer when colour begins to show in the
bud. Pests are only a problem because the young green leaves look so
appetizing between May and July. The RHS Wisley handbook calls

greenfly 'virus vectors', but the way to stop them vecting is to spray them early with Tumblebug. If the plants are unsprayed, leaf miners will also cause the leaves to curl up and look as though something is tunnelling through them. Again, Tumblebug keeps them away.

These foes are hazards, but are not inevitable. Can we also be lazy and keep these varieties through the winter? We can, if we remember that in November a parent plant should be cut down to about six inches, lifted and laid in a good peaty compost. It can then live in an unheated glasshouse and be brought back to growth by resuming the watering and increasing the heat in early March. Within three weeks, young shoots will be bursting everywhere and can be rooted easily as the cuttings for next year. Alternatively, you can order again from Halls in early spring and reckon that the time saved is worth the modest cost. If you cannot be bothered with lifting plants, you can cut them down, cover them with sandy soil, straw or peat to a depth of several inches and trust to luck. The early varieties will survive quite a heavy frost under covering and are a worthwhile gamble in light soil outdoors.

Alternatively, choose varieties from the hardy group, which flower from late September into early November and usually survive the winter. Excellent varieties are now being marketed again, after being rescued by keen conservationists. The single dark pink 'Anne, Lady Brockett' is a cracker but she had to be rediscovered by expert nursery-men at Monksilver Nursery, Cottenham, Cambridge. Her ladyship had decamped to France, where healthy plants were duly found and repatriated. Admittedly, she had always had what nursery lists call a 'running habit'. Two of the commonest hardy varieties are good value too, yellow-apricot 'Mary Stoker' and the double red 'Duchess of Edinburgh'. The prettiest is the late-flowering 'Emperor of China', which grows up to four feet high and combines a red flush on its leaves with beautifully shaped flowers of pale double pink. I look on these fine chrysanthemums with eyes formed not by China but by the unsurpassed *Tale of Genji*, the Japanese classic which was written by Lady Murasaki at the start of the eleventh century. Such a sensitive work is unimaginable in dreary old northern Europe at that date, but in Japan it was already traditional to debate the relative merits of gardens in spring and autumn. Fashions were fickle and as Lady

Murasaki neatly puts it: 'Women who are seduced by the spring garden (so it is in this world) are now seduced by the autumn.'

In his youth Prince Genji, she tells us, prepared to sing and dance for the court during their autumn excursion. He had been wearing a branch of maple in his cap, but as the leaves fell, 'it seemed at odds with his handsome face'. An unlikely character called the General of the Left replaced Genji's branch with chrysanthemums, which 'stood in his cap, delicately touched by the frost, and gave new beauty to the prince's form and motions'. Everyone was profoundly moved. 'Even the unlettered menials', who were thinking of 'rocks and branches', were stirred to tears at the sight. I picture Genji with 'Anne, Lady Brockett' in his hair and can well understand the menials' reaction.

Genji's cousin was a concubine of the emperor, and in her garden an entire 'chrysanthemum hedge would blossom in the morning frosts of early winter'. In the tale translated as 'The Ivy', a prince who is believed to be Genji's son attempts to seduce a secluded daughter of the Eighth Prince. She casts a quick look at him from behind a silk curtain and starts to cry behind her fan. He pities her, but he knows that her charm will bring other men flocking and, as a result, his 'doubts come back and also his resentment'. He turns away to the nearby chrysanthemums and notices how the better they are culti-vated, the slower they are to show their last, prized flush of colour. As he looked, one flower was already turning to its grand finale and the prince was moved to poetry. 'I do not love among flowers the chrys-anthemum only,' he began, quoting a famous old Japanese poem. Neither do I, but it was he who then had the luck. He captivated his young target and stayed on with her among the flowers for some days, 'with music and other diversions to break the monotony'.

At Home With Hellyer

Not until 2002 did I break one of the most welcome treaties of my life. It ran for twenty-five years and protected me from exposure to serious expertise. During its lifetime, I shared the role of writing weekly gardening columns for the *Financial Times* with a senior partner, Arthur Hellyer. His career as a gardener and writer had begun more than fifty years before mine. Born in 1902, he was the supreme expert when I began to write in 1970, but the treaty was his suggestion.

The terms were beautifully simple. Neither of us would visit the other's garden during our tenure of the job. Perhaps Hellyer did not wish to be interrupted. Perhaps he was shy of one of my first pieces, which attacked the entire family of flowering heathers. He knew far more about them than I did and grew some fine varieties near his own house. As I moved around in earlier life, I was glad he never came to see my less established efforts. He eventually visited the gardens of my Oxford college, but told me later that he did not know I was in charge of them. He never expressed an opinion.

I finally visited his garden, Orchards, in Rowfant, near Crawley, West Sussex, about ten years after he had died. In Arthur's older age there had had to be economies of scale, but since his death in 1993, his daughter Penelope had done her best to cope with the framework and the inevitable replanting. I found my visit extremely touching. It reflected the history of a particular era, now lost. As a schoolboy in Dulwich, the young Arthur Hellyer had had a sound, practical mind. He then contracted tuberculosis and for his health's sake was advised to work in the open air. During the First World War, emphasis was soon laid on the need to 'dig for victory'. Many people were digging for death in their trenches in France, but behind the lines, civilians were encouraged to grow vegetables to help feed the nation. Hellyer once told me that his early interest in gardening owed much to the need to dig up the family lawn and try to save Britain in 1916.

Arthur and Gay Hellyer in their Jersey garden

His garden at Orchards survived as a witness to the sort of self-sufficient vision which returned to fashion in the dark days of the early 1970s and was brilliantly satirized in the TV series *The Good Life*. Arthur's lifelong partner was certainly no Penelope Keith. He married Gay in 1933 when he was thirty-two and she was working at the John Innes Research Institute. Gay had a BSc and the clear mind of a natural teacher. She was an ideal match for Arthur's own practical and scientific outlook and his faith in the possibility of a self-sustaining life. In 1934, they did what many of us once dreamed of achieving: they bought seven acres of bare land, which was to be their home for the rest of their life. On it Arthur the gardener planted excellent magnolias, camellias and acers in a design which he developed on the ground rather than on the drawing board. He also built the house at Orchards. He continued for many years to work to a routine which makes life in a modern office seem a cushy number. In summer, he would begin the day at 5 a.m. He would garden until 6.45 a.m. He would then make cups of tea, one of which would be given to his young daughter, Penelope. He would leave at 7 a.m. for the daily train to London. Whenever possible, he would take with him some home-grown fruit and produce to sell to the greengrocer in Crawley on his way to the station. In London he would edit the immortal magazine *Amateur Gardening*. He would return home just before 7 p.m. to take an early supper. Then, he would write, breaking only for one programme on the television, the *Nine O'Clock News*.

An old black-and-white photograph from the 1930s captures the resolution of this pair of pioneers, he pushing a plough through virgin soil, she following it to beat the ground into shape. At the time, Arthur and Gay were living in a temporary shed on the lower slopes of Orchards. I found it enchanting that their early settlement survived seventy years later with orange blossom, lily of the valley, raspberries and indestructible shrubs around it. Of course, there had been a goat, a cow and various chickens. Arthur managed the heavy machinery, but Gay would help him with every other garden job. Once in the hot summer of 1976 she too contributed to the *FT*, publishing her excellent recipe for cucumber soup. Behind it lay her own practicality and hard work as a scientifically minded land girl.

Sometimes, I look back at old copies of *Country Life* magazine, published between 1935 and 1955, whose house prices make one sick with envy – 'offers around £5,000 for an enchanting Georgian rectory with two cottages, stables and 10 acres of land' in what is now the M25 corridor. Articles in these magazines reflect the Hellyer ethic, the bravado of 'back to the land' and the virtue of growing one's own vegetables and becoming a self-sufficient unit. Like that era's house prices, these assumptions now seem a distant echo of history. Most of us now 'pick our own' somewhere else or scour the supermarket. The old *Country Life* assumptions, however, were ones which guided Hellyer's life, but in his case, they had a further depth. For a while, in his youth, he had inclined to the sect of Jehovah's Witnesses, a group whom he abandoned only with difficulty. His settling at Orchards marked his personal escape, but the Witnesses' values of personal responsibility, work and dedication stayed with him throughout his life. Only once, when I had published a book on ancient religion, did he remark to me how fearful he had remained of his former sect, worrying that they would come to harass him while he worked on devotedly to transform his corner of the natural world.

There was a shared culture of science between Arthur and his wife which shaped their outlook and their clear way of teaching. He was profoundly uninterested in spin, though quietly appreciative of style. This clear, practical modesty gave him a style of his own. It also made him aware of gardening's many pitfalls, and generous, therefore, about others' efforts. If he had broken our treaty and called on me, I would have learned so much, and somewhere, he would have found something to admire.

Selecting Salvias

Twenty-five years ago my garden was living in an autumnal Dark Age. Since then plant-hunters and breeders have transformed the range of late-flowering plants from which we choose. One of the best transformations has been the discovery of so many new salvias. The best are not really hardy, but they are so free-flowering from mid-July onwards, in such exceptional colours, that it seems a small effort to protect them from extreme frost.

If I could choose only five out of more than 100 on the market, which would I pick? The colour might be startling, but I think the vivid *Salvia involucrata* would make it into the top group. The flowers of this vigorous Mexican are a marvellous shade of lipstick rose-magenta. It will withstand quite a sharp frost and continue to flower into late November. I have learned its special value in border plantings, where the art is to dot individual plants at intervals down a bed and let them develop their full potential so as to draw the eye down the bed's entire length. Each involucrata is best staked on a central cane, but there is no need to tie in the upper stems, as they are prettier if they spread out naturally at a horizontal angle. They grow furiously to a height of four feet and will even put up with light shade.

Also from Mexico, my favourites for small pots are the various forms of a natural hybrid, *Salvia × jamensis*. 'La Luna' is an excellent yellow, and there are fine pinks and shades of cream, including 'Moonlight Over Ashwood', which has yellow leaves and very pale yellow flowers. These fine little plants are not hardy in an English winter and need to be kept alive in the dark months as rooted cuttings sheltered indoors. Among the blues, my favourite is *Salvia cacaliifolia*. Its spikes of blue flowers have an exceptional depth and intensity, deserving the description 'royal blue'. It has two cardinal needs. It must have plenty of water and as it is spoilt by the first few degrees of frost, it needs to be sheltered. I simply take it indoors. At a growers' lunch at Chelsea Flower Show, I learnt that the easiest way to propagate it is to heap a mulch of compost round the central root stock and then pull off the root-bearing stems which emerge from the base.

Salvia microphylla also has to feature in the top five, but only in a form with a true red to its flowers. 'Kew Red' is excellent, flowering freely above shiny mid green leaves. For years now, I have also grown 'Newby Hall', which is tall enough to reach five feet and has bright red flowers with yellowish leaves. These plants tolerate a lack of water for up to a fortnight, allowing one to go on holiday with a clear conscience. At a recent RHS Autumn Show in London, I bought plants of the small *Salvia chamaedryoides*, a pretty number from Texas which has small deep blue flowers and grows to a foot in height. On balance, I think I prefer the tender *Salvia darcyi* which has big bright red flowers until late October. The leaves are quite sticky and the plant needs to be staked to show itself well at a height of three feet. The inevitable first frost in a modern November or December will ruin it, but salvation for all these salvias is easy. From late October onwards I bring the likes of *Salvia darcyi* and *cacaliifolia* into the house in pots and enjoy them for another month or two as indoor plants. If they are dead-headed there, they will go on flowering until December. They then go into a greenhouse and produce dozens of rootable cuttings when they start to grow again in spring. If you shelter these vivid new arrivals, you will never be short of stock to carry you cheerfully through a winter.

Goodnight at Gamberaia

The end of each season of flower gardening lives on in thoughtful gardeners' memories. One of my most memorable endings occurred on a hill outside Florence, the setting for the garden of the Villa Gamberaia, which has been widely praised as a supreme example of a garden with features in a Renaissance style. The site is easily reached by the number 10 bus from Florence's main railway station, which takes you up into the hill town of Settignano, once the home of distinguished sculptors and artists. The Villa Gamberaia's garden owes its continuing evolution to a series of dedicated private owners, and nowadays paying visitors are welcome. In its well-defined space, the final scene in my year of flower gardening involved China roses, lemon trees and some boisterous ladies.

First, I should explain the Villa's celebrated garden and its history, which has had admirable attention in recent years. In 1944 the house and garden were heavily damaged when a German officer set fire to the place, before abandoning the site. Three years later, despite the ruin and neglect, the sensitive eye of the great art critic Bernard Berenson described the place as still able to 'inspire longing and dreams, sweet dreams'. I do not think that Berenson had much knowledge about flower gardening but he had an eye for design, and it was Gamberaia's design which had endured. In his lifetime the place had become widely known in English circles through the book by the novelist Edith Wharton, *Italian Villas and their Gardens*, which described it as 'the most perfect example of the art of producing a great effect on a small scale'. Even if the villa had no garden it would still be a fine place to visit for the sake of its views across an enchanted landscape. It is hard to believe that the great urban sprawl of modern Florence lies so near, concealed beneath it in the valley. From the lawns, the views to the distant hills of Chianti country are unspoilt and, on one side, the landscape is fit to be included in a great Florentine painting from the fifteenth century.

What we see nowadays is only a temporary point in a long history. As so often, an admired garden makes nonsense of simple ideas of historical conservation. The garden which we admire has continued to be altered, and to what point in the past would purists for garden history now want it to be restored? The villa's name, 'Gamberaia', goes back to the old Italian word for a crayfish, and as there has always been good water on the site, the name suggests to some that the villa began life as a simple farmhouse on a property where this fish was farmed. There may have been a link between the fishponds and the nuns of a nearby convent, but others believe the name merely came from a like-named Florentine family. The villa which we see today took its main shape rather later, in 1610.

As experts on Edwardian gardening remarked, the villa garden is confined. On one side, the main distinction is the superb view over Florence. On another, it is a long green vista of grass which was once a bowling green and now ends in an imitation grotto. There is still some dispute about the origins of this pretty walk, which appealed to English visitors' love of lawns. In the Edwardian era, a visiting American student ascribed it to a member of the Lapi family in the later seventeenth century. Others think, as I do, that the credit goes to a later owner, Scipione Capponi, a member of a great Florentine family. He was a man of taste who admired classical antiquities, and his brother helped to fund the Botanic Academy in Florence. Certainly Scipione changed and improved the site and a map from the mid eighteenth century suggests that the best-known part of today's garden already had a formal outline during his ownership. It shows some twisted evergreen embroidery and a circular island for rabbits, confined by water.

What we now see and admire is due to very different hands. In 1896, the villa was bought by a Romanian, Princess Giovanna Ghika, who had studied arts and sculpture in Paris. She took over ground which had been given to vegetable gardening and introduced an attractive plan of formal water ponds which she edged with roses and oleanders in order to make a parterre. She planted a concluding wall of evergreen cypress beyond it and may already have cut tall windows into their green mass. These interludes of open space give brilliant views through the hedge to this day.

During the Princess's lifetime, the Oxford aesthete and historian Harold Acton lived at the fine villa La Pietra on the opposite line of hills. He loved the atmosphere at neighbouring Gamberaia and recalled how he 'began to frequent this paradise, then belonging to a narcissistic Romanian who lived mysteriously in love with herself, perhaps, and certainly with her growing creation, the garden'. At this point Acton's memory has airbrushed out of his text the Romanian's most beloved companion, the elusive Mary Blood with her blue-grey angora cat. I think there was more to these ladies' relations than narcissism. The Gamberaia garden should be recognized as a fore-runner of Britain's Sissinghurst in histories of female love and the landscape. It is not that Acton suppressed Miss Blood on purpose. On another occasion he recalls her and describes her as 'a great artist'. He even preserves what are some of her only surviving words. She told him as a boy to 'plant umbrella pines. You can never have enough of them.' It is not bad advice. The Princess and Miss Blood did most to make the parterre garden which visitors still admire, but in the mid 1920s the next owner, Baroness von Kettler, simplified some of their planting and introduced more evergreen yews. None of these ladies, however, were the ladies in the scene which concluded my year.

In the late November sunshine I climbed Gamberaia's stairway to the garden's upper levels where the planting is more formal. In sum-mer, the big terracotta pots here contain handsome lemon trees, but over the garden wall came something else: an operatic chorus of laughter, cheering and occasional swear words. The olive trees were swarming with women in aprons who were shaking the branches and pushing off their crop of fruits with long-handled mops. The olives then fell on to large sheets around the tree trunk, no doubt to be gathered and pressed. The female pickers played up to my male gaze, but they did not know that I was thinking of the unchanging tech-niques of olive-gathering. On ancient Greek vases, Greeks are shown up olive trees shaking fruits on to similar sheeting. They have sticks, not mops, and significantly, they are all men.

In front of me the big lemon trees in their heavy pots had just gone into the lemon house, the *limonaia*. They stood there in rows, sheltered from the November frost. On the sloping ground towards Florence, a line of China roses was still in pink flower, showing how good this sort of rose is in a dry and difficult season. The November light began to fade and suddenly the bells struck the hour in the town below. I felt part of the evolution which is every great garden's history. The landscape architect Geoffrey Jellicoe once described the Villa Gamberaia as 'more Italian than the Italians'. He ought to have seen my Italian ladies expressing their Italian natures and recanted his patronizing view. They were the right finale for a year of flowers outdoors, and I quietly covet them up the trees. Their singing would be most welcome as I set about pruning my avenues of ornamental pears.

Sophie's World

As Christmas approaches, old readers of my gardening column always resurface with news of their gardens' progress. Young ones join them, propelled by new ambitions, so I end this book with two young hopefuls whose public debut earned them many fans. The first of them represents my claim to have invented Facebook as early as 1997, although I was too unworldly to pursue the most lucrative idea in this book.

The years of the dotcom boom were hectic for all of us, but for none of those with whose gardens I keep in touch were they half as hectic as for the young Sophie Click-Portal. I can hardly believe that it is already fifteen years since that snowy afternoon in December when we rejected her application to read for a degree in Classics at New College, Oxford. My notes at the time said her spelling was appalling and she believed that the Elgin Marbles were carved in the second century BC. In her translation test she twice mistook an active for a passive. She went on to Cambridge, much as we expected, and two years later I heard from a colleague that she was taking their newly designed option called Classix instead.

Sophie's world turned out to be social rather than intellectual. When her graduation loomed, her friends were adamant that her choices lay only between headhunting or helping to write an agony column in the weekend press. They were not reckoning with Derek, Sophie's boyfriend, who had been working during her degree as a partner in a technology start-up in Cambridge's silicon fen. Every Sunday, she would commute to his flat in Biggleswade. It was there that she was introduced to the World Wide Web.

In 1997, Sophie decided to try agony-aunting online and set up a website for social and personal encounters and photos, the area where her strengths lay. On friends' advice, she approached nearby celebrities for venture capital and after she had been in touch with a number of offshore trusts, the funding was sorted out, although part of it arrived as banknotes in an envelope. By autumn her site was up and running and her plans for Intimate.com were born. Or, rather, they would have been born but for Sophie's talent for mis-spelling. By one of those lucky chances which lie behind most successful entrepreneurs, the name which she actually registered was Intermate.com instead.

The name suggested its own agenda and Sophie has developed it into Britain's most exclusive online encounter and dating service. Intermate is now the City's best-kept secret. If you think your financial adviser has been underperforming, the reason is that he has been obsessed with time on Intermate instead. The service is available only on subscription and only to individuals of high net worth or otherwise impeccable assets. On the site Sophie soon introduced a Call Option which went like wildfire. Her move into spread-betting was also inspired, but it had to be suspended when two European users misunderstood what it meant. Meanwhile, Intermate roared secretly ahead on Wall Street despite severe anxieties about security. When a very exclusive brokerage house discovered that its senior male partners were starting to date each other online, they decided that the only way to hush up the rumour from the private clients' ears was to buy Sophie out, monopolize the service and give her a vice-presidential role.

What do you do aged twenty-six with a pay-out of £60 million and a lifetime stretching in front of you? Sooner or later, you go back to your roots, and the Click-Portal roots go deep into northern Nottinghamshire. There, Sophie remembers a golden haze of childhood set in a dreamy summer garden of old-fashioned roses and scented jasmine. The memories, too, are hazy, because her mother could not face the Nottinghamshire winters and the obligatory shooting lunches, so she decamped to the South of France without Sophie's father when Sophie was only six. Thanks to her new-found riches Sophie can at last begin to integrate her past. She will recreate those golden afternoons and update them on a site of her own choosing.

She could afford to buy a house almost anywhere, but she liked the sound of the special section called Desperate To Impress on Britain's coolest internet start-up, lastminute.com. Among dozens of tempting offers she found a magnificent Georgian villa in Twickenham whose gardens slope down to the Thames near historic Marble Hill House. She bought it with one click of a mouse and became the proud owner of a long-neglected garden site. However, even in our enterprise culture, massive riches incite the envy of workers in the old economy. Her sister, Cathy, is the brains of the Click-Portal family and is slowly writing a doctoral thesis on early Georgian landscape poetry. When Sophie set up in Twickenham, Cathy sent her a moving-in card with a message inside from a malevolent poem written by Jonathan Swift in 1727. Impersonating a Georgian house in Twickenham, Swift had written as follows: 'Some South-Sea broker from the City / Will purchase me the more's the pity, / Lay all my fine plantations waste, / To fit them to his vulgar taste.' Cathy had scratched out the words 'South Sea' and 'his' and written 'online' and 'her' instead. She has not been invited to stay at Christmas.

Her sister's conscious plan, meanwhile, is to ride the new wave in gardening and take it forward beyond the stereotypes of the pre-electronic age. Her guiding design concept is to represent the telecosm in natural materials, and link the garden and the new global village by a subtle use of allusion. Her front door leads out on to some avant-garde wooden decking which she has had painted with red and yellow wavebands to suggest intercontinental communication. Beyond the decking visitors pass through a living 'portal', a block of evergreen hedging made from clipped leylandii conifers to symbolize rapid growth. Beyond the portal, students from Kew have worked at the weekends to lay out a complex web of clipped box. It is web-like to symbolize the internet and golden, not green, to symbolize the bags of money which can be made from it. Beyond her golden web, Sophie has sited an echo of her Classix training and her studies of the 'appro-priation' of the ancient world by modern taste. On a pedestal she has put a statue of Hermes, the ancient god of rapid messages, or heavenly e-mail. To move with the times, Hermes' sandals are no longer winged: they are webbed.

Beyond the telecosm the ground slopes down towards the River Thames where Sophie has fertility-stripped the turf and replaced it with hundreds of plants from the category of ornamental grasses. This part of the design is to be known as the Wild West, symbolizing the open frontiers which stretch beyond the telecosm for the next gener-ation of Sophies who are quick enough to see where they lie. In mild, wet winter weather, the top growth of these grasses looks much

New frontiers at Le Jardin Plume

dirtier and drabber than Sophie expected. She is still hoping for a
sharp frost over Christmas to make it look like the glistening photographs in her colour books of garden design.

Sophie sees it all as cool gardening at the cutting edge, but it looks
much less effective than the adjacent rectangular garden where
Sophie, unwittingly, has gone back to her dislocated roots. Drifts of
campanulas from her father's Nottinghamshire garden mix with pale
yellow evening primroses, the lovely white peony 'Kelway's Glorious'
and a range of purple-blue summer salvias which hark back to the
times before Sophie's mother bolted to France. The part of the garden
with the most personal warmth is the part which evokes a fractured past.

In Sophie's eyes, the only problems in the landscape are two
unanticipated visitors. Her elderly father, Tommy Click-Portal, has
invited himself for Christmas and expects to be entertained with
something as old fashioned as conversation. He has never got on with
Derek, and Sophie was not anticipating that Derek would migrate

from Biggleswade and set himself up on the top floor in Twickenham, near his beloved rugby football, with plans to telecommute by long-range terminal to Cambridge without ever leaving the house. Derek's motto is copied from the American head of Intel, who told the world that 'only the paranoid survive'. Sophie has always believed the opposite: 'only the extrovert succeed'. It has occurred to her that as she no longer owns the site, she can advertise herself on Intermate as a seasonal Christmas Call Option, keep quiet about the details and check the back-to-back offers. Deep down she knows that by the end of the holiday season she will have had more than enough Face Time with Derek, especially if he spends most of the day entrenched upstairs with his computer-game called *Heads Down*, which is advertised online as 'better than the best rugger scrum'.

As Intermate is so secure, Derek will never know that Sophie has put herself up for a cyber-relationship, under the general description of 'a multi-millionairess in her twenties with an ever-open portal'. As ever, Sophie is confident of success. She is only a mouse click away, she believes, from someone with whom to take telecosmic gardening into the new age. Deeper still, she is farther from what she needs, a soulmate to repair the past and join her in scattering bonemeal on the ground which her parents ploughed and buried in her heart.

À La Carte de Tendre

Post-Christmas tension is also the subject of prolonged telephone calls from my column's favourite readers, and over the years none has been more prolonged or enjoyable than my calls from Annabel Swift-Decking. She has always had a sharp financial brain, and nine years ago in March she did something truly last-minute: she took a vast short position in a dotcom company and made so much money that it changed her life. She then cashed in her holding in Asset.missmanagement, the one-stop website for high-flying women, and bought herself a charming Georgian rectory in my nearby Gloucestershire village of Upper Quartile. Friends in fund management had never thought of Annabel as anything so interesting as a 'wild card'. The most interesting thing about her was her string of unsatisfactory transatlantic boyfriends.

In January, everything changed, the way life can, when she met Thierry over dinner in a friend's flat in Onslow Gardens. Seven months later, he left Paris and came to spend a year in the depths of the English countryside. At first sight, anyone would fall for Thierry Taille Chic. His business is selling time-dated options on the pound's precise moment of entry into the euro and as sterling has fallen steeply, he has done a cracking business down in Gloucestershire. It is surprising how many of the local members of Business for Sterling have secretly opened positive positions in Thierry's book. His charm is still stronger than his English, but both are very much stronger than Annabel's French. This gap explains the recent fuss over Christmas presents.

In the summer, Thierry began to complain that Annabel was spending more time on her flowerbeds than she was spending on him. It was not very tactful, but in November he was pleased to find the perfect peace-offering in the Hatchard's Christmas catalogue, a book called *The Constant Gardener*. It will not go down well, because Annabel hates spy-writing. However, she cannot claim the high ground, either. Friends told her that the way to convert Thierry to Britain's

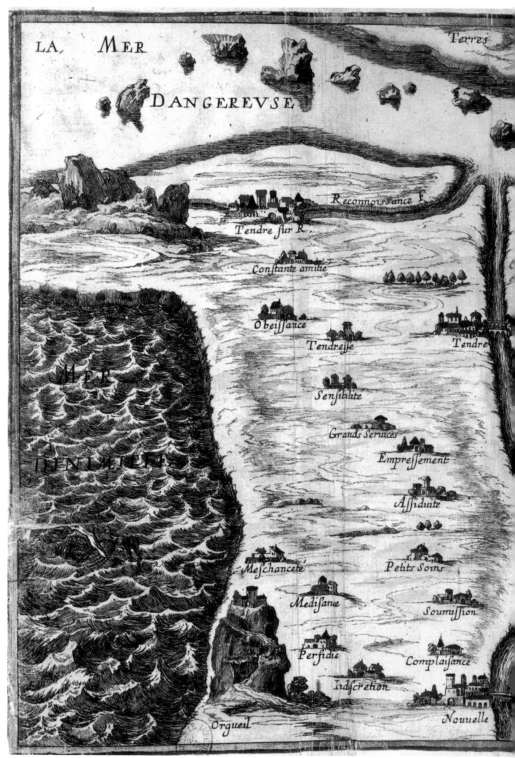

La Carte de Tendre

Estime F.

Tendre sur E.

Bonté

Respect

Exactitude

Generosité

Probité

Grand Cœur

Sincerité

Oubli

Billet doux

Legereté

Billet galant

Tiedeur

Iolis Vers

Inesgalité

Negligence

LAC D'INDIFERENCE

Fleuve

F.C.

| 2 | 4 | 6 | 8 | 10 |
Lieues d'amitié

national pastime was to buy him a book in French on gardening, so she went to Paris and looked for one. Much the best catalogue of gardening books is issued by the Maison Rustique in the Rue Jacob, and among some very scholarly treatises, Annabel found the perfect thing in the Maison's personal collection at the end of its list. It was called the *Livre des Caresses*. She imagined something sweet about flowers and the language of kisses, and the thought of them awoke pleasant memories. After her first lunch with Thierry, he had touched her heart by faxing to her office a sort of map which was called a 'Carte de Tendre'. Apparently, it was dreamed up in the 1660s by the authoress of an unreadable French novel called *Clélie*, whose heroine had forthright views on the pitfalls of a woman's love-life and the problems of feminine emotion. On the 'Carte de Tendre', the River of Inclination runs northwards between two well-mapped bits of country. The right bank is the Land of Reason, settled with such solemn virtues as Sincerity, and leads away to the Lake of Indifference. The 'rive gauche' is the land of emotion, tenderness and *'petits soins'* in which a woman risks being swept away to the left-hand side of life. Emotionally, Annabel has always felt decidedly Left Bank, and never more so than when Thierry drew a little route for himself entirely on the map's left side.

When Thierry opened his present at Christmas, the *Livre des Caresses* turned out to be something altogether different. Gardening in France is a broader subject, it seems, and this book from Paris's leading catalogue turned out to describe the *'géographie sensuelle'* of the female of the human species. Thierry took it as a hint and an insult but it was only the beginning of a very bad day. There were the usual problems over the morning's church services, because Thierry's Catholic service took place in a tin shed on the outskirts of town, while Annabel sang 'Glory to the new-born King' in the grand church in the centre of Cirencester. When they returned home, Annabel knew better than to suggest watching the Queen's Christmas Message after all the dreadful things which *Paris Match* has said about royalty in the past fifty years. They went straight in to lunch and Annabel thought she was justified in assuming that traditional Christmas pudding is now an acceptable currency Europe-wide. Thierry took one mouthful, spat it out and started talking in fast French about the joys of 6 January, the Feast of the Epiphany, and a pudding called *galette des rois*. After lunch, Annabel searched high and low in her kitchen bible, *Constance Spry's Cookery Book*, but this particular cake was never one which was taught to English debutantes in their dreamy days at Wingfield.

Christmas evening was definitely more right bank and reasoned than full of '*empressement*' on the left. There was more hope for Boxing Day, as Annabel had promised Thierry that they would go to watch a meet of Gloucestershire's famous Beaufort Hunt. She ended by wishing that Parliament had been more decisive and passed an act against Hunting With Dogs which actually worked. Thierry had seen the sport in France and was most put out not to be offered a plate of *fraises des bois* at the meet. He was expecting an array of horn-blowers to play something by Poulenc, but the elderly Beaufort huntsman, an ex-captain of little military distinction, blew three flat notes on his hunting horn and everybody moved off. Seeing his disappointment, a tweed-wrapped woman in mittens assured Thierry that it was not real hunting anyway because the 'unentered hounds' had not been able to go cubbing properly in the autumn and the legislation was beginning to bite. 'Unentered hounds' conjured up an alarming image in Thierry's mind, which was not helped when the woman added that everything had been ruined by fears of foot-and-mouth. When he looked completely blank, she explained in her best county French that it was all the fault of '*pied-bouche*'. Thierry was horrified, thinking it must be something that minor royalty do with their financial advisers on holiday.

To jolly things up Annabel had arranged lunch with her cousins, Julian and Veronica Sloane-Wally, in their nearby Old Rectory. She explained to Thierry that the Sloane-Wally garden was famous, but in winter he could only admire the golden thuja hedge. Lunch went off well enough, with devilled turkey on the menu, but when conversation returned to the topic of hunting, Veronica exclaimed that the government had very odd priorities as it had given so much parliamentary time to a ban on the noble art of fox-hunting but so little time to debate before reversing the admirable ban enshrined formerly in Section 28. Thierry again looked puzzled and when Veronica briskly explained the sexual behaviour which '*Section vingt-huit*' was supposed to discourage, he shrugged his shoulders and said that in Paris, these things were '*plus chic*'. Veronica looked as if she had been given a euro in her small change in W. H. Smith. Matters did not improve when Thierry later remarked that in Paris, he lived in the rue des Francs-Bourgeois in the Marais. Veronica muttered audibly that if so, it was the first time she had ever heard of a pansy living in a swamp. Soon after, they left, but their hosts' wariness about kissing anyone goodbye caused a slight unease in Annabel's mind.

For some weeks, Thierry had been talking fondly about the imminent arrival of his beloved Delors, the dog which lives with a friend in Paris and which Annabel has not yet seen. He has been telling her that it represents one of his two infidelities. During their early exchanges of local vocabulary, Annabel was charmed to discover that the French for a 'fox terrier' is the same as the English but pronounced in the French way. She assumed that they would be collecting '*le fox-terrier*' from Heathrow next week, but on the morning after Boxing Day she opened a parcel from Paris. Inside it she found a thick collar with big metal studs and an inset portrait of something which looks alarmingly like a Rottweiler. Worse, there was a medallion on the collar, engraved with the following words, '*Titi: baisers, Jules*'. Am I the second infidelity, she has begun to wonder, and if so, am I second after the dog or after whom? In matters of her personal 'Carte de Tendre', her cousin Veronica has a maddening way of being right. When Annabel last wrote to me, therefore, she was anticipating a grim time of further researches which would take her way out to the right of the River of Inclination. Down in Upper Quartile, it has been a poor Christmas for European union, but Annabel is determined to get to what she calls the bottom of it, even if it involves plumbing the right bank's Lake of Indifference.

The thoughtful future: my son and grandson plant their first tomato

Further Reading

I owe special debts to several older books, now mostly out of print, to which I continue to refer. I especially recommend J. Coutts, *Everyday Gardening* (London, 1945), which first taught me techniques of gardening, and the two masterpieces by A. G. L. Hellyer, *Your Garden Week by Week* (London, 1936) and *Amateur Gardening Pocket Guide* (Feltham, 1971). Christopher Lloyd, *The Well-Tempered Garden* (London, 1970) is also full of practical advice, based on experience, and remains essential. I find these practical books cheaper and more use than subsequent encyclopaedias written by many authors and diluted by too many colour pictures. As wide-ranging guides to particular types of plant, the titles by Martyn Rix with the photography of Roger Phillips are in a class by themselves, uniting expert knowledge of every plant discussed with superb colour pictures, frequently of the plants in their wild habitats. Roger Phillips and Martyn Rix, *Bulbs* (London, 1989), *Perennials* (London, 1994–6), *Roses* (London, 1988), *Shrubs* (London, 1989) and the remarkable *Summer Annuals* (London, 1996) are outstandingly good value. Among more specialized books I turn often to Paul Picton, *The Gardener's Guide to Growing Asters* (Devon, 1998) and only slightly less often to the other titles in this excellent series, all of which are worth reading. In the old, now defunct series of Penguin Handbooks, E. B. Anderson's *Rock Gardening* (London, 1960), Lanning Roper, *Hardy Herbaceous Perennials* (London, 1960) and E. B. Anderson, *Hardy Bulbs, volume I* (London, 1964) are unsurpassed. Peter Beales, *Classic Roses* (London, 1985) is invaluable and has greatly widened my love of this fine family of plants. Helen Dillon, *Helen Dillon on Gardening* (Dublin, 1998) and *Helen Dillon's Gardening Book* (London, 2007) combine great wit and clear, direct sense from one of our greatest flower gardeners. Among books on designing gardens I have written a preface to Russell Page, *The Education of a Gardener* (New York, paperback edn, 2008) and also to Vita Sackville-West, *The Illustrated Garden Book, A New Anthology by Robin Lane Fox* (London, 1986). Tracy DiSabato-Aust, *The Well-Tended Perennial Garden* (London, new edn, 2006) is a valuable encouragement to try new ways of cutting back border plants and changing their seasons. Jane Taylor, *Plants for Dry Gardens* (London, 1993) is very well founded and makes good use of earlier German reference books. Among the many recent accounts of making a garden as a beginner or an ignoramus, I like Roy Strong, *The Laskett: The Story of a Garden* (London, 2003).

My fellow journalists and broadcasters in Britain continue to produce many books which address aspects of gardening in accessible styles, sometimes reprinting their selections of their newspaper columns. Ursula Buchan, *Good in a Bed* (London, 2001) and *Better Against a Wall* (London, 2003), Monty Don, *The Ivington Diaries* (London, 2009) and Hugh Johnson, *Hugh Johnson on Gardening: The Best of Tradescant's Diary* (London, 1993) are recent collections of such articles, compiled from differing starting points. More general works include Stephen Anderton, *Rejuvenating a Garden* (London, 1998), Rachel de Thame, *Gardening with the Experts* (London, 2003), Jane Fearnley-Whittingstall, *Peonies: The Imperial Flower* (London, 1999), Mary Keen, *Creating a Garden* (London, 1996), Stephen Lacey, *Real Gardening* (London, 2002), Anna Pavord, *Anna Pavord's Gardening Companion* (London, 1992) and Alan Titchmarsh, *The Complete How To Be a Gardener* (London, 2005).

Selected References

I have begun from the *RHS Plant Finder 2009–10* when checking the plant names in this book and only departed from it when the names proposed are newly revisionist or manifestly at odds with general nursery lists and gardeners' practice. Most of the plants I discuss are listed in it with UK suppliers to whom readers should turn. There is also the helpful website www.britishplantnurseryguide.co.uk, which gives details of British nurseries of all sizes and lists their current plants and events. More generally, the website www.gardenersclick.com is a network of value for keen gardeners who are 'digitally included'.

Of the gardens I mention, two in France need further detail. Shamrock Garden (pp. 241–5) is at Route du Manoir d'Ango, 76119 Varengeville-sur-mer, and from the UK the telephone number is 0033-02-35-04-02-33. Brécy (pp. 264–7) lies between Caen and Bayeux to the west of the departmental road 82 between Rocqueville and Saint Gabriel-Brécy. Opening times currently include afternoons from 14.30 to 18.30 on Tuesdays, Thursdays, Sundays and (in June) Saturdays, from Easter to All Saints Day. The fax number in France for further details is 02-31-80-11-90.

An excellent way to visit these and other French gardens is to take a tour with French Gardens Today (www.frenchgardenstoday.co.uk), a meeting place for many keen gardeners. I am grateful to the founder and admirable organizer, Clare Whately, for all I have learned from her and her team.

In Britain the gardens which I discuss are open at times listed in the current *RHS Garden Finder*, but Kiftsgate Court in Gloucestershire, just down the road from Hidcote Manor, also has a particularly helpful website at www.kiftsgate.co.uk.

In Ireland the superb garden of Helen Dillon at 45 Sandford Road, Ranelagh, Dublin 6, mainly opens on afternoons in March, July and August but on Sunday afternoons only from April to June and in September. Times can be checked by calling 01-497-1308 within Ireland.

Specific references to other texts in this book include:

Thoughtful Gardening (pp. 1–7): L. Wittgenstein, *Zettel*, ed. G. E. M. Anscombe and G. H. von Wright (Oxford, 1967), sections 100–107 on 'thoughtful activity'. L. Wittgenstein, *The Brown Book*, in *The Blue and Brown Books* (Oxford, 1960), 178, discusses pansies, a reference which I owe to Peter Hacker. Erasmus describes flowers in literary terms in his *Colloquia*, in his *Opera Omnia 1* (Amsterdam, 1972), 235, which I owe to William Marx, *Vie du Lettré* (Paris, 2009), 78.

Jardin Majorelle (pp. 69–72): for Majorelle, see Alain Leygonie, *Un Jardin à Marrakech: Jacques Majorelle, Peintre-Jardinier, 1886–1962* (Paris, 2007).

'Oh dear, I do love gardens!' (pp. 73–6): the geraniums are described by Katherine Mansfield in J. Middleton Murry, ed., *The Journal of Katherine Mansfield* (London, 1954), 156–7, a reference I owe to Laura Marcus. The letters are superbly edited by Vincent O'Sullivan and Margaret Scott, *The Collected Letters of Katherine Mansfield*, Vols. 1–5 (Oxford, 1984–2008), and for her last days see Vol. 5, 303–48.

Let Them Eat Squirrel (pp. 97–9): Julia Drysdale, *Classic Game Cookery*, is itself a classic in paperback (London, 1983). It first appeared in hardback in 1975 as *The Game Cookery Book* (London, 1975).

Harassed by Perpetual Bother (pp. 115–18): the unsurpassed letters of John Clare are best available in Mark Storey, ed., *The Letters of John Clare* (Oxford, 1985), and I quote from pp. 630 and 643.

When Connie Met Oliver (pp. 133–6): I have used D. H. Lawrence, *Lady Chatterley's Lover*, in the Cambridge edition, ed. Michael Squires (Cambridge, 1993), and then for the earlier versions *The First and Second Lady Chatterley Novels*, ed. Dieter Mehl and Christa Jansohn (Cambridge, 1999).

Corona's Imprint (pp. 141–4): Altamont is signposted off the main N80 road from Carlow to Wexford. The garden is near Tullow, Co. Wicklow, and the weekly opening times can be checked on the Irish telephone and fax number 0503-59444. They include Saturdays throughout the gardening season.

Valerie Finnis (pp. 148–54): I have drawn on Ursula Buchan, *Garden People: Valerie Finnis and the Golden Age of Gardening* (London, 2007), which ends with an invaluable survey of individual 'garden lives' by Brent Elliott.

Separate Beds on the Bay (pp. 165–8): I refer to Statius, *Silvae*, 2.2, 2.7 and 3.1, which are brilliantly interpreted by R. G. M. Nisbet, '*Felicitas* at Surrentum (Statius, *Silvae* II. 2)', *Journal of Roman Studies*, LXVIII (1978), 1–11.

Irises on Drugs (pp. 177–80): Aldous Huxley, *The Doors of Perception* (London, 1954).

The Tivoli Garden (pp. 221–4): David R. Coffin, *The Villa in the Life of Renaissance Rome* (Princeton, 1979), gives the facts of the Villa d'Este's history. I quote Horace, *Epistles*, 1.8.12; and for the Sibyl and floods, see J. L. Lightfoot, *The Sibylline Oracles* (Oxford, 2007), 116–17 and 416–17.

Asphodels of the Negroes (pp. 228–31): I allude to the poem 'Stratis Thalassinos Among the Agapanthi', in George Seferis, *Collected Poems*, trans. Edmund Keeley and Philip Sherrard (Princeton and London, 1995), 144–5. It was written in Transvaal on 14 January 1942.

Gendered Landscape (pp. 236–40): an excellent survey of Englishwomen in the garden is given by Sue Bennett, *Five Centuries of Women and Gardens* (London, 2000), which I draw on with gratitude. It accompanied the fine exhibition at London's National Portrait Gallery in 2000.

Rosemary Revisited (pp. 255–60): Rosemary Verey, *A Countrywoman's Notes* (Gloucester-shire, 1989), collected some of her monthly articles for *Country Life* magazine, written between 1979 and 1987. It has been reprinted in miniature editions in London since 1993.

Forcing Nature (pp. 264–7): Eric T. Haskell, *The Gardens at Brécy: A Lasting Landscape* (Paris, 2007), gives a full historical account of the garden.

The Haunt of Ancient Peace (pp. 296–9): Robin Whalley, *The Great Edwardian Gardens of Harold Peto: From the Archives of Country Life* (London, 2007), is a magnificent account of Peto's work.

Space Invaders (pp. 300–303): I refer to John M. Randall and Janet Marinelli, eds., *Invasive Plants: Weeds of the Global Garden* (New York, 1996).

Á La Carte de Tendre (pp. 341–6): George de Scudéry, *Clélie* (Paris, 1661–5), is the source of the Carte de Tendre, my knowledge of which is owed to the kind help of Dr Wes Williams. The author was in fact female, Madeleine de Scudéry. The Carte is discussed in fascinating detail by James S. Munro*, Mademoiselle de Scudéry and the Carte de Tendre* (Durham, 1986).

Picture Acknowledgements

I am particularly grateful for the help of Peter Beales, supplier of so many fine roses through Peter Beales Roses, London Road, Attleborough, Norwich NR17 1AY, and of Thompson and Morgan Ltd, suppliers of so many fine seeds at Poplar Lane, Ipswich, Suffolk. Paul Picton has helped me with excellent pictures of the asters and autumnal plantings which are exemplified in the Picton gardens at Old Court Nurseries, Colwall, near Malvern, Worcestershire WR13 6QE. Anne Chambers has provided the pictures of Britain's finest garden flourishing in long family ownership, Kiftsgate Court in Gloucestershire, whose regular opening times for visitors are given on the website at www.kiftsgate.co.uk. Andrew Lawson, king of English garden-photographers, has been a patient source of images from his archives. Lucy Waitt and staff at the RHS Lindley Library have made available the pictures taken by Valerie Finnis (Scott), now in the RHS's keeping. Clare Whately has been an invaluable help with the pictures from France, whose gardens I know through her organized tours, available at www.frenchgardenstoday.co.uk. I have made every effort to trace underlying copyrights, but if any has been overlooked, it will, if possible, be acknowledged in future editions.

The following sources apply for pages as listed: Michael Walker ii, viii, 17, 21, 39, 205, 229, 234, 243; Didier Wirth 8, 172, 265; Thompson and Morgan 13, 14, 123, 201, 220, 233; Caroline Thomas 25; Robin Lane Fox 24, 51, 59, 71, 79, 99, 105 (top), 121, 143, 197, 211, 223, 263, 269, 285, 291, 294, 297, 319, 342–3; Valerie Finnis (Scott) and RHS Lindley Library 29, 103, 149, 151, 153, 154; Melissa Wyndham 31; Anne Chambers 43, 217, 274; Andrew Lawson 45, 63, 112, 113, 117, 170, 187, 213, 219, 239, 257; Kim Wilkie 46; John Fairey 85; Arabella Lennox-Boyd 95; Marquis of Lansdown 100, 127; David Astor 105 (lower), 114; Patrick and Sylvie Quibel 107, 125, 247, 248, 249, 273, 339; Melinda Manning of the New York Botanical Garden 139; Isabelle Brunetière 178; Peter Beales 183, 194; Robert Mallet 244–5; Paul Picton 253, 272 (top), 313, 315, 316; Peter Moore 279; Ayletts 309; David Hall 323; Peter Hellyer 327; Tara Lane Fox 347.

Index